# THE PLANTFINDER'S
## GUIDE TO
# EARLY BULBS

# THE PLANTFINDER'S GUIDE TO
# EARLY BULBS
## Rod Leeds

David & Charles

Timber Press
Portland, Oregon

## PICTURE ACKNOWLEDGEMENTS

All photographs are by **Marie O'Hara**, except pages 17, 24–5, 28–9, 42–3, 52–3, 62–3, 72–3, 78–9, 88–9, 116–17, 124–25, 146–47 and 160–61 by **Karl Adamson**, pages 135 and 136 by **John Fielding** and page 132 by **Geoff Stebbings**

Illustrations on pages 16-19, 71, 115 and 145 by **Reinhild Raistrick**

**Note:** Throughout the book the time of year is given as a season to make the reference applicable to readers all over the world. In the Northern Hemisphere the seasons may be translated into months as follows:

| | |
|---|---|
| Early winter – December | Early summer – June |
| Midwinter – January | Midsummer – July |
| Late winter – February | Late summer – August |
| Early spring – March | Early autumn – September |
| Mid-spring – April | Mid-autumn – October |
| Late spring – May | Late autumn – November |

First published in the UK in 2000 by David & Charles Publishers
Brunel House, Newton Abbot, Devon
ISBN 0 7153 0805 X
A catalogue record for this book is available from the
British Library

First published in North America by Timber Press Inc.,
133 SW Second Avenue, Suite 450, Portland, Oregon 97204, USA
ISBN 0–88192–443–1
Cataloging-in-Publication date is on file with the Library of Congress

Art Editor: Alison Myer
Project Editor: Caroline Smith
Book design by Ian Muggeridge
Printed in China by Hong Kong Graphic and Printing Ltd.

Photographs: page 1 *Fritillaria pyreniaca*;
page 2 *Trillium chloropetalum giganteum*;
page 3 *Muscari pseudomuscari*;
page 5 *Galanthus caucasicus* 'John Tomlinson'

# Contents

# Preface

The intense colours produced by bulbs in the garden's more sombre season are an immense fillip to our spirits. It might seem that there is very little on offer, but on closer inspection the beauty of each flower and its structure reveals an intriguing diversity that many gardeners have collected and treasured for hundreds of years.

In this book, I hope to explore this diversity and to trace the origins of these bulbs back to the work of those early gardeners. Back to the Victorians and Edwardians who, with the advent of world-wide plant collection, were able to begin gardening with many of the plants we take for granted today.

In my garden in Suffolk, in the east of England, winter seems to arrive by the last week of November, when the gales are wrenching the last few leaves from the trees and the first air frosts are reducing other foliage to shades of brown. From then until early spring, any colour in the garden is so welcome, whether it's from a single flower or a drift of thousands under the canopy of the leafless trees.

The winters in temperate climates (places where the temperature is 10°–20°C (50–68°F) for four or more months in the year) vary from place to place and so gardeners can consult a map to determine which hardiness zone they are in. The experiences and plant descriptions that follow are all based on a garden in Britain which is within Zone 8, that means a minimum winter temperature between −7°C (20°F) and −12°C (10°F), and with an average rainfall of 54cm (22in), fairly evenly spread throughout the year.

The gardener can, by experimentation, extend what is growable by improving drainage, using and creating shelter and by the selective use of mulches. In Britain the maritime influence renders the hardiness zones of academic interest only. Experience has shown that the stormy but mild western extremities of Britain can be home to plants from the warm temperate regions of the world. Gardens such as Tresco, Logan and Inverewe are renowned for growing a range of plants that can only be grown under glass elsewhere in the country. Throughout this book, the timings I have given for flowering can only act as a guide, since local weather plays such an important part in determining the actual date of flowering, as does the garden's site.

The word bulb is used loosely to cover all storage organs and so includes true bulbs, corms, tubers and rhizomes. These storage organs have evolved to enable the plant to grow very quickly for a short growing period, sometimes to beat the onset of drought or the shading from a leaf canopy in summer. It is more convenient for the gardener to use 'bulb' as an umbrella name, since nurseries, most gardening literature and, more importantly, gardeners themselves don't differentiate between the different storage organs. However, when propagation is considered they do need to be identified correctly so the right methods can be used.

Early bulbs need not be confined to garden borders and beds: the addition of raised beds, with their extra drainage; bulb frames, where control of rainfall is achieved, and greenhouses, which can be heated to protect against frost, means that an even wider range of bulbs can be grown. Each of these constructions also serves to bring the flowers nearer to the grower so they are more easily enjoyed; especially in the greenhouse where even winter sunshine can lift the temperature enough for flowers to open.

The aim of this book is to show the range of plants that can be grown quite easily in temperate gardens. By utilizing a knowledge of the environment together with tried and tested methods of cultivation, the gardener can get great enjoyment in almost cheating winter and in so doing eradicate those winter blues by growing some of the most diminutive and beautiful plants in the world.

An early hoar-frost enhances the beauty of *Cyclamen coum*, as it mingles with the leaves of *Achillea*.

# *Part One* Introducing Early Bulbs

# Influential Gardeners

Over the years, many gardeners, both amateur and professional, have played a part in the development of early bulb cultivation. Thanks to their efforts, both as plant hunters and breeders, we can enjoy some beautiful and refined named selections as well as rare and unusual species.

## EDWARD BERTRAM ANDERSON 1886–1971

In his book *Seven Gardens or Sixty Years of Gardening*, E.B. Anderson wrote about his gardening philosophy; 'the true gardener is one who enjoys the manual work involved, the skill required and the observation essential to satisfactory results and the beauty of the resulting picture or of the individuals composing it.' A research chemist by profession, he brought this intellect to gardening, making him one of the most skilful growers of dwarf bulbs and alpines in his day. His unrivalled knowledge in this field led him to be a founder member of the Alpine Garden Society and later its president. In 1960 he was awarded the Victoria Medal of Honour, the highest award the Royal Horticultural Society (RHS) can bestow.

He had a number of gardens in Britain ranging from one at Porlock in Somerset, just a mile from the sea, to Rickmansworth in Hertfordshire, close to the most notorious frost hollow in England. Anderson himself likened it climatically to the Aberdeenshire Highlands.

Typical of Anderson's skill was the approach he brought to growing *Scilla rosenii*, a species from the Caucasus. This snow-melt bulb has a most stunning white and sky-blue flower which, unless triggered by melting snow water, tends to grow slowly and then flower at ground level. In Britain, this beauty is usually lost and it is soon mud splattered and eaten by slugs. Anderson, in his last garden in the limestone Cotswold Hills, conceived the idea of removing the rubble that filled the

(Pages 8–9) A sparkling of raindrops adorn the leaves and flowers of *Erythronium tuolumnense* 'Pagoda'.
(Below) The ever-reliable *Iris* 'Katharine Hodgkin'.

dry-stone walls in his garden and replacing the top 23cm (9in) with a soil mix. This was, in effect, a very fast draining bed and a very successful home for many bulbs; it was also the perfect position for *Scilla rosenii*. The cold and dryness inhibited growth until spring was well advanced so the plant grew normally with a flower in character, well above the soil.

Anderson will always be associated with three winter-flowering bulbs of great merit, two of which are snowdrops. One of Anderson's greatest friends was John Gray of Saxmundham in Suffolk, who on becoming infirm asked Anderson to take any plants he wished from his garden. Anderson found two labels next to some snowdrop foliage marked XXX, one he named *Galanthus* 'John Gray', after his friend, and the other, *G.* 'Mighty Atom'. Both these selections are still amongst the finest snowdrops available today. It was typical of the man that within a few years these plants were grown by enthusiasts the length and breadth of the country.

In 1955 he deliberately crossed *Iris histrioides* 'Major' and *I. danfordiae*, with *I. danfordiae* as the pollen parent. (However, the yellow parent may have been *I. winogradowii*, not *I. danfordiae*, see chapter 8, the A-Z of Early Bulbs) Two seeds resulted and one germinated to flower in 1960; it was named 'Katharine Hodgkin' after the wife of another gardening friend, Eliot Hodgkin. The colour was unique, with bluish green standards and yellowish green falls, veined slate blue.

## SIR CEDRIC MORRIS 1889–1982

A painter and plantsman, Sir Cedric Morris lived for over forty years at Benton End, a sixteenth-century house near Hadleigh in Suffolk. Here, he developed both a plant collection and the East Anglian School of Painting and Drawing, so fondly remembered by many artists for its individuality and inspiration.

The garden at Benton End had been neglected for over a decade and in wartime 1940, when Morris moved in, the first priority was food production. There is a painting, *Wartime Garden*, of about 1944, that shows the walled garden with row upon row of vegetables, all within box-lined paths. Once World War II was finished, Morris was able to continue his southern European painting and plant-hunting forays. His garden soon became a mecca for plantsmen. The sheltered garden had excellent drainage, and with Morris's flair and eye for a good plant, the collection increased, so much so that one expert declared that some plants had 'no right to exist' in

Whatever the weather, *Narcissus minor* 'Cedric Morris' will brighten up the dark days of winter.

that part of the world. Bulbous plants thrived in this imitation of the Mediterranean in East Anglia, and whether apocryphal or not, the Californian *Fritillaria recurva* was said to flower in the open garden.

The plant most connected with winter is *Narcissus minor* 'Cedric Morris'. This amazing bulb flowers outside at Christmas without any protection. A few bulbs were collected from a roadside verge in Northern Spain by a friend and surprisingly always flowered around the winter solstice when back in Britain. Further searching for the original site proved fruitless, as the road had been widened. Like so many gardeners, Morris was very generous with plants and consequently many plants have 'Benton' or 'Cedric Morris' as a cultivar name.

## JAMES ALLEN d. 1906

A Victorian gardener from Shepton Mallet in Somerset, Allen was growing snowdrops in the latter half of the nineteenth century, and was always alert to the new and rare species that became available at this time. It seems likely he did not made intentional crosses, but collected and sowed all the naturally occurring seed set in his garden. He did record the seed parent and make an informed guess as to the other. He certainly had an 'eye' for a good plant and this legacy can still be seen among the outstanding snowdrops in the garden today. *Galanthus allenii* was named after him by Mr Baker of Kew, from one plant imported from an Austrian nursery. Robust and still with us, no trace has ever been found of a similar plant in the wild.

In 1891, the interest in snowdrops culminated in the RHS organizing an event, with Allen and other notable growers reading papers. Allen's paper was by far the most comprehensive. William Robinson, in his epic *The English Flower Garden*, added in later editions a précis of Allen's paper, so continuing the interest well into the twentieth century. E.A. Bowles became the custodian of Allen's manuscript so further glimpses of his collection can be gleaned from Bowles' chapter in *Snowdrops and Snowflakes*, by F.C. Stern published in 1956. Tantalizingly, of Allen's two favourite selections *Galanthus* 'Charmer' and *G.* 'Galatea', only 'Galatea' has survived to this day. Even in 1891, Allen was very concerned about the appearance of snowdrop fungus (*Botrytis galanthina*) in his garden, which resulted in many of his choicest bulbs being sadly lost.

However one of his selections is still amongst the most robust and distinctive snowdrops in cultivation, *G.* 'Magnet'. The seed parent is recorded as *G. nivalis* 'Melvillei'. This snowdrop is tall, a prolific grower and indeed can be naturalized in suitable areas. When a mild mid- or late-winter day with a gentle breeze lifts the outer segments of the flower to the horizontal, the effect is most eye catching. They sway more than other snowdrops as there

Among the older snowdrops is *Galanthus* 'Galatea', a very distinct and vigorous Victorian selection.

is an unusually long pedicel connecting the stem to the ovary, rivalled only by *G.* 'Galatea'.

Still to be found are other distinctive and healthy *Galanthus* of Allen's selection, 'Anne of Geierstein', 'Merlin' and 'Robin Hood'. It is fun to speculate what 'Lazybones', 'Leopard' and 'Majestic' would be like had they survived to this day.

## EDWARD AUGUSTUS BOWLES 1865–1954

E.A. Bowles' name is still regularly heard today wherever gardeners gather to talk of plants and their properties, nearly fifty years after his death. In his obituary written by The Hon. Lewis Palmer, vice-chairman of the RHS council, he wrote '[Bowles] was nearly the last of a generation of great gardeners … and in some ways [was] the greatest of them all'.

He was a dedicated gardener, with immense patience, and the author of many books still consulted regularly today. They were often illustrated by his beautiful drawings and paintings. He disliked using herbarium specimens, much preferring 'living' plants as a basis for his botanical writing. To this end he grew an amazing array of hardy plants at Myddleton House in Enfield, his family home. He specialized in *Crocus*, *Galanthus*, *Narcissus*,

*Crocus sieberi* 'Albus' was one of E.A. Bowles' selections and was, until recently, known as 'Bowles' White'.

*Colchicum* and *Anemone*, but also wrote three books, mostly about his gardening experiences at Myddleton House aided by his regular European plant-hunting trips. These books, *My Garden in Spring*, *My Garden in Summer* and *My Garden in Autumn and Winter*, are so authoritative that they have been reprinted regularly, although of course the first editions are much sought-after.

Crocus was an early passion and at the beginning of this century he grew every species available and many more hybrids, usually crosses of *C. chrysanthus* and *C. biflorus*. Today some of his cultivars are still with us; 'Blue Jay', 'Kittiwake' and 'Snow Bunting'. *C. chrysanthus* 'Snow Bunting' can be found at most garden suppliers and in catalogues, and is still holding its own against modern cultivars, seventy years its junior.

*C. tommasinianus* was a prolific grower at Myddleton House, so much so that Bowles wrote; 'it conquers new territory at a surprising rate, being a great seeder and also by splitting into many small offsets from the larger corms.' He took great delight in searching through his spreading swarms and selecting promising varieties. *C. t.* 'Bobbo' is one such selection grown to this day, each segment has a white tip above a pale lavender of an almost Wedgwood-china hue. Another species that he loved was *C. sieberi*. In *My Garden in Spring* he wrote very fully and

encouragingly about pollinating crocuses. However, it was with chagrin that he found nature had produced two beautiful albino forms of *C. sieberi* in his garden well away from the crocus frames. One of these albino seedlings was known as 'Bowles' White' (it's now 'Albus') in recognition of his prowess in picking outstanding plants. The corms of this crocus used to be expensive but now it has been commercially propagated and is widely available at a modest price.

In later life he began working on a book with F.C. Stern, *Snowdrops and Snowflakes*. Bowles was to write the history and background to the garden cultivars, using as illustrations some of his definitive snowdrop paintings. In the event we are frustratingly left with only a short chapter and only two paintings as Bowles died before the book was published in 1956. Luckily his paintings and some manuscripts were bequeathed to the RHS Lindley Library and are an invaluable source for the identification of some of the older snowdrop cultivars.

## OLIVER E.P. WYATT 1898–1973

Oliver Wyatt was a man who loved gardening, even in childhood, where he learnt a great deal from his family's Edwardian gardener. He became a headmaster at twenty-nine and in 1933 moved to Maidwell Hall in Northamptonshire, where he gardened with great distinction until his retirement in 1964.

The name Maidwell Hall is synonymous with the excellent cultivation and breeding of lilies, but will also be remembered for selections of crocus and snowdrops. Wyatt grew and loved *Crocus tommasinianus*, being very careful to grow them in isolation, wary against ever mixing them with other crocus, in case, as he wrote 'they would flood them out'. From the drifts of 'tommies' he selected colour variants of which we still grow; *C. t.* 'Claret' has a rich deep rosy purple flower. Two snowdrop selections, *Galanthus* 'Maidwell C' and *G.* 'Maidwell L' are still treasured by enthusiasts and are available commercially. 'Maidwell L' has a large green X on each inner segment and very glaucous convolute leaves. 'Maidwell C' has plicate leaves and fine rounded flowers, below a large ovary. The inner segments have a small, but long V marking and separate paler green lines near the base.

## ALEXANDER GREY 1895–1986

Alec Grey, who worked at Camborne in Cornwall, will always be associated with miniature daffodils, of which he registered around one hundred. The first was in 1937, the last, *Narcissus* 'Little Sentry', was in 1984. In 1955 he wrote *Miniature Daffodils*, the first and until recently, the only book on the subject. Still a very useful and practical book it can be found in second-hand lists and shops. Early spring would not be the same without *N.* 'April Tears', *N.* 'Jumblie', *N.* 'Bobbysoxer', *N.* 'Picoblanco', *N.* 'Segovia' and the universal *N.* 'Tête-à-tête'.

These miniature hybrids gave the gardener the chance to place daffodils in the rock garden, and in tubs and pots where previously size had precluded their use.

## BRIGADIER LEONARD AND MRS WINIFREDE MATHIAS

After World War II, this husband and wife partnership began to interest gardeners in snowdrops, initially from the garden they bought in 1947. This garden, near Stroud in Gloucestershire, had been neglected for much of the war and on clearance they found drifts of robust snowdrops. One in particular, later identified as *Galanthus* 'S. Arnott', stood out, but there were others that had been collected by the garden's previous owner, Walter Butt.

In 1951 they issued their first catalogue as The Giant Snowdrop Company, which continued to trade very successfully until 1968. The company became renowned for its annual catalogues, with cover photographs of the snowdrops, and set a trend in the horticultural trade in post-war Britain. During this period the company regularly mounted inspirational displays at the RHS Westminster shows, winning over new converts to winter gardening, as well as many awards. Selections have been made from their garden and some have proved to be vigorous and distinct forms. One attractive selection of a *G. plicatus* ssp. *byzantinus* seedling, called 'Armine' was named after the the couple's daughter. There is also *G.* 'Winifrede Mathias', with a slim pale green ovary and delicate flowers over almost grey leaves. Although The Giant Snowdrop Company is no more, the name, itself so memorable, and the plants will continue to delight gardeners for many winters to come.

Drifts of *Galanthus* 'S. Arnott', naturalized in the grounds of Colesbourne Park in Gloucestershire.

# 2 What is a Bulb?

As he or she plants or propagates bulbs, the gardener is handling the result of millions of years of evolution. The survival of all these plants has been because of their ability to adapt to adverse weather situations by storing food in the optimum conditions, ready to grow and flower very rapidly when either the drought breaks or the temperature rises. Exactly how the different plants have developed to achieve these amazing features varies, but the results are similar.

## TRUE BULBS

A bulb is a very reduced stem seen as the basal plate, underneath which grow the roots which are usually of annual duration. Each year from near the centre of the plate a new stem, with or without a flower bud, is formed surrounded by a number of fleshy scales. Each scale is either the swollen leaf base of the aerial foliage or thick fleshy scale leaves which never grow upwards. Many bulbs such as *Narcissus*, *Tulipa* and *Allium* are

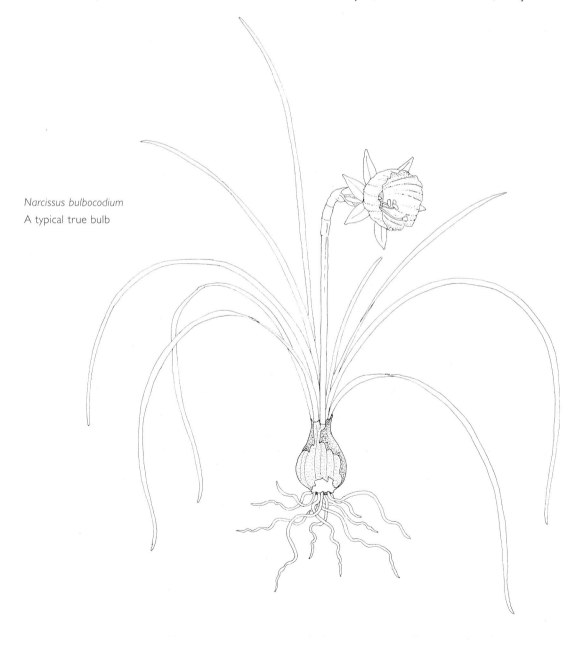

*Narcissus bulbocodium*
A typical true bulb

*Iris kuschakewiczii*, clearly showing the perennial roots of the Juno iris.

## CORMS

A corm is a solid food-storage organ made from the swollen base of the stem. It is usually covered by a tunic formed from the dried-up leaf bases of leaves; again this will protect the corm from damage and drying out. In dry climates some corms of *Crocus* are encased in a tunic composed of many year's worth of old leaves, as there is little moisture to rot them, so ensuring very good protection from desiccation.

In the family Iridaceae, a new corm is usually formed annually on top, or beside the old one which gradually fades away and disappears. In Liliaceae, the new corms are developed as offsets, enlarging the colony and leaving the parent to grow larger. Most cormous plants develop cormels (young corms) during the growing season, which are very useful for propagation purposes.

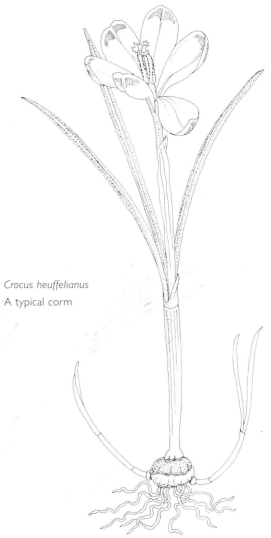

*Crocus heuffelianus*
A typical corm

enclosed in a papery tunic which is usually the remains of the previous years scales and acts as a protection against drying and surface damage. *Fritillaria* and *Lilium* do not produce any tunic covering, so must not dry out when dormant. Their structure varies from just two scales in most fritillaries, to a large number in most lilies.

Within these true bulbs there are three distinct types, based on the differences in the annual growth cycle. In the very popular genus *Narcissus*, for example, the bulb persists year after year. This is because it is composed of scales retained within the bulb and the swollen leaf bases and so can continue to grow and produce offsets annually. In *Tulipa*, the bulb shrivels and dies after flowering and is renewed each year from buds formed at the base of the scales where they join the basal plate. The last type is less common and is found in species like *Hippeastrum*, where the bulb is composed of swollen leaf bases, within which are produced embryonic bulbs for up to three years ahead; a true perennial.

*Anemone blanda*
A typical tuber

## TUBERS

Generally speaking, a tuber is not the base of a stem but a swollen root, which develops buds on the upper surface. As the season develops, new tuberous roots will form to carry the plant through the winter as the old tubers die after flowering. These tubers include some very important early flowering plants, such as *Cyclamen*, *Ranunculus asiaticus* and some anemones. A 'true' tuber, however, is really an underground or occasionally above ground stem. These structures are rarer but include the ubiquitous potato and, ornamentally, many *Tropaeolum* species. In *Cyclamen* it is not absolutely clear whether they are stem or root tubers as the root positions vary greatly from species to species although they are all perennial, and in fact some must live for many decades to judge by their size.

## RHIZOMES

These food storage organs are modified elongated stems, that wander on the soil's surface or just beneath it, and which at intervals send up shoots and put down roots. As it expands, the oldest part of the rhizome becomes exhausted and dies, ensuring that the nutrients in the soil are not exhausted. The rhizome of *Anemone nemorosa* is a good example of a woodland plant that grows very early in the year taking advantage of the bare forest canopy to grow and flower before shade sets in for the summer.

## BULB FAMILIES

Bulbs are nearly all monocotyledons, that is they have only one seed leaf in the embryo, whereas most flowering plants have two; these are dicotyledons. The monocotyledons are represented by three main families;

*Anemone × seemannii*
A typical rhizome

Amaryllidaceae, Liliaceae and Iridaceae. In early bulbs, these different families can be recognized by certain features. These can easily be seen by close inspection of an open flower. A simple hand lens is not essential but may helpful, and a closer examination of plants will often give a new perspective on their beauty and complexity, which can so easily be overlooked by the amateur gardener.

## AMARYLLIDACEAE

Many of this very large family of bulbous plants are found in the tropics, but there are very important exceptions, like *Narcissus*, which is found mostly in southern Europe, with members of the genus extending into western Asia. The bulbs of this family are scaly with a papery tunic. The flowers have six separate or joined perianth segments (often referred to as petals), with some, like *Narcissus* again, with a corona. There are six stamens with an inferior ovary, that is where the other floral parts are inserted above it, which develops into a three-valved seed capsule.

## LILIACEAE

The largest flowering monocotyledon family, this has recently been broken down into smaller groups to ensure greater uniformity, such as Hyacinthaceae, Alliaceae and Colchicaceae. However for our purposes the unifying elements of the family are as follows. The 'bulb' can be a true bulb, rhizome or tuber. The flowers are regular but show great variation in size and shape, and can be solitary as in *Tulipa*, or in long spikes or umbels, as in *Allium*. The perianth segments are separate or joined, even to the point where the segment divisions are merely teeth, as in *Muscari*. There are six stamens with a superior ovary, usually forming a three-valved seed capsule.

## IRIDACEAE

This family consists of true bulbs, rhizomes and corms. The perianth segments are six and often, as in *Crocus*, the inner three are smaller than the outer three. Here there are only three stamens, with an inferior ovary and a style with three or more branches.

A number of the 'bulbous' plants included in this book come from families where a few have evolved storage organs but are not monocotyledons The main families are Primulaceae (*Cyclamen*), Ranunculaceae (*Anemone* and *Ranunculus*), Araceae (*Arum*) and Oxalidaceae (*Oxalis*). All these plants belong to the far more numerous dicotyledons that have two seed leaves at germination.

# *Part Two* Growing Early Bulbs

# 3 Microclimates in the Garden

Naturally every gardener talks of, say, the sunny wall, the sandy bed or the windy corner when describing their garden and these considerations guide most plantings and their ultimate success or failure. The microclimates that exist in our gardens can be our allies and a closer look can help us to grow certain plants without the aid of artificial heating.

If you are going to be growing early bulbs, such as those covered in this book, then you are more likely to be gardening in a temperate climate zone without great extremes of temperature or wind. My own experience is of a garden in East Anglia, in Britain, where, because of our maritime climate, the winter winds have, to some extent, been warmed by crossing some water before rushing across our country. This, combined with an intelligent use of microclimates within the garden, allows for a great range of plants from many countries to be grown. King Charles II said of our island's weather; 'The English climate is the best in the world. A man can enjoy outdoor exercise on all but five days in a year.'

## ASSESSING YOUR SITE

Most early bulbs grow close to the ground and their survival depends on being able to cope with every type of weather. As bulbs take up such a relatively small growing area, it is quite possible to adapt a small part of the garden to give them the best chance to perform well. If you want to make an effective use of microclimates, you will first need to assess the site. The soil type and structure and the way in which is cultivated play their part, as does the slope of the garden and the direction of that slope. It is also important to consider any obstructions, man-made or planted, to the movement of the air above the garden and any cover that will lessen the night-time radiation of hard-won daytime heat. Such cover should be designed so that light and heat from the sun are not obstructed. Most of the considerations that follow deal with how to avoid or lessen the risk of frost damage.

The forecast of frost for the night ahead is always based on the temperature over 1m (3ft) above the ground. The ground where our bulbs will be growing will be subjected to a temperature some two to three degrees lower. This is because as cold air cools it becomes denser and

slides downhill, so even on a level site the ground frost is always harder than the air measurement. Most gardens slope in one direction and so unseen at night the air will move towards the lower end of the garden. If you live in the very bottom of a valley there is little you can do to avoid damaging frosts but for others there are ways of avoiding the worst. A barrier such as a wall or fence can deflect the air around your site, as can an evergreen hedge. If this can be at an angle to the flow then the air will slide around it, but if you have no choice then the air will build up on the highest side and eventually spill over. Even so there will be some lessening of the effect. In notorious frost hollows tests have been carried out showing that the air moves at about 2mph downhill, but if the slope becomes very steep there is a reverse of this cooling. The moving air, with a rapid loss of height, rises in temperature due to an increase in pressure, which counteracts the cooling by radiation. This may account for the ability of gardens like Kiftsgate Court in Gloucestershire and Powis Castle in Wales, with their steep sloping gardens, to grow many tender plants.

Any obstruction to air movement that you create can also become a very useful windbreak as the season of early bulbs also coincides with the greatest incidence of storms. In Britain, those storms which do the greatest damage have come from the east, sometimes as far away as Siberia. As they rush westwards, they warm only slightly and arrive at a sub-zero temperature that can even damage plants in the warmer Scilly Isles. A solid barrier, such as a wall, does give good protection in its lea, but the wind then strikes with great turbulence a little further into the garden. A dense evergreen hedge like yew, however, will diffuse the wind, giving slightly less immediate protection but without any induced turbulence. Planting or constructing barriers to the movement of cold air can lessen the damage the wind can wreak.

In Britain, on average, the coldest weather occurs well after the winter solstice (21st December) when the sea has cooled and the sun hasn't the strength to warm the soil that it has in spring. This is when any retention of warmth in the soil is so vital for early plants. The air is hardly heated by the sun and the temperature each day and more critically at night, is influenced by the earth and sea. Soils vary in their ability to retain heat. Sandy soil with its open texture soon radiates heat and is renowned for low temperatures. Clay, although seeming cold, contains little air and is usually quite wet, and so is slowest in radiating heat and therefore has higher night temperatures. Whatever your soil, it should not be loosened by cultivation in these critical times, as any air incorporated in the surface will radiate heat very quickly at night. If for any reason the soil is dry it must be watered, as this will aid heat retention.

In northerly countries like Britain, the south- or southwest-facing wall is the most favoured planting site. Without extra protection, it provides a 2°C (4°F) uplift and with glass covering this can give up to 5°C (9°F) protection. This lessens the potential damage caused to plants to just a few nights, when extra covering, such as sacking will be needed. In these really low temperatures it is often the strong wind that causes fatal damage. The wind, and in Britain the east wind in particular, can bring a very low humidity, causing the plant to wilt. As the ground is frozen, the plant can not transpire in the normal way and so it dies, of drought. The protection given by a wall is narrow but effective.

(Pages 20–21) *Muscari azureum nestles* among the attractively marked leaves of a cyclamen.

(Below) *Anemone apennina* surrounding a hypertufa trough.

Equally effective elsewhere, can be the canopy provided by deciduous trees and shrubs. Here, with the wet soil covered with a loose mulch of leaves, the ground rarely freezes to any depth. The hardy bulbs like snowdrops and *Eranthis* thrive here, looking very natural in these surroundings. In natural woodland, you will often find some dell or ditch that makes the most of the winter sun and has very early plants in flower, long before the rest of the wood has woken from winter's slumber. Such natural plantings are always good to copy in the garden.

As to the plants, it is always interesting to experiment with plantings. I have seen *Cyclamen libanoticum* flourishing under the west wall of a cottage without any protection and *C. graecum* doing the same with some glass covering just to ensure a good ripening in summer. If you have snowfall in winter this can, when evenly spread, be a very good blanket for plants. It contains a great deal of air and is a very poor conductor of heat from the soil beneath, and so shields the plants from very low night-time minimum temperatures. Unfortunately the very siting of your best microclimate site will also be the first to thaw, so a little shovelled snow or extra sacks will be required until the cold spell finishes. Even if you do not attempt an experimental or daring planting, the use of your microclimate can extend your enjoyment of hardy bulbs by inducing earlier flowering than the rest of the garden and by keeping the blooms in good condition with its added protection.

# PLATE I

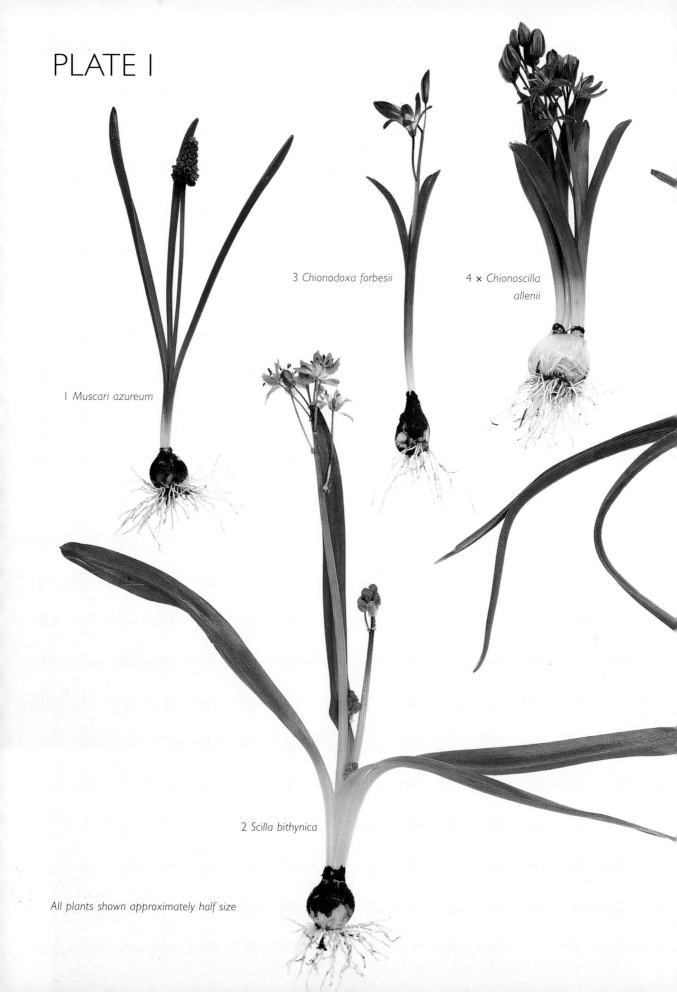

1 *Muscari azureum*

2 *Scilla bithynica*

3 *Chionodoxa forbesii*

4 × *Chionoscilla allenii*

*All plants shown approximately half size*

6 *Scilla siberica* 'Spring Beauty'

5 *Muscari pseudomuscari*

7 *Chionodoxa cretica*

8 *Scilla bifolia* 'Rosea'

9 *Muscari azureum* 'Album'

10 *Chionodoxa sardensis*

11 *Scilla siberica* 'Alba'

# 4 Cultivation and Care

When you've decided which early bulbs you want and where you're going to plant them (see Chapter 5), avoid buying any that show signs of disease or deterioration; look out for damage to the tunics or scales, any unusual marks or any soft spots. Always buy from a reputable source to ensure that you are getting bulbs from cultivated stock rather than from the wild. (For more information about the conservation of bulbs in the wild, see Appendix I.)

Generally speaking, you buy bulbs in their dry, dormant state and for early flowering bulbs, these are usually available from late summer. You should aim to plant them as early as possible, as soon as they become available, before growth begins. The exception to this is *Galanthus* and *Eranthis*; if either of these are bought as dry bulbs

The South African, cliff-dwelling *Cyrtanthus falcatus* is equally at home in a pot.

then there is a high chance of mortality. Both are best planted 'in the green', that is, just after flowering when the bulb, complete with leaves and roots, will be dispatched by nurseries for immediate planting.

When planting your bulbs, the general rule is to plant them to a depth two to three times the length of the bulb. An ordinary garden spade will usually be adequate, but if you are aiming to plant a large number of bulbs in grass, then a bulb planter, looking rather like a tall pastry cutter, might be better. Long-handled versions are also available, to help ease the strain on the gardener's back!

As a rule, bulbs prefer slightly alkaline to neutral soil but the more important consideration is drainage, since most require a dry summer rest period in soil that will warm up quickly in winter. If you know that you have a problem with heavy soil, then digging in grit and well-rotted organic matter before planting can go a long way towards improving your conditions.

Once planted, the care of early bulbs is fairly simple, although much will depend on where and how you choose to grow them. They will need little in the way of fertilizer; just an occasional application of low-nitrogen, high-potash feed to encourage flowering if necessary. However, one of your main concerns will be keeping track of where the bulbs are in the open garden when the foliage has disappeared.

## MARKING BULBS IN THE GARDEN

If where you have planted your bulbs is left to memory then there is a strong chance that the evolving shape of the garden will play tricks on you and the actual position will be a hazy supposition. That is, of course, until your fork impales at least two bulbs as you excavate for a new planting. There is no perfect solution and much will depend on how much time you can devote to this chore. The easiest marker to use is the ubiquitous white plastic label, which is practical until it snaps, as it most certainly will. More durable labels are made of metal – aluminium, zinc or copper – and though they are more expensive, they are less garish. Although they are not likely to break, they still can be moved by animals of all types and even the most careful gardener can scoop up a label when clearing a border in autumn. One solution is to fix the

A pot-grown *Ipheion sellowianum* can be moved outside to brighten up a shady corner of the garden.

metal label to looped piece of galvanized wire, which is pressed deep into the earth, so avoiding accidental removal. It is possible to nearly bury the wire and label, thereby lessening the 'tombstone' effect of labels dotted all over your garden. Another small but important point, is to decide which side of the planting to fix the label and then make it a rule of the garden; this will put a stop to any expletives being heard from deep in the shrubbery, when you forget where your bulbs were in relation to the labels!

Your labels can be most simply marked with a good quality HB pencil. Equally long lasting are the chinagraph pencils, the type that write on glass, however they blunt quickly and the lines produced tend to be too thick. You can buy a laminated plastic label with black overlying white, which you scratch with a stylus to give a very clear and immovable engraved name. Again, the only drawback is the brittle nature of the plastic. There are label-making machines available that produce tapes,

which can be stuck on metal or plastic labels. For many years a mechanical hand-held version has been used where letters are punched into the tape, which is then cut off. More recently a computerized edition, looking like a miniature keyboard, has become available. This produces thinner but equally useful tape to fix to labels.

Still seen in a few older gardens are lead labels produced by the Serpent label maker. Now treasured, these machines are reminiscent of old wind-up toys. They were slow to operate but in the pre-plastic era both machine and label were virtually indestructible. Finding a source of lead strips proves to be a problem today. An ideal modern-day and very long-lasting solution, is to use a hand-held electric hobby drill with a small diamond-tipped bit to engrave metal labels. Just before leaving this subject, mention should be made of the use of miniature computers in mapping the garden in grids. Rather than fiddling about in the mud and cluttering the garden with labels, the clean and dry gardener can log the position of the bulbs, their number and when they were planted on the computer plan. It sounds ideal, but whether it works in reality may be another matter!

# PLATE II

4 *Ranunculus ficaria*
'Brazen Hussy'

1 *Anemone* × *seemanii*

2 *Anemone nemorosa*
'Royal Blue'

3 *Anemone
ranunculoides*

*All plants shown approximately actual size*

5 *Anemone nemorosa*
'Bracteata Pleniflora'

9 *Anemone nemorosa* 'Wilks' White'

6 *Anemone nemorosa* 'Pallida'

8 *Anemone nemorosa* 'Leeds' Variety'

7 *Anemone nemorosa* 'Wyatt's Pink'

# 5 Where to Plant Early Bulbs

The great attraction of early bulbs is their ability to give colour when all around is so drab and damp. They are also an extra incentive for the gardener to don an extra sweater and get outside in cold weather. Once out, the pleasure and fun of searching out the emerging leaves and buds of old friends and the surprise of finding a precocious bloom takes over, and time and the cold are soon forgotten.

## A CHRISTMAS BED

The siting of these early flowers is a matter of choice and nearly all garden sites can accommodate at least a few to give early colour. Before the description of how best to display them in the usual garden situations, I would like to describe the planting and siting of a Christmas bed. This is specifically designed to provide interest at the very darkest time of year and is the perfect antidote to the seasonal excesses and commercial hype that are so hard to avoid at Christmas.

In choosing the site for your Christmas bed, try to place it next to a regular walkway, or possibly near the kitchen door, so that the colour and scents can be enjoyed, albeit fleetingly, as you pass. It is also possible that an area like this will be lit at night, giving you a greater chance to see the plants. Aspect is, to a certain degree, less important than drainage. Most of summer's shading, in the form of leaves, will have left the trees and be beginning to mulch the beds. So light will be adequate. Drainage can be improved by building a raised bed. The planting will not be exclusively bulbs but can include a few other plants that provide both additional interest and a background that will compliment and possibly protect the bulbs.

A selection of snowdrops could include *Galanthus caucasicus* 'Barnes' and *G. c.* 'Earliest of All', these two span two months of flowering and one or the other will always be in flower. A larger selection from John Morley is the aptly named *G. plicatus* ssp. *byzantinus* 'Three Ships', a stunning large-flowered selection which reliably flowers in early winter. Continuing with the white theme, the Christmas rose, *Helleborus niger* can be ready for Christmas. Unfortunately some seedlings wait until spring, so careful selection is needed and it is a good idea

to buy when in flower or prevail on a friend to split an authentic Christmas rose. There are also a few other notable hellebores, like the *H. atrorubens* of gardens, which reliably flower near Christmas. There are a number of different plants with this name, all very attractive, but none actually *H. atrorubens*, so do try to buy them when in flower to be sure.

An excellent *Narcissus* at this time of year is *N. minor* 'Cedric Morris', which is proving to flower reliably without any protection from early winter into early spring. It has the marvellous capacity to completely straighten up after a hard frost has prostrated both stem and leaves. A plant to place just under the *Narcissus* is *Crocus laevigatus* 'Fontenayi', a selection of the Greek crocus that blooms in the middle of this species' flowering period; different forms can be found in flower from mid-autumn through to early spring. Again to provide a contrast in colour the winter-flowering *Cyclamen coum* is worth a place. If a number are grown from seed that

*Crocus laevigatus* 'Fontenayi' is a Christmas-flowering selection of a very variable species.

One of the best snowdrops, *Galanthus plicatus* ssp. *byzantinus* 'Three Ships' reliably flowers at Christmas time.

comes from different sources, a great range of leaf colours and markings will occur. Also, the time of flowering will vary from early winter through to early spring. Choose the ones you like, from shiny dark green marbled leaves to ones that are nearly silver. The choice is vast and selecting an early flowering form will bring a strong magenta to this Christmas bed.

Not bulbous, but some of its relatives are, *Iris unguicularis* is a must for this bed. They are untidy growers with long linear leaves that refuse to be pulled up even when apparently dead, but an occasional severe haircut in late summer overcomes this problem and gives the flowers room to emerge in winter. Two selections that flower early are *I. u.* 'Walter Butt' and 'Abington Purple'. The blooms are very large by winter's standards and admittedly are frost tender when in flower. However, the wise gardener cuts the flowering stem the evening before a hard frost is forecast and puts them in water indoors. The bud unfurls very quickly to display the beautiful flower to perfection. *I. u.* 'Walter Butt' is a very pale lavender colour, almost white in sunshine, with a sweet fragrance, whereas 'Abington Purple' is a rich velvety purple.

In the NW States of the USA, at the first sign of spring and as soon as the snow begins to melt, *Sisyrinchium douglasii* pushes through with its delicate purple and sometimes white flowers, which can be so prolific they stud the ground. In Britain, even without the snow, the first flowers begin in the depths of winter. They were formed and ripened the summer before and although not bulbs, have been dormant for some six months, waiting for the first sign of warmth and moisture. This plant is uncommon and often overlooked, as the slender leaves are all that remain come spring. One other plant that is rarely considered for this season is *Anemone coronaria*. This Mediterranean plant has a long flowering season, with some forms in flower by late autumn, but most waiting until spring. These early forms will need a sunny well-drained site to induce short growth and regular flowers of purple through to pink.

The magnificent architectural leaves of *Arum pictum* make a real show in the garden in midwinter.

If the weather does become very cold with severe frosts many of these selections are able to withstand the onslaught, and even if some flowers are damaged, there will be others to take their place as soon as the temperature rises. One plant unaffected by the weather is *Iris foetidissima*, an evergreen species which is grown not for its flowers but the large orange seeds which hang exposed in the seedpods for months. The flower stem is dead but the seeds seem so tightly packed that they do not fall until spring. There are selections that are yellow, as well as a rare white form; all are surrounded by thick sword-like evergreen leaves. Before leaving this small bed the wintergreen leaves of the true *Arum pictum* are a worthy addition. This plant is not the rather fast spreading *Arum italicum* 'Pictum', but a seemingly tender species from the islands of the western Mediterranean. In fact it has survived temperatures as low as −8°C without any sign of damage. The leaves are a glossy dark green with silver veining with great substance.

The whole bed can be top dressed with a fine bark mulch, to provide a good contrast to flower and foliage and also prevent mud being splashed on this most select little grouping.

Now to the general garden and how early bulbs can transform borders that are usually dull with only the remains of last summer's foliage to be seen. Growing these early treasures ensures that you tidy up the borders in the autumn and give some thought to their planting. The bulbs need to be easily viewed and given suitable positions with regards to neighbouring plants which may

*Fritillaria meleagris* with *Cyclamen repandum*, both of which revel in light shade and will seed profusely.

provide shelter from the severest weather as well as creating a cameo planting. A good example of this being a group of snowdrops placed next to an evergreen fern and *Ophiopogon planiscapus* 'Nigrescens', with its tough, near-black, grass-like leaves.

## HERBACEOUS BORDERS

In winter these borders are usually empty of flower colour, but obviously full of plants and, more importantly, full of roots. Bulbs will be of secondary importance here and must not detract from the herbaceous display in high summer, but bays and corridors between plants can be taken up by different bulb plantings. Many bulbs thrive in these positions if selections are made from those that do not require a completely dry summer.

In the days when people could afford a jobbing gardener to do all the hands-on work, early bulbs were planted in autumn and lifted in late spring as soon as the flowers had faded and either stored till next season or replanted in a reserve bed to grow on as best they could. In most people's gardens today, bulbs are usually planted and left for many seasons, only lifted when they become congested or need attention. If your border includes a few shrubs then the areas around them make ideal islands

for planting bulbs, as disturbance will be limited. Similarly, plant bulbs next to perennials that are rarely split, like *Paeonia* and *Helleborus*. If possible, plant in groups or drifts as individual plants can create a 'spotty' picture. When planting, incorporate plenty of grit and insert the bulbs more deeply than usual so any surface cultivation will miss them. There is nothing more annoying than spiking a bulb as you weed a bed or make any other plantings. One unusual planting I have seen that worked well was in an open-plan front garden, where a simple rectangular bed of hybrid tea roses was underplanted with *Fritillaria meleagris*, which flowered and set seed long before the first rose appeared.

In late winter, when you can see the 'bare bones' of the garden, it is always a good time to asses the structure and it is then that the planting of those bulbs last summer and for many summers before, becomes very important. In late summer or early autumn, it is hard to find a space among the season's more rampant growth, and we tend to plant bulbs in any gaps there are, which may not always prove to be the best site some six months later. Shrubs and sturdy herbaceous plants have already been mentioned, but some individual perennials make good backdrops for early bulbs. The grass *Stipa tenuissima*, with

The soft blades of the grass *Stipa tenuissima* act as an ideal foil for the fresh flowers of *Galanthus* 'Atkinsii'.

its billowing seed heads and bleached leaves, blends well with strong snowdrops like *Galanthus* 'Atkinsii'. When tidying the garden in autumn do remember to leave the ornamental grasses until early spring for their annual cutback. The emerging leaves of fennel are dark and also display the glaucous leaves of snowdrops very well. Hellebores flower with the snowdrops and they make good companions, as long as last year's hellebore leaves have been cut off. Otherwise, on a windy day, these hard evergreen leaves with their serrated edges, might make short work of the emerging snowdrop buds.

Other small-scale planting combinations could include snowdrops with *Carex oshimensis* 'Evergold' and any *Bergenia* cultivar that has beetroot-red leaves. The fertile fronds of *Onoclea sensibilis* stand 30cm (12in) or more high and remain when they have withered to become dark brown, fluted and twisted spires. The unusual fronds are highlighted against a planting of snowdrops, when otherwise they may have been overlooked against the brown earth. Above these plantings, the stems of a dogwood or willow, selected for the colour of their bark, will

The delicate pale flowers of *Corydalis cava albiflora* bring light to the shady spots that this plant prefers.

complete the picture, especially if they are pruned annually to keep the colourful bark at eye level.

The front of an herbaceous border is ideal for *Eranthis*, the easy *Crocus* species and hybrids and *Galanthus*, with the taller *Narcissus* and *Fritillaria* further back. Some bulbs can be invasive and generally *Muscari*, *Crocus tommasinianus*, *Ornithogalum umbellatum* and some *Allium*, like *A. triquetrum*, are best placed in a wilder setting. This is not to say that the sight of sheets of *C. tommasinianus* in late winter is not beautiful and a swathe of *Muscari* contained within a restricted bed is quite stunning; but you can have too much of a good thing. An effective contrast I saw in a Norfolk garden was *Magnolia stellata* underplanted with *Muscari neglectum* and as this was in an island bed, the *Muscari* had nowhere else to go. On the two occasions I saw this garden in spring, the two together looked very beautiful.

However, any diktat about rampant plants is always vulnerable to criticism as gardens vary so much in their soil structure and pH. These bulbs are not so keen on acid soils and in gardens like this will certainly not become weeds. In fact, if you look to the wild you will see that limestone areas are far richer in bulbous plants that those of acidic rock formation. Plantings will not thrive either in very exposed and windy spots, where the stems are constantly bent over in one direction by the prevailing wind, which is often accentuated by buildings or the contours of the garden.

## BEDDING WITH BULBS

This is an intensive form of gardening most usually associated with summer and parks, but not exclusively. After the riot of summer bedding, beds are often left fallow until next year, or planted with wallflowers or the inevitable winter-flowering pansy. In place of these standards, or incorporated with them, a planting of early bulbs can greatly enliven the scene. They can be planted in autumn with the bedding plants and removed with them in spring to make way for the tender plantings of summer. Here many genera are very useful planted as single colour blocks: *Crocus*; *Muscari*, like *M. armeniacum*; tulips; hyacinths; *Narcissus*, and the taller *Fritillaria imperialis* can be used very effectively.

As the seasons roll by it is inevitable that a few bulbs will be left behind to gradually spoil the effect in years to come. One way to avoid this problem would be to plant the bulbs in large plastic aquatic pond baskets which are then buried, making it an easier task to retrieve the bulbs in spring. It also helps the bulbs to continue growing if they are replanted into a reserve bed and left to die down naturally without damaging the roots. In summer the bulbs can be taken out of the basket and sorted ready for the next season. In a formal setting, a bedding of hyacinths is still a stunning sight in mid-spring, with upright ranks and blocks of strong colour. Planting is getting later; once late summer was the prescribed time, but now late autumn planting is shown to produce sturdier flower spikes at about the same time next spring.

## BULBS IN GRASS

Naturalizing bulbs in grass can be one of the most effective plantings, but does need to be carefully planned. Grass planted with bulbs has to be left well into summer before it can be cut, so the site needs to fit into a wilder part of the garden or under trees in some shade. Whatever bulbs are planted, they need at least six weeks of growing after the last flower has faded before the grass can be cut, so the leaves can build up the food supplies for next year. If seed is required then it will be necessary to wait a little longer before mowing as the seeds are not immune to damage from the mower blades. The seed can then be deliberately scattered before cutting the grass with the mower.

*Narcissus* and *Crocus* are the favourites for naturalizing in grass, increasing well and giving a great display year after year with very little effort on the part of the gardener. A group planting of a single colour is most effective with these larger bulbs but some smaller ones can be mixed to good effect. When the site is selected an assessment of the grass has to be made; if it is coarse then only large bulbs will succeed, but if it is thin or composed of fine grasses then a wider choice is available. In any case it is best to cut the grass before planting, to lessen any competition for the bulb in the first autumn of growing. Planting for most is best carried out in late summer or autumn, either using the standard circular bulb planter, or by slicing off the turf and planting in the usual way in the soil beneath. The turf is then replaced and firmed down with the foot to expel air and deter mice. Plant the bulbs deeply, at least three times their own depth. There are two exceptions to the autumn-planting rule; these are the two stalwarts of the early spring, snowdrops and *Eranthis*; both are best planted 'in the green', that is just after flowering.

A carpet of naturalized *Eranthis hyemalis* in light woodland at Anglesey Abbey, in Cambridgeshire

The unusual bicoloured *Muscari macrocarpum* looks well with the red of the *Tulipa montana* in a sunny raised bed.

Both *Galanthus* and *Eranthis* succeed very well under the canopy of deciduous trees, where the grass is sparse, because of poor light in summer and the associated drought. In late winter and early spring, these unpromising spots can be the highlight of the garden. At Anglesey Abbey in Cambridgeshire (a National Trust garden), there is a magnificent display of naturalized snowdrops, which are not the usual *Galanthus nivalis*, but rarities like *G. lagodechianus* and *G. reginae-olgae* ssp. *vernalis* which have proliferated on the banks of dried-up stew ponds, where the monks used to keep carp. This marvellous collection was originally found in and around a Victorian garden rubbish dump in the 1960s by the head gardener, Richard Ayres. Since then the collection has been sorted and named, but still the old Victorian site full of *Galanthus* and *Eranthis* is quite outstanding, with the tantalizing hope that more new cultivars may emerge.

Turning to other bulbs that succeed in grass, the large Dutch crocuses, which can look rather blowsy in the open garden, tend to loose their vigour in grass and seed around, gradually looking quite natural. Other commonly and cheaply available crocus, like the selected forms of *C. chrysanthus* × *C. biflorus* and *C. sieberi*, do very well in short turf, as do seeding *C. tommasinianus*. However, they can be a little lost in grass but once in the garden seem to go where they will. The selections *C. t.* 'Ruby Giant' and 'Whitewell Purple' have stronger colours which stand out well in any planting. The beautiful snake's head fritillary, *Fritillaria meleagris*, is native to damp meadows, but in cultivation, is surprisingly tolerant of drier conditions and will grow well in any area of grass that is not too dry in summer. They are amongst the most attractive of fritillaries, with bell-shaped flowers that have a variable background of purple or white, overlaid with a dark chequering, and which hang modestly over a slender stem. They are not brightly coloured but nevertheless can look stunning on a breezy day in early spring. Let them set seed, then shake the seed head around the parent and be patient. Alternatively, sow the seed in pots (see Chapter 6 on propagation) and add to the colony in three years time.

The choice of *Narcissus* is vast, so it is best to select from those that do well in your local area and order accordingly. Species *Narcissus* look very effective in many notable gardens like Wisley and Savill Gardens, but I doubt many ordinary gardens have Wisley's damp sloping meadow, that suits *N. bulbocodium* so well, or a large wild area that can accommodate *N. cyclamineus*. This last species is an aristocrat among daffodils, but it demands an acid soil to do well. However *N. cyclamineus* hybrids have mostly lost this intolerance to lime, at the same time gaining some extra height. And don't forget, these plantings in grass need not be exclusively bulbous, plants like primrose and sweet violet will happily grow in grass as long as it is not cut too short and they can add interest without competing with the bulbs.

## RAISED BEDS

As soon as you raise the soil 20cm (8in) or more above the surrounding land, a greater variety of bulbs can be grown because of the improved drainage. If the garden area is formal then the walls of your raised bed can be built of bricks or blocks to match the surroundings, but if the position is more informal then treated timber, such as old railway sleepers, is appropriate. If you use treated timber, it will give you added peace of mind to line the inside with a plastic membrane, just in case creosote is still seeping from the wood.

Once the supporting edges have been built, spread a good layer of hard core at the bottom and in fill the gaps with gravel. If possible, cover the stone with a single layer of turf, roots uppermost, this will prevent the drainage becoming blocked for some time. Next, an equal mix of loam and coarse grit to which some fertilizer like bone meal has been added, will provide a good home for many bulbs. Top dress with grit to a depth of about 5mm (¼in); this will help prevent rain splashes on the plants and help stop the soil drying out in times of drought. The plantings need not be exclusively bulbs, but any additions need to be chosen carefully to avoid those plants that spread too freely or seed profusely. Small shrubs like *Daphne oleoides* and *D. collina* will remain in scale and if in semi-shade, the small willows like *Salix* 'Boydii' and *S. lanata* remain compact for many years. Alpines like *Pulsatilla*, *Hacquetia* and *Hepatica* are plants with little tendency to spread and can help bring an early raised bed to life. Evergreens are harder to chose as most 'dwarf' conifers are only dwarf if compared with the American *Sequoia* and soon are in need of moving.

However *Ilex aquifolium* 'Hascombensis' and some *Cryptomeria*, like *C. japonica* 'Tenzan-sugi', do remain quite small for many years. The temptation to plant low, carpeting alpines like thymes has one drawback – the mat of wiry stems is a haven for small slugs throughout the year. They do not seem to damage the thyme, but prefer the fresh foliage of your bulbs.

The site of your raised bed will, to some extent, dictate the planting. For instance, in full sun a good selection of Mediterranean bulbs will think they are at home and grow well. *Crocus* immediately spring to mind with species like *C. corsicus*, *C. etruscus*, *C. sieberi* in all its forms, *C. imperati*, *C. korolkowii*, *C. minimus* and *C. × luteus* 'Stellaris' (an old sterile clone) being ideal choices. None of these are hard to grow and in this sunny bed will thrive with little attention and give years of pleasure. They are not always available from every garden supplier but all good bulb merchants can supply them. So far the genus *Iris* has been barely mentioned but one or two of them will look perfect in this bed. *I. histrioides* 'Major' and *I.* 'Katharine Hodgkin' will flower very early in the year, closely followed by the forms of *I. reticulata*, like 'J.S. Dijt', 'Harmony' and 'Cantab'. The leaves follow, as the flowers are fading, stiff and not unattractive for a few weeks. Miniature *Narcissus* will do well as long as the

*Narcissus* 'Gipsy Queen' is a delicate-looking hybrid that is ideal for a rock garden.

drainage is not too fierce and the species *N. minor*, *N. asturiensis* and *N. bulbocodium* will settle down. The choice of hybrid *Narcissus* under 30cm (12in) is less daunting than for the larger brethren. Look out for 'Gipsy Queen', 'Little Beauty', 'Hawera' and 'Minnow', all of whom will add a touch of spring, and as raised up in the bed, will be closer to the eye.

*Corydalis* are in vogue at present, particularly the tuberous types. Many are rare and quite expensive but are proving to be excellent early flowers with intense colours and strong constitutions. For the raised bed, there are many E European and W Asian species that thrive in conditions with damp springs and dryish summers. Once established, they will self-seed and soon establish a colony. *Corydalis malkensis*, with its creamy white flowers and ferny foliage has taken over a 3m (10ft) square bed in my garden for early spring, after which it sets seed and by late spring has virtually disappeared, retiring below ground to the small tubers about the size of marbles. The seed only remains viable for a short period, which explains why this stunning little beauty is so rare. Other forms of *Corydalis*, such as *C. solida*, can unfortunately be

*Corydalis malkensis* is a marvellous colonizer for the garden in early spring.

rather drab, so look out for the named clones like 'George Baker' and 'Highland Mist' which are really vibrant selections. Quite often these clones are nurtured under cold glass, but when planted in the open their superior colour seems to have an even greater quality. If seed is collected and sown immediately it germinates next spring and by the following year will flower, one of the fastest of the 'bulb' world.

Most snowdrops would not do well in full sun and fast drainage but there are a few that do demand this treatment in order to flower well. *Galanthus gracilis*, with its twisted leaves, loves all the midwinter sun it can get – conditions it enjoys in its native habitat in Greece and the Balkans. *G. fosteri* from the E Mediterranean seems to enjoy sun and the extra drying that the close association of shrub roots provides. A site to the south west of a choice shrub would be ideal. If sufficient bulbs are available, it is always worth while experimenting with different growing conditions.

## ROCK GARDENS

The traditional rock garden is similar in many respects to the raised bed; in fact many raised beds are built primarily for alpines and are equally adaptable as homes for bulbs. The rock garden can provide some good sites for

*Cyclamen coum* is a very reliable species and provides vibrant colour early in the year.

bulbs but care has to be taken with the scale of the flower and more crucially the size of the leaves that follow. These can detract from the alpines that are generally planted in rock gardens and will disfigure them with decaying foliage. The larger *Narcissus* and *Iris* fall into this category and are best avoided, but the rock garden will have shadier aspects suiting small snowdrops like *Galanthus rizehensis* and *G. nivalis* selections. The small but very tough *Cyclamen coum* will revel in a little shade as would the even smaller *C. parviflorum*, provided the growing pocket can be kept moist the whole year. These smaller cyclamen do not present any problems with their decaying leaves as these shrivel in summer and rarely act as a wet blanket to adjacent plantings. Species crocus will do well but do not let *Crocus tommasinianus* in to this specialist area – it is an excellent early bulb, but for a wilder area of the garden.

*Corydalis solida* 'George Baker' brings a splash of red to a raised bed.

## A BULB FRAME

This method of growing bulbs is very simple, low in maintenance and effective. It is really a raised bed covered with glass, which is usually a permanent structure over the bulb-growing area. It can be arranged so that the glass is removable and does the job when needed, only to be taken away when protection is not required. The ability to remove the glass means the bed can be sited anywhere in the display garden. A permanent bulb frame is not particularly attractive and is better suited to a working area, where it can be positioned to get maximum light and with paving all round for easy access. The moveable bulb frame enables the grower to enjoy a few, very choice bulbs just where they want, but I would not recommend having too many areas like this in the garden, as they are labour intensive. An old Pluie frame could be used to protect the early scarlet *Anemone pavonina* and the white *Crocus hyemalis*, together with some autumn-flowering bulbs. If a temporary moveable cover is used do make sure it is windproof by fixing it securely.

The usual bulb frame provides an excellent method of growing bulbs and once established, maintenance is reduced to a minimum with just the occasional need for watering. Many frames are fitted on to rectangular beds built up to waist level, which is usually achieved with concrete blocks, bricks or railway sleepers, however they need only be 30cm (12in) high, just enough to give good drainage. The compost used is similar to the raised bed, but with one major difference. Once the planting height has been achieved, instead of planting directly into the soil mix, use is made of the plastic lattice baskets normally used for pond plants, which make perfect growing containers for the bulbs. The bulbs are planted in the standard frame mix (equal parts loam and coarse grit, with a little added bone meal or similar) in the baskets and planted into the frame, then the whole frame is top-dressed with 5–7mm (¼–⅓in) grit. These baskets give the roots a free run beyond the confines of the container and also make retrieval easy when the bulbs are dormant. It is well worth attaching a label to the rim of the lattice basket at planting. Aluminium labels are ideal for this.

Before choosing your plants, do consider the respective heights, planting the tallest in the middle. It is wise to exclude any that have rhizomes or increase by stolons. These plants will move out of their original basket and into the next and in the case of some tulips that have stolons, like *Tulipa saxatilis*, through the entire frame, necessitating a complete overhaul. It is also good practice

to collect the seed, as fallen seed soon mixes your stock and overcrowds the bed. Besides, the gathered seed can be sent to amateur seed exchanges or given to gardening friends. It also helps management if the planting is well mixed, making the identification of any plants that 'escape' that much easier.

The type of frame you choose depends on your budget. The simplest and often the best are Dutch lights on a frame or against a wall. They are quite large so a good method of anchorage is needed. Their size does give a useful growing area and the height can be arranged to accommodate any size of bulb foliage. There are popular aluminium frames, with sliding sides and top lights, which give excellent control; it is best to avoid hinged aluminium frames, as they are very susceptible to wind damage and do not allow side ventilation. During mid- and late spring the covers can be left off the frames to let any natural rainfall in, but in countries like Britain, which have regular summer rainfall, the covers need to be put in place, come early summer, to imitate a Mediterranean climate. However, during some more recent summers here in Britain, we have had very hot spells, during which it has been advisable to take the covers off, as the ripening process would be too severe and bulbs could become wizened. It is worth remembering that in the Mediterranean there are occasional thunderstorms and when we consider the rocky soils and the depths at which the bulbs grow in the wild, many are not quite as dry and baked as we originally might think.

Maintenance is needed when a group becomes con-

*Cyclamen cyprium* will sweetly scent a greenhouse or conservatory in late autumn or early winter.

gested, so in summer the basket can be found and emptied, with the best bulbs being replanted in fresh compost and returned to the frame. Only very rarely will you need to empty everything out and start again. Any necessity for this would be signalled by a gradual loss of vigour in the annual growth.

## BULBS IN POTS

This is a highly controlled method of gardening, which lets the grower really get to know the plant, with the regular attention to watering and inspection for pests and disease that is necessary. To succeed, the pots of bulbs will need sorting into groups with similar requirements. Factors to bear in mind would be; when to water, frost tolerance, soil type and sunny aspect or shady aspect. They will need a greenhouse, frame or at the very least a plunge bed to grow them well.

To begin with let us consider the pots; plastic or clay? Either is fine but when mixed together it can be difficult to get the watering right. If plastic pots are used, they obviously only allow water to pass in and out of the drainage holes. Clay, however, is porous and can remain quite moist, especially in winter and if in a damp plunge. Clay is heavier, more expensive and liable to break if frozen or dropped, whereas plastic, especially the square varieties make excellent use of valuable space. In spite of this I use clay, and probably aesthetics play a part here, but the ability to keep soil-living creatures like worms out is very useful. In clay pots a piece of zinc gauze or aluminium mesh cut and placed over the drainage hole before any compost is added will keep unwanted visitors out. This is not so easy to achieve with plastic as there are many drainage holes.

Having chosen the pots, the compost is usually similar to the sort used in a bulb frame. Many growers, however, either buy John Innes composts and add grit, or sterilize their own sieved loam and add grit and sphagnum peat or leaf mould. For the majority of bulbs, soil-based composts are best. They are more easily wetted after the dry period and retain plant food longer without the need to always use liquid feed. Most bulbs are potted in late summer, planting them twice their depth in the pot, covering with compost and finally topping with 5–7mm (¼–⅓in) grit to a depth of 1cm (⅜in). Most bulbs are not repotted every year, and indeed do not need it. Instead, when they are dormant the compost above the bulbs is removed, the bulbs inspected, fed with a feed like bone meal and restored to the pot with compost and

grit. While doing this, I always sit the bulbs on a layer of coarse sand, believing it aids drainage but the real help is in locating the bulbs while repotting, especially if there are small offsets or bulblets around the parent. For most bulbs it is quite sufficient to repot in alternate years and if you happen to find great deal of overcrowding it is an easy matter to repot instead of top dressing.

Most pot-grown bulbs will grow best in full light during winter and early spring. For those hardy bulbs, a cold greenhouse or frame is the best home, where at least there is protection from damaging winds and precipitation. In midwinter, although the sun is low in the sky, warmth will build up under glass, but after a sunny day the temperature drops and frost may penetrate the pots. It is good cultivation practice to try and lessen the range of temperature as much as possible, by plunging the pots up to their rims in a water-retentive medium like sand. This keeps the roots cool by day and less cold at night, which is as near as we can get to imitating the growing conditions in the wild.

Next comes the frost-free greenhouse, where the temperature should never fall below 1°C (34°F), and this can be achieved by the installation of an electric fan heater. It also helps in circulating the air; in cold weather the air is often very still and any movement will help to prevent fungal diseases developing. Many growers are installing this kind of minimal heating, even for hardy bulbs, as a precaution against any damage.

Then comes the cool greenhouse, where the temperature minimum is set at 5°C (41°F). This is the traditional

*Fritillaria pudica* 'Richard Britten' is a vigorous selection that first came to attention in the 1950s.

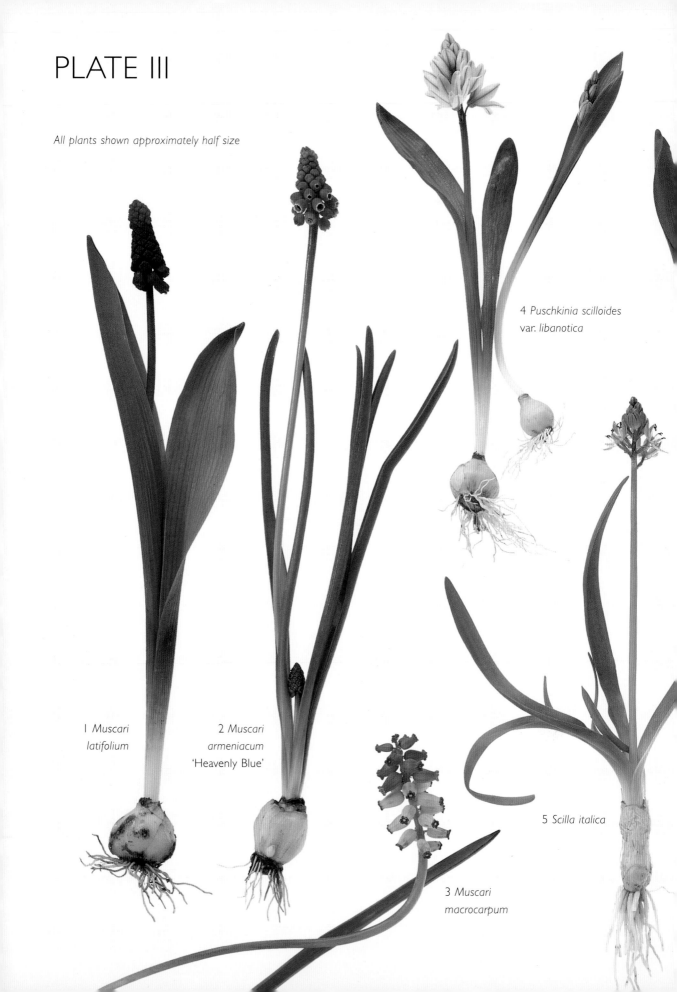

# PLATE III

*All plants shown approximately half size*

4 *Puschkinia scilloides*
var. *libanotica*

1 *Muscari*
*latifolium*

2 *Muscari*
*armeniacum*
'Heavenly Blue'

5 *Scilla italica*

3 *Muscari*
*macrocarpum*

6 *Chionodoxa forbesi* 'Pink
Giant'

8 *Tulipa kurdica*

9 *Tulipa saxatilis*

10 *Tulipa montana*

7 *Tulipa neustreuvae*

next step in greenhouse cultivation and enables a very large range of bulbs to be grown. It would be interesting to see whether, now that thermostats are so sensitive, many of the plants which we traditionally grew at 5°C (41°F) would grow just as well if the temperature never went below 1°C (34°F). The saving in fuel bills would be quite significant. Bulbous plants from South Africa, South America and Australia give tremendous colour in these cool greenhouses.

Within each kind of greenhouse there will be types of plants flowering nearly all the year, so the grower has to work out how best to deal with their requirements. For our purposes the winter bulbs need to be in prime positions for both light and viewing. They will need regular watering which increases in frequency as spring

advances. The amount and length of the foliage is a good guide to how liberal you need to be with the water; the more abundant and longer the leaves, the more water they will need. *Narcissus*, in a good free-draining compost, requires very regular floods to imitate the melting snow of the wild. With all the pots, it is helpful to give a dilute liquid feed on alternate waterings.

## BULBS IN BOWLS

Specially prepared bulbs of hyacinths, daffodils and a few other species are grown for indoor display during winter. The popular hyacinth bulbs will be of flowering size, bought early in the autumn and then planted in bulb fibre within a bowl or pot. Once watered they need to be placed in a cool dark place for two to three months, where the roots must develop or the eventual flower will abort or be malformed. After this period they need full light, in a cool room at about 10°C (50°F), until the

The nickname of *Oxalis versicolor*, candy cane, aptly describes the appearance of the half-opened flowers.

flower colour begins to show after which they can be place in their chosen site in the home for flowering. It is very important to buy your bulbs as soon as they come into the nursery as the producer has cooled them to induce early flowering and a dry, hot wait in a box full of shavings is going to undo all that preparation. Another, rather novel method of growing hyacinths is in special glass or plastic, shaped vases, known as hyacinth vases. This is nothing new, but it is still fascinating to see the large amount of root produced before the leaves begin to grow and it's an ideal way to help young children learn about plants, and bulbs in particular.

The *Narcissus* generally used in forcing, like *N.* 'Soleil d'Or' and *N.* 'Paper White' are not so susceptible to temperature changes prior to planting and will grow very quickly and flower within six weeks. They do grow somewhat laxly and need staking to look attractive. When hyacinths have finished flowering they can be planted out to flower in subsequent years in a sunny border. If the weather is very severe keep them in a greenhouse until they die down and then they can be planted out. In succeeding years, the flowers will be fewer and more widely spaced and look less formal.

The large-flowered *Hippeastrum pratense* hybrids (generally known as amaryllis) are often sold in a box, complete with pot and compost. They do require a constricted root run to flower well, so do not be surprised by the relatively small pot. They will flower at any time of the year but fit best into a cycle starting with repotting or potting (if newly acquired) in late autumn and then being kept moist and warm (16°C (61°F) or more) but in not too dry an atmosphere. They can flower within six to eight weeks, after which they need frost-free conditions and feeding with a liquid tomato fertilizer until the some of the leaves begin to turn yellow. This is usually in late summer and for the next two months the bulbs can be given a cool, but still moist rest, until late autumn when the cycle starts again. This treatment is a convenient growing regime for nurseries and growers but is not really necessary, as in the wild the plants have no dry rest period. The one advantage to the grower is the freshness of the foliage, which starts into growth just after the flower bud and then matures after the flowers have finished. The leaves are the equivalent of caviar to slugs, so do protect them if plunged outdoors during summer. There is are new, more dwarf selections available, which would suit the smaller windowsill, as a well grown *H. pratense* hybrid can be 60cm (24in) plus tall, with leaves

that spread even further. These new, smaller varieties are hybrids of *H. gracilis* and come in a range of colours, from white through to red, and have a greater number of smaller flowers to a stem.

## CUT FLOWERS

If you are a flower arranger then bulbs are a favourite source of material, with almost anything available at any time of the year from the florist. But if you look in the garden in the early part of the year, it still can provide plenty of material for arrangements. Cut flowers can be gleaned from *Crocus, Cyclamen, Hyacinthus, Muscari, Narcissus* and *Scilla*, but to last longer in water the stems will need conditioning first. The flower stems need to be cut at an angle, to expose the inner tissue, so water can be drawn up more efficiently. The stems need immersing in shallow tepid water for a few hours in a dark room – the arrangement, with flower preservative added to the water, will then be longer lasting.

## A TUSSIE-MUSSIE

Some of the inspirational gardeners of modern times have resurrected this archaic fifteenth-century word, formerly meaning a posy or nose-gay, to become the name for a collection of cut flowers and foliage, simply arranged to lift the spirits in winter. Vita Sackville-West seems to have been the first gardening writer to mention a tussie-mussie, in the weekly articles she wrote for the *Observer* newspaper around the middle of the twentieth century. Others have followed, often making this a collection of flowers just for Christmas.

The tussie-mussie, or tuzzy-muzzy, can be quickly gathered, or if you wish to escape from the household chores, then a longer and more interesting search of the garden can be made to glean all the unexpected treasures from around the beds. I have been gathering a winter tussie-mussie for over ten years, always finding over twenty flowers and in 1988 managing forty-two. Bulbs always add variety to the bowl and usually include the snowdrops, crocus and cyclamen mentioned earlier, plus early flowering *Narcissus bulbocodium* and *N. cantabricus*. If the season has been kind, then *Sternbergia lutea* can still be found, as well as the last flower spikes on *Allium callimischon*, the little delicate Greek onion.

This collection of winter colour can be set in a shallow bowl and kept in a cool place until needed. It is not long lasting, but is not intended to be, it is just a special gathering for a special day.

# 6 Propagation

Most gardeners use some method or another to increase their plants – the cost of buying new plants, bulbs and seeds every time that you want to improve or expand your display, is enough to encourage anyone to brush up on their propagation techniques. With any luck, you will also be left with enough spare plants to give away to friends and relatives.

With bulbous plants, you have a wide choice of methods, depending how many you want and whether you want an exact clone or something similar. Producing bulbs from seed is very rewarding but is not an option if you wish to propagate a hybrid, as the resulting progeny will all vary to some degree. However if you want to increase a species, sowing seed is a very effective if somewhat slow method. Here, we'll look at the best ways of propagating bulbs for the amateur gardener.

## PROPAGATING WITH SEED

Most bulbous plants will set seed and pollination is usually by insects. The seed cases will, according to their natural method of seed dispersal, vary greatly in position and structure. Once seed has been set the method of dispersal varies according to natural habitat. Evolution has diversified the way species, even within a genus, attract insects. Dispersal is often down to the wind or insects. Many bulbous plants, by their very design, have evolved to cope with a dry period each year. During this dry and often warm season, the seeds are dispersed, sometimes as light single seeds, or as large wind–catching seed capsules and occasionally by the aerial parts of the plant being rolled around by the wind. Fritillaries and lilies have seed capsules held aloft on stiff dry stems, which shake in the breeze and so disperse the seed. This is easily collected by shaking the seed head into a paper bag (but not plastic as any dampness may cause rotting).

Ants are the unwitting distributors of many seeds, attracted by their fleshy coating. Such seed capsules are, as you would guess, found close to the ground, or when ripe collapse on to the soil surface. Genera that have this method of dispersal include *Crocus, Cyclamen, Puschkinia* and some *Iris*. The gardener has to search around the base of the plant in order to find the capsule, and to get there before the worker ants do!

In general, it is best to sow seed as soon as it's ripe, so viability is not lost and germination is quick, giving the young plant the longest growing period possible before dormancy. For a few genera such as *Corydalis* and *Eranthis*, immediate sowing is essential to stand any chance of a good germination. However, if you cannot sow straight away, store the seed in the salad compartment of the refrigerator until ready to do so. Seed you purchase will either be hermetically sealed or have been stored at 5°C (41°F) with a relative humidity of fifteen per cent. If a modest amount of seed is sown, the standard 7cm (2¾in) pot is adequate for the purpose.

The compost is important, with a choice between soil- or peat-based. If conservation of peat is a concern, a soil-based compost should be used. There is the tried and tested John Innes seed compost, which is soil based and from a good source; the addition of a similar volume of coarse grit makes this an ideal base for your potting compost. Alternatively, you can use sieved sphagnum peat, mixed with an equal of amount of sharp sand to which you have added a proprietary base fertilizer.

Fill a clean pot with compost, to within 1cm (⅜in) of the top, and level gently. Never press too hard or the compost will become compacted and lose aeration, a vital ingredient. Sow the seed thinly and evenly over the surface and cover with sieved compost of approximately the depth of the seed. If the seed is large and flat, as in the case of *Fritillaria eduardii*, it is a good idea to use forceps or a pair of large tweezers to gently insert the seeds vertically into the seedbed. Fill the remainder of the pot with 5–7mm (¼–⅓in) grit and water well to settle the seeds in. The grit will also reduce the disturbance caused by heavy rain and lessen the annoying growth of liverwort and moss. Unfortunately, sharp grit doesn't seem to deter grazing by slugs and snails, and at night, with the dew to aid their slithering, they seem to get everywhere. Do remember to label the pots; here plastic is quite adequate, especially if pushed well down the side of the pot to lessen the chance of being broken.

The pots should then be moved to a cold frame or the north side of a greenhouse where the weather can induce germination. Temperature fluctuations are fine but prolonged rainfall is best deflected by closing the lights. Of course if the bulbs were from a warm temperate climate they need a frost-free home to ensure germination. Spring is the time of most germination but not exclusively, so regular inspection will be necessary throughout the year. It is always exciting to find the first thin seed leaf of the monocotyledon as it emerges through the grit. Once germinated the young plant needs some protection, so removal to a shaded position under glass is necessary. Here they will spend two growing seasons before being tipped out during the next period of dormancy.

It may have been three years before germination so the compost will be very low in nutrient, as most will have been leached out in the intervening time, making feeding necessary. A dilute liquid feed is ideal, used at half strength and given in place of a watering. The packets of feed have three numbers to show the ratio of the three main fertilizers – nitrogen, phosphate and potash (or NPK). For bulbs, a ratio of 12:10:27 or similar is ideal; the extra potash will aid bulb growth. Some so-called 'tomato' fertilizers fit this category.

An attractive selection of *Crocus vernus* from the Tatra Mountains in Poland.

There are a few bulbs that can not be left until the second season, as they grow rapidly and to leave them would inhibit their growth badly. They can be identified by their large leaves and by any roots that extend well beyond their container. Pot on after one year, as you would after two years, into larger pots or a prepared bed outside. The positioning of the bed and placement of the pots will depend on the type of bulb; for example, *Galanthus* need some shade, whereas most fritillaries like a well-drained sunny position. Compost now needs to be soil based, so that any transition to the open garden is more easily achieved.

When the seeds and young bulbs are in pots it is essential to keep the earthworms out. Although they are vital in the garden, when they decide to live in a pot they will soon compact the soil until it becomes an impervious mud in which nothing can thrive. A piece of gauze placed over the drainage hole under the compost or a polythene membrane under any sand plunge reduces this problem considerably.

## SIMPLE DIVISION

Whether in the ground or in a pot, there will come a time when a group of bulbs becomes very congested, sometimes to the point where flowering ceases and you are only left with leaves every season. The simplest method to restore flowering is to lift the whole clump of bulbs and replant, thus extending your colony. In an ideal world this division in most species would be undertaken during the period of dormancy, but since the actual position of dormant bulbs is hard to pinpoint, the saying 'out of sight is out of mind' proves very true.

With pot culture it is an easy task to divide the congested bulbs during dormancy. The whole pot of compost can be knocked out and the largest bulbs repotted in fresh compost, with any excess bulbs being planted out or potted on as well. At this time it is interesting to note the different methods bulbs have evolved to reproduce. Some, like *Galanthus* and *Narcissus*, which are 'true' bulbs, have grown 'daughter' bulbs from the basal plate. As long as the young bulb has a piece of this basal plate attached, it can be snapped off and grown on. In some corms, like *Crocus*, there may be tiny cormlets produced, which can be removed and potted on as usual.

In the garden, it is possible to very carefully lift a group of bulbs just as they show leaf, usually in spring. Great care should be taken not to damage the roots as they do not re-grow when damaged. The bulbs should be gently

*Galanthus plicatus* ssp. *byzantinus* seedlings growing in a walled garden in Chelsworth, Suffolk.

teased apart and replanted immediately. The planting area needs forking over with some fertilizer and compost added. It is a good idea to look out for any larvae that eat roots and bulb tissue and to dispose of them. Even in spring, do water the newly planted bulbs well as it will settle the roots and soil back together, as well as help the foliage remain turgid.

*Galanthus* and *Eranthis* are treated a little differently. After flowering but before the leaves die down the groups are carefully lifted, so called 'in the green', separated and replanted normally. This method is far superior to planting dry bulbs in summer; these have a high mortality rate and may still be sourced from material collected in the wild. *Eranthis,* when lifted, may need to be snapped into usable pieces, making sure each has a growing point before replanting. This is a good time to assess the stock and if any disease or abnormal growth is noticed, discard it or better still, burn it.

Some plants are very slow to divide, so in order to get more plants the gardener has to be more direct in getting what he wants. In the genus *Fritillaria* some species have bulbs composed of two scales which naturally separate year by year, spawning new bulbs, only in some cases very slowly. In dormancy, the two sections can be snapped in two, dusted with a fungicide like flowers of sulphur and replanted normally. With luck you may have two flowering stems the following year. In a similar way, some tubers such as begonias can be cut into large pieces when dormant. Each piece with a growing point can be potted on. Again treat the damaged faces with a fungicide to lessen the chance of infection.

## ARTIFICIAL METHODS

There are occasions when natural reproduction is very slow or even non-existent. For example, if you have only one rare bulb it may need pollen from another to produce viable seed, or you may have a hybrid whose seed is useless if you want to produce an exact replica. To overcome these problems gardeners have tried many direct methods that are more akin to the laboratory than the potting shed. However, once the soil is washed off and a few simple items brought from the chemist and hobby shop you are ready to begin. You will need a craft knife and a bottle of a sterilizing fluid like Isopropanol, which you will probably have to obtain from a pharmacist. Lastly a cutting block is required; a surplus piece of kitchen work surface is adequate.

## Chipping bulbs

This technique and other similar methods are best undertaken in summer when dormancy has just begun and before any new root growth begins. Chipping is very useful for propagating *Narcissus* and similar bulbs. Clean off all the old roots and any loose scales, then with the knife blade just dipped in the sterilizing fluid cut off the top quarter of the bulb, so that the bulb has a flat top. Then cut downwards, dividing the bulb into segments (four, eight or sixteen), depending on the size of the bulb, and making sure there is a bit of basal plate on each segment. Wash or dust the cut surfaces with a fungicide and put the chips into a clean new polythene bag containing a mix of damp peat and perlite or vermiculite. Seal the bag, leaving as large an air space as possible under the tie and put in a dark place at about 20°C (68°F) for two to three months – an airing cupboard is ideal. Inspect the bag every so often and throw away any bulbs that show signs of mould. In early autumn the bag can be carefully emptied and the chips examined. Along the cut basal plate, there will be one or sometimes more, tiny bulblets. Do not detach these but pot the whole thing in well-drained compost and grow on in frost-free conditions for the first winter. After one growing season the bulbs can easily be separated from the old chip and treated as an ordinary bulbs. This method is very easy and there is a good increase in the stock.

## Scales

A common procedure for propagating lilies, this method will also work with any bulb that is composed of many scales, such as some fritillaries. This is best undertaken late in summer or even in early autumn as these forms of bulb seem to start growth later in the year.

These bulbs are made of concentric rings of scales, all attached to the basal plate. On lifting the bulb a few of the scales can be snapped off, making sure that a vestige of the basal plate is still attached. The parent bulb should be replanted immediately and if only a few scales have been removed, this bulb may well flower as usual next year. If a large number of new plants are required then the whole bulb can be stripped and used for propagation. Check that all the scales are firm and without disease before coating them with a fungicide and putting them in a clean new polythene bag with damp peat and perlite or vermiculite. As before, the bag needs a temperature of 20°C (68°F) and leaving for two to three months in a dark place. After this time, remove the bag

*Hyacinthus orientalis* 'Blue Orchid' shows the less crowded flower spikes indicative of outdoor cultivation.

and put it in the salad box of the refrigerator for a further two months. At the end of this time, bulblets will have formed along the top of the basal plate at the base of the scale. Pot on into a free-draining compost with the tops of the scales just showing above the compost and keep frost free for the first growing season. After this time, the bulblets can be removed from the old scales and potted up as young bulbs.

## Twin-scaling

This is a very useful and productive way to reproduce *Galanthus*, *Hyacinthus* and *Narcissus*. Sterile conditions are essential or all your efforts will be in vain, which is usually very annoying as the bulbs you cut are bound to be either rare or expensive or both! This task is best carried out in late spring and early summer.

As in chipping, the bulb is cleaned and the top quarter cut off. Cut downwards through the bulb making segments like an orange and making sure each piece has a piece of basal plate attached, up to sixteen segments are usually possible. Next is the tricky bit; ease back the two outer scales and with the tip of the knife cut downwards

through the basal plate. This will give one twin scale from the outside and a smaller, but equally productive piece, from the inside. Treat in the usual way with fungicide and put in a clean new polythene bag with vermiculite. It is important that the vermiculite is barely moist, so to every 300ml (11fl oz) of vermiculite add 25ml (1fl oz) of de-ionized water. A bag 22 × 18cm (8¾ × 7in) will take the 300ml (11fl oz) of vermiculite easily and leave room for an air space beneath the tie.

After sealing, store the bag for up to three months at 20°C (68°F). On inspection, you may find that up to three bulblets have formed on each basal plate. Do not disturb the union and pot on into a well-drained compost placing them in a frame or greenhouse for the first growing season. After this season they can be separated from any old scale residue and treated as normal bulbs.

### Cutting and scooping

Large bulbs such as *Hyacinthus* and *Fritillaria imperialis* and *F. eduardii* have large basal plates, which can be cut to induce the formation of bulblets. Make a 5mm (¼in) deep cut in the basal plate. If the bulb is large enough a cross can be incised. Place the bulb in a clean new polythene bag with sterile compost and leave for up to three months at 20°C (68°F); when you look in the bag then, there should be many bulblets formed along the damaged basal plate. Take the bulb and plant upside down in a well-drained compost and keep in a frame or greenhouse until late summer when the bulblets can be separated and potted up on their own.

In a similar way, hyacinths can have their basal plate scooped out, leaving a depression, which must be dusted with a fungicide. Place each bulb upside down in a tray of moist sand or similar and place in warm dark conditions. Eventually numerous small bulblets known as spawn will form all over the wound, they can be separated from the mother bulb and potted up.

### Stem cuttings

A few tuberous plants can forced into making early growth that can be taken as cuttings without affecting the later flowering potential of the parent plant. This method is often used to produce new tuberous begonias, but it is also useful for propagating tuberous and rhizomatous *Ranunculus* and anemones. Small pieces of tuber or rhizome can be cut off in late winter and potted into pots or trays of propagating compost (50:50 sharp sand and peat or perlite). They should be watered and kept at about 16°C (61°F). In early spring the rooted pieces can be potted on and in a few weeks they can be planted out, once they have new leaves and a good root system. This is a surer method than simply snapping off pieces of tuber or rhizome and planting them straight back in the garden – such a small plant might easily be overlooked as spring unfolds.

*Fritillaria imperialis* 'Rubra', the red crown imperial, is a good bulb to provide height in an early border.

The yellow European wood anemone, *Anemone ranunculoides*, is just as much at home in the garden.

# PLATE IV

*All plants shown approximately actual size*

1 *Fritillaria elwesii*

2 *Fritillaria davisii*

3 *Fritillaria conica*

4 *Erythronium citrinum*

5 *Fritillaria carica*
(reflexed form)

6 *Fritillaria hermonis* ssp.
*amana*

7 *Fritillaria melaegris*

# 7 Pests and Diseases

It is always rather dispiriting to come to this section in a gardening book and it would be nice to think that early bulbs were in some way, perhaps because of the season, immune from attack. Unfortunately they are not, but some simple cultivation techniques and correct planting can at least help lessen the problems.

As gardeners we inadvertently invite hordes of invertebrates into our gardens by planting a huge range of flora and by exposing the soil to egg-laying creatures. You only have to compare the nearest 'wild' area with your garden to find that most of the native plants are unaffected by aphids and remarkably untouched by molluscs. But of course in the wild, only the toughest have survived – not a situation we allow in our gardens. Here, we go to great lengths to ensure the rarest and most capricious plants will survive. We would probably find that the common plants are easier to cultivate precisely because they are able to grow through many attacks and still thrive.

The old maxim 'prevention is better than cure' is very apt in gardening. Good drainage is beneficial, as is the movement of air through the foliage, especially through bulb frames and greenhouses when the weather is foggy. In these circumstances keep the air stirred by running a fan without the heating element. However, do not site it too close to a vent or it may draw in the very moisture you do not want. The slugs and snails that inhabit our gardens feed mostly at night and hide in cool dark crevices during the day. Eliminate as many potential hiding places as possible, and check plunge areas and pots, for instance, occasionally during winter and remove any hibernating villains. During the summer after dusk, and especially after rain, the offending molluscs always come out of hiding and can be collected for disposal. One famous Victorian lady gardener was renowned for her deft use of a hat pin, but today the more squeamish may prefer to drop them in a polythene bag for disposal by the refuse collection service.

In spite of physical efforts there will be occasions when chemicals can be helpful in controlling both pests and diseases, especially in pots and frames. Small rodents can wreak havoc; mice and short-tailed voles can acquire quite a taste for bulbs. If you keep a cat this can help keep the population down, otherwise the back-breaking placing of traps is an effective method of control; if you place the trap inside a piece of pipe you can avoid trapping birds. Poison can be used but increasingly there are environmental concerns about the possible effect of this on other wildlife; the shrew is an ally in the garden, as in its incessant hunt for food it eats many slugs and other invertebrates. The grey squirrel, however, is sometimes a problem and being so much larger is harder to deter, so it may be that a covering of chicken wire is necessary to protect the bulbs. This can be incorporated beneath the top dressing so is won't be too unsightly.

## UNDERGROUND PESTS

Slugs and snails are undoubtedly the greatest general dangers to the young foliage and, more insidiously, to the bulbs underground. Slug baits can be used but they do not prevent the tough keel slug attacking the bulb under the surface, where sharp grit and good drainage are the best defence. Also unseen are the larvae of insects that feed on the bulbs before pupating. There are some well-known ones, like the caterpillars of the large and small narcissus fly, which enter the bulb from the tunnel left by the decaying foliage of summer. One simple control is removing the leaves when yellow and then raking over the soil to cover the possible entrances. Another subterranean pest is the swift moth caterpillar, which has been distributed by random egg laying throughout the garden. Some plants will survive but not bulbs that are eaten from the bottom up leaving little chance for regeneration. This larvae is whitish with a brown head. The adult moths are rather drab and pass unnoticed even if they rest near outdoor lights on an early summer evening.

All these pests can be alleviated to some degree by dusting the necks of the bulbs as they become dormant with a soil-pest killer. The names of the products available varies year by year as some are withdrawn and others take their place. It is really impossible to deal with a large collection in this way, so concentrate on the special bulbs you cherish most. Cyclamen are prone to attack by the vine weevil, both the adult and caterpillar. The adults' presence is seen by quite large bites taken out of the sides of the leaves. It is worth locating the culprit, probably after dark, as the female can lay up to a thousand eggs in

Miniature *Narcissus*, bringing colour to the greenhouse in the middle of winter.

a season. The small caterpillars, often many to a pot, are very destructive and eat away unseen until the plant collapses and it is too late. They seem to prefer peat-based composts, so there is another reason to keep to soil-based mixes. Wherever they are found, the whole pot needs to be carefully searched and the grubs destroyed. There are few insecticides available to the amateur that are effective against the vine weevil, however malathion used as a drench has had some controlling effect on the larvae.

## APHID ATTACKS

There are hosts of small sap-sucking invertebrates that when found in large numbers, may need controlling chemically. But if the numbers are small it is very worthwhile removing them by hand or tweezers. Aphids are the most infamous of this group and if left to multiply can distort growth and, rather as the mosquito spreads malaria, can transmit virus diseases from one plant to another. There are numerous methods of control from introducing predators to chemical sprays. If you try the predators it precludes the use of sprays and requires a fresh supply of aphids to keep the predators alive. However some chemicals are damaging to the foliage of emerging and even some developed leaves, so it is sensible to vary the chemicals used and use sparingly.

When the flowers have long finished it is easy to forget these early bulbs and leave them in inappropriate sites for the early summer. One of the worst is in airless warmth where the tiny red spider mite thrives, causing premature drying of the leaves. Spraying with water helps to keep the pest away and it best to site the pots in an airy place and keep side lights open on frames and greenhouses so the environment hinders its multiplication.

The possible diseases of bulbs are legion but luckily most pass the garden by or more likely only attack weak or badly grown plants. This includes plants that have been over-fertilized and have grown out of character, being far too lush and so proving susceptible to fungal attack. Good cultivation again is essential to lessen these problems, but a few diseases still manage to damage early bulbs. Vigilance is the best defence, so at the first sign of the problem the leaf or bulb can be isolated from the rest. Botrytis, often specific to a family of plants, can be fatal. *Botrytis galanthina*, for instance, has been known to damage snowdrop collections for over a century. A spray of systemic fungicide can halt the spread but infected bulbs are best destroyed and the site not used for bulbs for some time. If any leaf looks out of character, then it is essential the whole plant is lifted and checked and unless the damage can be traced to some obvious problem like drought, then the plant needs isolating at the very least and most probably destroying. It may be a virus disease which is incurable, so it is better to be cautious and start again. Seed-grown stock at least starts life free of disease but when dry bulbs are acquired or repotted they need a close inspection for any marks, odd colours or softness that could spell ·trouble later; if you have any doubts it is best to discard them there and then. If you need further information then consult one of the many books available or, in Britain, contact the RHS at Wisley about their advice service.

# Part Three A Choice of Plants

# 8 A–Z of Early Bulbs

Since early bulbs are generally grown for their flowers, the heights given here refer to the size of the plant when in bloom, rather than any subsequent height the foliage may reach. You will find information on the height the plants can reach in either the introduction to the genus or at the end of each plant entry.

The Award of Garden Merit (AGM) is given by the Royal Horticultural Society (RHS) to the most outstanding plants for garden decoration, grown both in the open and under glass. In this section, those plants are indicated with the symbol ♔

## AMANA

### Liliaceae

This small genus is closely related to *Tulipa* and found only in Japan, Korea and China; tulips are found no fur-

(Above) A close up of *Anemone apennina*.

(Pages 56–57) A combination of *Narcissus pseudonarcissus* ssp. *moschatus*, *Muscari azureum* and *Chionodoxa sardensis*.

ther east than Kashmir in the W Himalayas. The differences between the two genera are quite small, but most obvious are the two small leaves (linear bracts, in fact) held on the stem just below the flower. These plants grow at quite a low altitude along river valleys but appear to be quite hardy. As they are small, less than 10cm (4in) tall, they are best grown in pots in a cold greenhouse or on a sunny raised bed where they can be best appreciated.

### A. edulis

This is the most common *Amana* found in cultivation, with star-shaped flowers, about 3cm (1¼in) in diameter, formed by white petals with yellow centres, that appear in early spring. When in bud the segments exhibit white edges and a reddish veined centre. The leaves are dark green with a pronounced channel and pointed apex.

### A. graminifolia

Similar to *A. edulis* in many ways, this species is the earlier flowering, appearing in midwinter. The flowers have a darker shading to the outside of the segments and the leaves are of unequal width.

### A. latifolia

Flowering early, in late winter and early spring, this species has segments that are purple on the outside. The flowers are 3cm (1¼in) in diameter. The broader leaves have a silver line along the centre. A Japanese species, it is found in sunny woodland glades.

## ANEMONE

### Ranunculaceae

Anemones can provide the garden with a huge range of colour very early in the year, for very little effort, once they've been planted. Not that gardeners are lazy, but many of the tuberous and rhizomatous anemones have the advantage of being good colonizers, seeding and spreading very freely. Also known as windflowers, some species of *Anemone* look like exotic daisies and the best come from the temperate regions of the Northern Hemisphere. The tuberous species generally come from climates with a dry summer and winter rainfall and so need well-drained positions in full sun. The further east their native home, the drier they need to be kept during summer; the Middle Eastern species are best grown in bulb frames or in pots in a cold greenhouse.

*Anemone apennina* 'Petrovac' is a good, deep blue selection from the Balkans.

The rhizomatous plants are frequently woodlanders, native to Europe, and are very tolerant of damp, semi-shaded conditions. Most anemones are easily grown from seed, especially if it is sown as soon as it's ripe. In general, the seedlings of plants belonging to the Ranunculaceae family, like anemones, dislike being pricked out while in growth. Leave them until early spring the following year when there is a better chance of success.

### *A. apennina* ♛ (see picture also p.23)

A woodland species from S Europe which is quite happy in the open garden in full sun or semi-shade. The flowers are 3cm (1¼in) in diameter and made up of between ten to eighteen petals. They are found in every shade from dark blue to white, even with some rare double forms, which have a pinkish tinge. This anemone will colonize widely and is usually flowering just after *A. blanda*, in early spring. The rhizome is a solid, nearly black cylinder with projections that can be snapped off for propagation. This is not for the faint-hearted, however, as these rhizomes are very tough and it is hard to tell the top from the bottom! Height: 15cm (6in).

### *A. biflora*

An attractive species with flowers that are globose and which never fully open; the segments are red or a bronzy yellow and are some 2–4cm (¾–1½in) across. The leaves are made up of three stalked lobes, which are in turn deeply divided. A native of Iran, Afghanistan and Kashmir, where it grows on sunny stony hillsides, it needs a dry rest and so should be grown under cold glass. Height: 10cm (4in).

### *A. blanda* ♛ (see picture p.60)

This marvellous early 'bulb' sometimes flowers as early as midwinter, but usually waits until early spring. It is actually a tuber found wild in shady places in the Balkans and Turkey. In the garden, *A. blanda* will self-sow, forming truly eye-catching drifts of flowers in spring. The flat daisy-like flowers open in the sun and can be up to 5cm (2in) in diameter. They come in many shades of blue, purple, pink and white, many of which have been selected and named. Many gardeners keep the different colours apart, which is worth considering before you plant, as once a mixed planting has settled in, it is impossible to separate any of the muted and dull-coloured seedlings that soon appear. The leaves are finely divided into three leaflets. Height: 10cm (4in).

*Anemone blanda* is a superb colonizer, bringing a bright patch of purply blue to gardens in late winter.

Some of the named forms (see pictures plate V) are: 'Atrocaerulea', with deep blue flowers; 'Charmer', a smaller pink form; 'Ingramii' ♀, which has the darkest blue flowers; 'Radar' ♀, with very strong magenta flowers with a white centre – it needs careful placing, it does not seem as strong as other varieties; 'Scythinica', a very beautiful variety from N Turkey with blue on the outside of the petals but opening to reveal white inner surfaces, and 'White Splendour' ♀, with large white flowers that are slightly flushed with pink on the outside.

### A. caucasica

A smaller version of *A. blanda*, this species has blue flow-ers, only 2cm (¾in) across. It needs a trough or raised bed to be appreciated and does not seed as freely. It grows in rocky meadows up to 2000m (6560ft) in the Caucasus and adjacent countries. Height: 3cm (1¼in).

### A. coronaria

This Mediterranean species has been crossed with other anemones, like *A. pavonina*, *A. hortensis* and *A. × fulgens*, to create the many florists' anemones available today. The species has flowers in various colours; red, crimson, blue, mauve and white. Some forms can begin to flower in mid-autumn, but most wait until the spring, needing a hot sunny spot to do well. The flowers, which are 3–6cm (1¼–2½in) across, are made up of between five and eight segments, which almost overlap. The foliage is highly dis-sected, with the stem leaves sessile and jagged. These tubers are often used in repeat plantings to give a succession of colour. They are planted in mid-spring for flowering in early and late summer, in early summer for early autumn flowering and in mid-autumn for late winter or spring flowering. These plants need a well-drained spot in rich soil and the availability of cloches for the winter plantings, if the winter is severe. Often these plantings are discarded after flowering, but a few will survive to become perennial and make attractive additions to the garden. Height: 60cm (24in).

There are many forms available, including *A. c.* **De Caen Group**, a selection of single flowers of mixed colour, and *A. c.* **Saint Brigid Group**, a semi-double selection from the Victorian era with three rows of segments in several colours. Individual forms that have been named include *A. c.* **De Caen Group 'Hollandia'**, a double scarlet with a white base and black centre and, in contrast, **'The Bride'**, a single pure white form.

### *A. flaccida*

This rhizomatous plant from E Asia starts to grow quite early in the year. The spring flowers are creamy white, usually with five petals and up to 3cm (1¼in) across. The leaves are dark green marked with white and almost succulent. It is very susceptible to spring droughts and does need a moist situation to do well. After the flowers have finished the foliage continues to lengthen, up to 30cm (12in). Height: 10–15cm (4–6in).

### *A. × fulgens*

This hybrid of *A. coronaria* and *A. hortensis* from S France has narrower petals than those of *A. coronaria*; the flowers are a bright scarlet and up to 5cm (2in) across. They appear in early spring. Like most of these plants from the Mediterranean, they need a warm sunny situation. Height: 20cm (8in).

The form **'Annulata Grandiflora'** has red flowers with a yellow centre. In **'Multipetala'** the flowers have become semi-double.

### *A. hortensis*

Smaller than most of the tuberous anemones, this species has pale starry flowers, 3–4cm (1¼–1½in) across, with narrow pointed segments of pink or mauve and with a darker centre. They bloom in early spring. It is found wild from S France to the Balkans. Height: 30cm (12in).

The flower of **ssp. *heldreichii*** are pale pink or white and held above indented but quite entire foliage. Native to Crete, this diminutive but attractive plant reaches a height of 10cm (4in) and requires a bulb frame or pot culture under cold glass in Britain.

### *A. nemorosa* ♛

The wood anemone of Britain and Europe, its white, occasionally pink-flushed flowers are a beautiful sight in a springtime wood. In the garden they prefer semi-shade in humus-rich soil that does not dry out too much in summer. The thin rhizomes make a network of interlocking plants, colonizing large areas if the conditions are right. They are best moved when dormant, either in early spring or late summer, just as the leaves fade. The flowers are 2–3cm (¾–1¼in) across. Height: 10cm (4in).

Many selections of colour and size have been made over the years, often with flowers far larger than the species. James Allen of snowdrop fame also has a very good form of *A. nemorosa* named after him, **'Allenii'** ♛, with large lavender-blue flowers. Other notable selections include **'Bowles' Purple'**, with dark leaves and soft violet flowers, and **'Vestal'** ♛, pure white with a ruff of button-like segments in the centre. There are many 'blue' selections that do not quite deserve that name, but are attractive nevertheless. Two white selections worth looking out for are **'Leeds' Variety'** ♛ (see plate II, 8) and **'Grandiflora'**. **'Bracteata Pleniflora'** (see plate II, 5) is a historic form from the sixteenth century with a few green petals among the white while **'Virescens'** has petals that have become green bracts like a frilled ruff.

A beautiful form of *Anemone pavonina* with delicate pink petals and a white centre.

# PLATE V
## *Anemone*

2 *Anemone blanda*
'Scythinica'

I *Anemone
blanda* 'Radar'

3 *Anemone blanda*
var. *rosea*

*All plants shown approximately actual size*

5 *Anemone blanda*
'White Splendour'

4 *Anemone blanda*
'Atrocaerulea'

The bright red flowers of *Anemone pavonina* make a stunning show on a sunny day.

## A. pavonina (see picture also p.61)

This is the anemone with the 'peacock eye', as the quite large flowers have a yellow or white centre. It has between seven and twelve, broad overlapping petals of scarlet, purple or pink. The flowers are 7.5cm (3in) across and appear in spring. This species is also distinguished by the entire sessile leaves on the stem, which are hardly toothed. This can be an eye-catching plant in a sunny border and it is long lived and flowers regularly. Height: 30cm (12in).

## A. petiolulosa

The yellow flowers, 2–4cm (¾–1½in) across, are often backed with red and appear in late winter, above ferny looking foliage. A hardy tuberous species from Central Asia, it requires a dry summer rest. Height: 10cm (4in).

## A. ranunculoides ♛ (see pictures p.51 and plate II, 3)

Like a yellow-flowered *A. nemorosa*, this species has flowers 1.5–2cm (½–¾in) in diameter with five to eight petals that appear in early spring. A woodland species found in the wild from Spain, through Central Europe to Siberia in the east. Height: 10cm (4in).

The form most usually found is **ssp. ranunculoides**, which can reach a height of 25cm (10in), whereas **ssp. wockeana** is shorter and has a bronzy green colour to the leaves, which fades with maturity. There is a very neat double form of the species available, **'Pleniflora'**, with two to three times the usual number of petals, but normal stamens. It is a very satisfactory little plant for brightening a dull corner.

## A. × seemanii (see picture plate II, 1)

This hybrid between *A. nemorosa* and *A. ranunculoides* is sometimes found with the name *A. × lipsiensis*, but whatever the name, they all have pale yellow flowers of great charm and vigour. Up to 3cm (1¼in) in diameter, the flowers bloom in early spring. These hybrids are becoming more widely available and are often listed in specialist catalogues. Height: 10cm (4in).

### A. trifolia

Another woodland rhizomatous anemone, with very attractive and quite large trifoliate leaves, this is found wild from Portugal to Yugoslavia in scrub and woodland. The white flowers, 3cm (1¼in) across, stand out well above the dark foliage when they bloom in early spring. Height: 15cm (6in).

The flowers of **ssp.** *trifolia* can be white or blue but always have blue anthers, whereas the flowers of **ssp.** *albida*, from the Iberian Peninsula, are similar but with white anthers.

## ARISAEMA

### Araceae

Grown for their large hooded spathes, imposing leaves and interestingly marked leaf stalks, most *Arisaema* flower in summer but there are a few that emerge in early spring to provide a very different and quite bizarre feature unlike any other early 'bulb'. The tubers these plants grow from have often been thought of as tender, but by planting them deeply, 15cm (6in), they seem unaffected by winter conditions. However, the emerging leaves can be damaged by a hard frost in early spring, so a sheltered site is called for and the protection of a little fleece on the coldest nights. The genus is found in the wild in part of the Northern Hemisphere.

### A. nepenthoides

The leaves and flower stem of this species emerge together, looking reptilian, a russet-brown with purple streaking and without a trace of green. When the two pedate leaves break free from the sheath, they are dark green with a silvery white central vein and composed of five leaflets which are glaucous beneath. The stalk continues to grow for 15cm (6in) and is topped by a spathe which is mottled greeny brown, striped white and hooded like a snake. This species is found in the wild in Nepal, Bhutan and SW China, above 2000m (6560ft). Height: 20cm (8in).

### A. ringens

This species has two leaves which are divided into three large glossy green leaflets up to 20cm (8in) long with thread-like tips. The stalk is quite short, to 30cm (12in), and is topped with a 5cm (2in) long spathe of purple or green, striped white. It will grow outside but does better in a frost-free greenhouse, as frost can damage the emerging plant. Height: 35cm (14in).

### A. serratum

From Japan where it is grows in mountain forests, this is a hardy species. The spathe is 8–12cm (3¼–4¾in) long and pale green to dark purple or purple spotted and occasionally striped white. The two pedate leaves with five to eleven leaflets, are pale green and mottled with purple. Height: up to 1m (3ft).

### A. yamatense

This species has a green spathe that is yellow within and quite short. The two pedate leaves have seven to twelve leaflets with thread-like ends. It comes from Japan and is said to be hardy, but I have only been able to grow this under cold glass. Height: 40cm (16in).

## ARISARUM

### Araceae

Like *Arisaema*, the plants in this genus, with their attractively marked spathes and leaves, give us an interesting rather than beautiful feature in the garden early in the year. There are two species regularly grown in cultivation. They are tuberous and are native to the Mediterranean Basin, but from very different habitats.

### A. proboscideum

This species is nicknamed the mouse plant, because its spathe tapers to a long tail-like tip and so looks like a mouse diving for cover amongst the foliage. If the plant is left for many years this effect is lost in the tangle of stems, leaves and spathes, so regular division is necessary. There are masses of arrow-shaped dark green leaves, amongst which the browny purple spathes, some 2–3cm (¾–1¼in) long, are hidden – except, that is, for the long tails! This species is found in Italy and Spain growing where there is some shade. It is easily cultivated but grows best in humus-rich soil in a position with some shade. Height: 10cm (4in).

### A. vulgare

A widespread tuberous species growing in sunny places, in the Mediterranean, Canaries and Azores, it flowers throughout late autumn into spring and requires a sunny well-drained site, where it will send up the spathe in early spring. The leaves are arrow shaped and vary from plain green to some with silvery markings, up to 10cm (4in) high. The spathe, sometimes aptly called the friar's cowl, is striped green to silver-white, over a browny maroon; it is about 6cm (2½in) long. From this hood a purple spadix protrudes. Height: 15cm (6in).

## ASPHODELUS

### Asphodelaceae

A genus of rhizomatous perennials, just one of which is included here, because it flowers in winter. This plant has long, thong-like swollen rhizomes, which multiply and can form a tangled mass like a loose rope.

### A. acaulis

During winter, succulent linear leaves, up to 30cm (12in) in length, spread out to form a flat rosette. From the centre of this rosette, a succession of soft pink tubular flowers, about 4cm (1½in) long, emerge in late winter through to spring. Each flowers lasts for just a day but during the season hundreds are produced. After flowering each bloom does form a short stem, but rarely sets any seed in temperate climates. The plant needs good drainage in full sun to grow in character, It also needs a dry summer and so in countries with summer rainfall, it is best grown in a frame or greenhouse, where the drought of the N African Atlas Mountains can be copied. Height: 5cm (2in).

## BABIANA

### Iridaceae

The colourful flower spikes of this South African genus, appear over a long period in spring. They have narrow sword-like leaves that are pleated, slightly hairy and arranged in a fan shape. Some of the species from mountainous areas of South Africa are able to withstand a few degrees of frost, but it is best to treat the corms as tender. If you grow these plants from seed, which can germinate very quickly, then it is worthwhile experimenting by planting a few of the resulting corms outside, especially if you live in areas where the winter temperatures rarely fall below −5°C (23°F).

The corms need planting in autumn, deeply (20cm (8in)), in a sunny position. In the coldest period a loose mulch of straw or bracken will give all the protection needed. If grown in containers, *Babiana* need a free-draining sandy compost. Once watered in, they are left until growth is well underway before regular watering is commenced. When they are about to flower the small corms will need feeding with a liquid feed if they are to flower in subsequent years. Once the foliage begins to turn yellow, watering should stop and the corms given a dry rest until repotting in autumn. There are a few low-growing species like *B. pygmaea*, *B. ambigua* and *B. nana* that are best grown in pots, as they would be a little lost in a border.

### B. ambigua

The leaves of this species barely reach 10cm (4in) in length. It looks rather like a wide-leaved crocus with up to five mauve or pinkish mauve flowers, 3–5cm (1¼–2in) long, with the lower two segments having creamy yellow markings. It comes from the SW Cape and begins to flower in midwinter. Height: 20cm (8in).

### B. nana

A small species, as the name suggests, with velvety leaves reaching 12cm (4¾in) in length, but usually less. The fragrant flowers, 5–8cm (2–3¼in) long, are blue, mauve or pink, with yellow or white markings on two segments. It grows in sandy places in the Cape Province of South Africa. Height: 14cm (5½in).

### B. plicata

The simple or branched flower spike of this species carries four to ten fragrant pale blue to violet flowers, each 3–5cm (1¼–2in) long. The broad leaves are a little shorter than the flowerhead. From the Cape Province of South Africa, this plant blooms in early spring. Height: 30cm (12in).

### B. pygmaea

Another Cape native, the flowers of this eye-catching plant are held above the fanned leaves. The yellow flowers with maroon centres are up to 9cm (3½in) in diameter. Height: 10cm (4in).

### B. rubrocyanea

One of the most attractive species, this plant has a short stem, with an inflorescence of ten flowers, 3–5cm (1¼–2in) long, of deep cornflower blue with a crimson centre. The velvety leaves are 12cm (4¾in) long. From the Cape, where it grows at low altitudes in clay and gravel. In cultivation it is quick to develop corms, flowering in two years from seed. Height: 20cm (8in).

### B. sambucina

Known as the elder-scented babiana, this dwarf species has very fragrant pale blue to deep violet flowers, 5–8cm (2–3¼in) long, held in a spike. The leaves are also pungent and 20cm (8in) long, overtopping the flowers. It is found growing in fast-draining stony places throughout South Africa. Height: 20cm (8in).

### B. villosa

Known as the red babiana, this species has beautiful claret flowers with contrasting black anthers. There are up to eight flowers on a stem reaching 20cm (8in). There are five to seven, velvety sword-shaped leaves that are shorter than the flowering stem. From the SW Cape region of South Africa. Height: 20cm (8in).

## BELLEVALIA

### Hyacinthaceae

The plants of this genus are similar to those of *Muscari* but with open mouths to their flowers. They are easily grown, just requiring a sunny border or raised bed to flower regularly. Unfortunately, they do seem to attract slugs, which can soon damage the foliage, but otherwise they seem trouble free.

### B. dubia

This species has a raceme of small blue or violet flowers that turn to a bright green once they mature. This unusual combination is best achieved when grown in a sunny frame or a deep pot in full sun. This plant is found from Portugal eastwards to Turkey, where it grows in places like olive groves. Height: 20cm (8in).

### B. forniculata

This species has possibly the most stunning blue flowers of any plant; short and bell-shaped, they are held in a loose raceme. The two or three leaves reach 30cm (12in) in length. Although this plant is found in wet peaty meadows in NE Turkey at 2000m (6560ft) or more, it grows very well in a frame or large pot in a cold greenhouse. Height: 30cm (12in).

### B. pycnantha

Dark blue bell-shaped flowers, overlaid with a bloom of grey, are held in sturdy racemes, 4cm (1½in) long, in this species. It makes an arresting sight if a number are grown together, close to the path, or better still, in a raised bed closer to the eye. The channelled leaves are one of the most popular with nightly marauding slugs! A Middle Eastern plant from meadows and marshy fields in the mountains. Height: 30cm (12in).

### B. romana

The creamy white racemes, about 5cm (2in) long, are composed of twenty to thirty loosely held bell-shaped flowers. The leaves are crowded and can reach 30cm (12in) in length. This is a very easy species to grow as long as it is planted in full sun, where it will soon form a self-sown colony. This is a European plant from quite low altitude from France to Yugoslavia. Height: 20cm (8in).

## BULBOCODIUM

### Colchicaceae

A genus of just two plants, *Bulbocodium* is closely related to *Colchicum*. They differ most noticeably in that, in the flowers of *Bulbocodium*, the segments are divided down to the base. Both species are quite hardy; they can also be grown in a raised bed or bulb frame where the protec-

tion of the glass will keep the flowers in good condition longer. They reach no great height, flowering as they do, just at ground level.

### B. vernum

The starry flowers open up to 4cm (1½in) wide in sun. They are rose-purple with a white base and almost crocus-like as they open. The corm is nearly black and up to 3cm (1¼in) long. Three to four leaves appear with the flowers but only reach their full size, 15cm (6in) long and 1·5cm (½in) wide, later. The plant is widespread in the Pyrenees, SW Alps and in S Austria.

### B. versicolor

Similar to *B. vernum*, this species is smaller with narrower leaves. It is from S Russia and a few places in E Europe, where it grows in dry grassland. It requires pot cultivation, as there seems a need to regularly change the growing medium if it is to thrive.

## CHASMANTHE

### Iridaceae

The three plants of this genus are quite vigorous and need plenty of space for their roots to grow and their corms to multiply. The long tubular flowers, which end in spreading lobes, come in shades of yellow, orange and red and are held in long panicles. In western parts of the USA where these plants have been introduced, they can be pollinated by hummingbirds.

In their native South Africa, these plants are winter growers; in cooler climates they should be kept moist if they are to flower in late winter or early spring. Another method of cultivation is to change the natural growth cycle, so that the flowering coincides with summer in the Northern Hemisphere. To do this, the corms are treated as bedding plants, and lifted in autumn before planting in a pot or box of sandy loam, which is kept fairly dry in a frost-free place until replanting in spring. Their vigorous growth means they will need repotting every year.

### C. aethiopica

This species has orangey red flowers that tend to come from one side of the flower stalk. The sword-like leaves can reach a length of 1m (3ft) and are arranged in a fan shape. It comes from a damp shady habitat, but is very tolerant of conditions as long as it is moist. In mild climates this species can multiply to become a beautiful weed. Height: 1m (3ft).

### C. bicolor

A less vigorous, shorter species which has deep scarlet flowers with greenish lower segments. The flowers of this

*Chasmanthe* grow from both sides of the stalk, giving a flattened appearance to the plant. The leaves are bright green with a silky sheen, reaching to 70cm (28in) in length, and are produced with the flowers in midwinter. Height: 60cm (24in).

### C. floribunda

Like *C. bicolor*, this plant has a flowers that grow from both sides of the stem. It produces the largest flowers of the genus. Height: 1m (3ft).

The tubular flowers of **var.** *duckittii* are larger and more open. They are yellow with yellow-brown anthers. The flowers of the inflorescence open together. It is considered to be the most elegant and desirable form of the species. The flowers of **var.** *floribunda* are orangey yellow; this variety is found at the side of water courses in the SW Cape region.

*Chionodoxa cretica* is an perfect subject for pot cultivation, with its starry mauve-blue flowers.

## CHIONODOXA

### Hyacinthaceae

*Chionodoxa* comes from the Greek *'chion'* meaning snow and *'doxa'* glory and these plants do indeed glorify the melting snows of W Turkey, Crete and Cyprus. They are among the earliest flowering of small bulbs and are closely allied to *Scilla*, but distinct because the flower segments are joined at the base. All are quite hardy and easily grown in sunny well-drained positions, or in bulb frames or pots under cold glass, where their starry, brilliant blue, white or pink flowers, 1–2.5cm (⅜–1in) wide, will brighten up a dull winter's day. The flowers are borne in a loose raceme, up to 25cm (10in) tall. The leaves are strap shaped and appear with the flowers. Most of the species will grow best outside, but one or two from Crete are less strong and can be seen to perfection when grown under cold glass.

### C. albescens

This Cretan plant bears two or three quite delicate, pale

lilac-blue flowers with large white eyes. They do not open widely, remaining narrowly funnel shaped, and so a number are needed to produce a good show. For this reason they are often grown in pots in a frame or cold greenhouse. The leaves reach up to 20cm (8in) in length. Height: 10–15cm (4–6in).

**C. cretica** (see picture also plate I, 7)
The delicate blue or mauve flowers with clear white centres open more flatly than *C. albescens*. Another small species, this also does best under cold glass. From the White Mountains of Crete at about 2000m (6560ft). Height: 10–15cm (4–6in).

**C. forbesii** (see picture plate I, 3)
There is some uncertainty about the exact naming of this species as the wild stock from SW Turkey may be synonymous with *C. siehei*, but until that is sorted out, I will stay with the older namings. This is the largest plant in the genus and carries as many as fifteen flowers a stem. The flowers are violet-blue, with a large white centre. Height: 25cm (10in).

Among the named cultivars are **'Pink Giant'** (see plate III, 6), **'Blue Giant'** and **'Rosea'**. The dwarf variety **'Tmoli'** has a one-sided raceme with large, purplish blue flowers with large white eyes.

**C. lochiae**
This little plant is endemic to the Troodos Mountains of Cyprus, where it grows in stony soil under pines. It has one to four light blue flowers, without a white centre. It grows very well in a pot or in a bulb frame. Height: 10–15cm (4–6in).

**C. luciliae** ♛
This species is very distinctive with only one or two, large upright flowers, between 3–4cm (1¼–1½in) in diameter. The segments are a soft violet-blue with a small white central zone. A white form exists. This is another species with various synonyms and it will continue to cause confusion until the old names fall into disuse. Height: 20cm (8in).

**C. nana**
The flowers of this small species from Crete can be pale lilac, pale blue or white and open out flat like *C. cretica*. It is smaller than *C. cretica* and may be a high-altitude form. Height: 10–15cm (4–6in).

**C. sardensis** ♛ (see pictures pp.56–57 and plate I, 10)
An easy garden plant, this species will self sow and colonize wherever you wish, as long as the spot is not too shady. The flowers are a deeper blue than *C. luciliae* and only have a small white eye. The purplish brown stems,

up to 15cm (6in) tall, bear racemes with four to twelve flowers. Once the flowers have finished they quickly fall over and the fleshy capsules spill their black seeds around. This plant comes from the Anatolian Mountains of Turkey. Height: 15cm (6in).

## × CHIONOSCILLA

### Hyacinthaceae

The cross between *Chionodoxa luciliae* and *Scilla bifolia* has been attempted several times and has subsequently been named × *Chionoscilla allenii*. Several named varieties of this hybrid were grown at the RHS garden at Wisley for many years but these seem to have lost their different identities and today we have only × *C. allenii*. Wherever the two parent species are grown close together, hybrids will occur, so further selections can easily be made.

**× C. allenii** (see picture also plate I, 4)
This plant resembles *Chionodoxa luciliae*, with its segments joined at the base, but its flowers are a darker blue

Attractive both in bud and in flower, × *Chionoscilla allenii* makes an impact in late winter.

ageing to violet-blue. It is a stout but quite imposing plant with flowers of 2.5cm (1in) across. The original garden hybrid was noticed by James Allen of snowdrop fame, in his garden at Shepton Mallet in Somerset. Height: 20cm (8in).

## COLCHICUM
### Colchicaceae
Most gardeners associate colchicums with the large pink and white goblet-shaped flowers of autumn. Many of these are forms of *Colchicum speciosum* and are finished flowering by late autumn. However, there are many winter and spring colchicums that are little grown but deserve a wider audience. As in autumn, most flowers are in shades of pink and white, although there is one exception that has cream or yellow flowers. These early season corms are best in a bulb frame or pot, so that they can have a definite rest period in summer and the slugs and snails of spring can be more easily controlled. They are all hardy and once in growth like copious amounts of water, as many are springtime snow-melt plants in the wild. The corms have thick brown or nearly black tunics that protect them from extremes of drought and temperature.

### C. brachyphyllum
Found from Syria to the Lebanon, this species has pink, and occasionally white, globular flowers about 3cm (1¼in) across. It blooms in the depths of winter and the succession of up to fifteen flowers is finished by late winter. There are four to six, narrowly ovate to lanceolate leaves. Height: 10–15cm (4–6in).

### C. burttii
Only found in W Turkey, this species blooms in early spring. The flowers are up to 4cm (1½in) long, usually pink and funnel shaped, opening to a star as they age; the anthers are nearly black. The leaves are often hairy and appear silvery. Height: 15cm (6in).

### C. diampolis
In cultivation, this has white flowers, 3cm (1¼in) long, with quite wide segments and yellow anthers. The leaves lengthen after flowering. The plant sets viable seed and is proving to be very perennial. It comes from Bulgaria. Height: 15cm (6in).

### C. falcifolium
This is a name applied to similar group of plants found from Syria eastwards through Turkey, Iraq, Iran and into what used to be S Russia, growing on exposed rocky hillsides. There are many names in use but *C. falcifolium* is the oldest. The star-shaped flowers, 2.5cm (1in) long,

number up to eight and have white to pinkish purple segments and black or brownish anthers. The three to six leaves are narrow, linear and channelled, and grow on after the plant has flowered to become 20cm (8in) long. Height: 20cm (8in).

### C. hungaricum
This species makes a very easily cultivated little beauty for midwinter. There are both pink and white forms; the white is very pure with contrasting black anthers, which later do have the usual yellow pollen. Up to eight flowers can be produced, measuring 3cm (1¼in) long and just under 1cm (⅜in) wide. The flowers keep coming, week after week with the old ones still colourful but lying around the stem. At flowering the two to three leaves are quite erect and short, later reaching up to 20cm (8in) in length and 1-2cm (⅜–¾in) wide. The leaves are quite hairy and in good light appear silvery. The white form should be referred to as f. *albiflorum*. The plant comes from SE Europe. Height: 5cm (2in).

### C. kesselringii
A bright, neat little plant with small white flowers, striped with purple and 3–4cm (1¼–1½in) long. There are two to seven glabrous and quite erect leaves that extend after flowering to 10cm (4in) long and 1cm (⅜in) wide. It is always worth growing these 'bulbs' from seed so the very best forms can be selected; in this case, that will be the plants with the widest segments and darkest stripes. Native to Central Asia, it is found on stony hillsides and alpine meadows up to 3000m (9840ft). Height: 5cm (2in).

### C. luteum
The only yellow colchicum, this plant is found wild from Soviet Central Asia and Kashmir through to SW China, near the snow line. The yellow varies from straw coloured to bright orange, and at the moment the bright orange selection is widely available. In the wild, other forms have some darker markings on the outside of the segments. These flowers are up to 3cm (1¼in) long and of good substance, with the usual repeat flowering. It is quite easy to grow in a frame but does not like to be too dry during the summer. Height: 15cm (6in).

### C. szovitsii
A very good early colchicum, this snow-melt plant will flower in character if winter turns quickly into spring. This is with leaves just emerging, shorter than the small goblet-shaped flowers, up to 3.5cm (1⅜in) long, which can be anything from dark pink to white. The pinker forms stand out well, with their purplish to nearly black

anthers. Like so many colchicums, the leaves lengthen after flowering, reaching up to 25cm (10in) long and 3cm (1¼in) wide. They come from Turkey, Caucasus and Iran, growing in meadows that are very wet at flowering time. Height: 10–15cm (4–6in).

### C. triphyllum

One of the few European spring-flowering colchicums, this species has flowers that are purplish pink to near white. They vary in shape but can be goblet shaped. The anthers are darkish, between green and black. There are usually three leaves, lengthening after flowering to reach 15cm (6in) and 1cm (⅜in) wide. A widespread species found above 700m (2300ft) all around the Mediterranean basin and east through Turkey into E Asia. Height: 10–15cm (4–6in).

## CORYDALIS

### Papaveraceae

This large genus includes many herbaceous plants which fall outside the remit of this book. Here only the tuberous species and forms will be considered, of which many new ones have entered cultivation in the last decade. The cultivation of these plants falls into three categories. The first, group 1, are easily grown garden plants that can be enjoyed in an open border, a raised bed or trough. The second, group 2, need to be rested, as they come from areas with dry summers, and so are best grown under cold glass, but even here must not be dried too much.

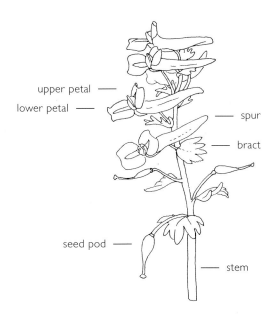

upper petal
lower petal
spur
bract
seed pod
stem

A typical *Corydalis* flower – *C. solida*

Lastly, group 3 are those from quite harsh continental climates where the tubers are larger, divide less and do really need to be kept dry for a few months in summer. The plants in all these groups are hardy. The corydalis in group 1, that can cope with moister conditions, have small tubers that divide every year when growing well. They also set seed, which is quite tricky to collect as it is shed while the pods are still green, although the seeds are usually a shiny black. It must be sown immediately or viability is lost, or at the very least impaired. This seed will germinate next spring.

It is best to grow corydalis in full light to bring out a greater depth of colour and to stop them stretching and loosing their attraction. Or put another way, when they are grown under glass in poor light they are quite anaemic and become stretched and out of character.

Corydalis flowers have four petals, two of which, the upper and lower, are the largest. The upper one extends back into a spur, which is often used for identification purposes, and the lower one seems to make a pouch. These two petals extend to look quite like a nettle flower or even an orchid. Each flower has a bract beneath it which again is helpful for identification. The flowers range from 1.5cm (½in) to 4cm (1½in) in length. Those plants included here bloom from late winter to midspring. The green leaves are usually alternate, except in the plants in group 3, where they are opposite. They consist of three leaflets which are often highly divided and glaucous, especially beneath.

### Group 1

These species are mostly from Europe and thrive in ordinary garden situations, whether it's a raised bed, rock garden or ordinary border, as long as they are not overshadowed by taller plants. The tubers are generally quite small and re-form every year. The best planting site will vary according to the rainfall and drainage of each garden, but in general they are very tolerant as long as the ground is not waterlogged.

### C. alexeenkoana

From the Caucasus, this robust plant has large creamy white to pale yellow flowers. Height: 20cm (8in).

### C. × allenii

This hybrid between *C. bracteata* and *C. solida* has creamy flowers with some pink veining. It needs frequent dividing and is a good garden plant. It has an invalid name which is over seventy years old and has yet to be replaced. Height: 15cm (6in).

# PLATE VI  *Corydalis*

2 *Corydalis solida*
'George Baker'

1 *Corydalis solida*
ssp. *incisa*

3 *Corydalis cava*
*albiflora*

4 *Corydalis*
*solida*
'Beth Evans'

6 *Corydalis
henrikii*

5 *Corydalis solida*

7 *Corydalis
malkensis*

*All plants shown approximately two-thirds size*

### C. angustifolia

The flowers have upright spurs and are whitish and quite slim; the inner, smaller petals are tipped with purple. The bracts have three divisions. Found in NE Turkey, Caucasus and Iran in shady places, where it also will do well in cultivation. Height: 9–14cm (3½–5½in).

### C. bracteata

This species is found in Central Asia where the severity of the winter keeps it dormant well into spring. In more temperate climates winter weather can vary considerably, from wet and mild one minute, to freezing cold the next. In such conditions, growth can be induced and then, just as quickly, stopped, causing the flowers to abort. This beautiful species prefers the more northern counties, where hopefully the large pale yellow flowers with enlarged lower lips will not emerge until late in the corydalis season, in early spring. Height: 15cm (6in).

### C. cashmeriana

This species has very attractive sky-blue flowers with divided bracts, held above pale green foliage. It does not have the circular tubers of most corydalis, it has small clusters of ovoid tubers. A native of Kashmir, that likes shade and an acid soil, it grows well in colder temperate countries. Height: 10cm (4in).

### C. caucasica

A good garden plant of easy cultivation, which has purplish pink to lilac flowers with a horizontal spur and entire bracts. The leaves have leaflets that are divided into two to three lobes. Height: 15cm (6in).

### C. cava ♀

This differs from the other plants in this group in that the tuber is perennial and enlarges, eventually becoming hollow with age. The tubers will draw themselves into the soil to a greater depth than might be expected, up to 20cm (8in) or more, making lifting a tricky task. The flowers vary in colour, with purplish red and white being the most usual. Found from Portugal eastwards to Iran, but mainly in Europe. Height: up to 30cm (12in).

The purple bracts and stems of *albiflora* (see pictures p.34 and plate VI, 3) contrast well with the white flowers.

### C. decumbens

Flowers that vary from white to pale pink, often marked with pale blue, are held on rather weak stems. A Far Eastern plant with abundant, slender and fern-like foliage, it does best in woodland conditions. Height: 20cm (8in).

### C. glaucescens

The short stem to is topped with pinkish flowers with upward pointing spurs above pointed bracts. A Central Asian plant from the Tien Shan and Pamir Mountains, growing in shady places, it does well in rock-garden conditions, needing the extra drainage of a raised site. Height: 8cm (3¼in).

### C. henrikii

A new introduction from S Turkey which is proving to be easy to grow in a raised bed. The pale purplish pink flowers, some 3cm (1¼in) long, are held on erect stems. The leaves are slightly glaucous. Height: 15cm (6in).

### C. integra

Twenty or so white to pale pink flowers, the inner petals tipped blackish purple, and with entire bracts, are held above beautiful foliage. This excellent compact garden plant is found wild from the Balkans to NW Turkey, growing on north-facing cliffs. Height: 10cm (4in).

### C. malkensis ♀ (see pictures p.38 and plate VI, 7)

A plant from the Caucasus, this is one of the most beautiful corydalis. It is white flowered, but primrose-cream in bud, the blooms held in large compact racemes. These begin to appear in midwinter, when they are especially welcome. The foliage is very divided and dark green. The species seeds around very freely, with the vast majority coming true to type, but it is fun to find the odd pink or purple seedling amongst the masses. It never becomes a weed as by mid-spring it has retired below ground for another year. If seed is to be given away, try to collect it while the pods are still green and sow immediately; with luck the paddle-shaped seed leaves will emerge early next spring. The seedlings soon inhabit the most unlikely spots in the garden, but seem to thrive everywhere. Height: 15cm (6in).

### C. nudicaulis

This is one of the more recent introductions from Central Asia, where it grows in shady north-facing slopes. In cultivation, it grows well in a sunny rock garden, which does give the tubers some chance of ripening in summer. The flowers are creamy white with a most attractive coffee-coloured nose to the two largest petals, and an entire bract. Height: 10cm (4in).

### C. paczoskii

From the Ukraine, this has purple flowers with the small inner petals tipped with purple-black. The leaves are dark green and deeply divided, with bracts that vary from being almost entire to deeply divided, but always a very noticeable feature on the stem. It is self-fertile and seeds around well in the open garden. Height: 15cm (6in).

### C. paschei

Another newly discovered species from SW Turkey, this

is already proving to be amenable to outdoor cultivation. It has substantial pink flowers, growing on long lax racemes, above small rounded entire bracts. The foliage has very long stalks to the dark green leaves with rounded lobes. Height: 15cm (6in).

*C. solida* ♔ (see pictures plate VI)

The most widely grown tuberous species, this has many subspecies and cultivars. If grown with faster drainage, in a raised bed or trough, for instance, this plant is more compact and flowers just as prolifically. The stems bear racemes of up to twenty flowers, varying from white, pink, purple to red with grey-green biternate leaves. The bracts are dissected. It is a widespread plant found in Europe, through Turkey, Lebanon and W Asia. There are some forms with very muddy purple flowers that are very fertile. These are probably best banished to the wilder parts of the garden or disposed of altogether. This may seem hard, but the other selections and subspecies are so much more attractive and they would be spoilt if diluted by drab seedlings. Height: 20cm (8in).

The following cultivars are all first-class garden plants for early spring. **'Beth Evans'** ♔ has pale pink flowers with a white spur. **'Blushing Girl'**, a selection by Janis Ruksans of Latvia, has rich pink flowers in a compact raceme. **'Dieter Schacht'** is a selection from the Munich Botanic Garden that is similar to 'Beth Evans' but with more vigour. **'George Baker'** ♔ (see picture also p.39) is a well-known name for a rich red form. **'Highland Mist'** has attractive glaucous foliage with smoky bluish pink flowers. **'Lahovice'** is a deep red strain. **'Prasil Strain'** is a seed-raised strain varying from salmon-red to pink in colour. **'Snowstorm'** is another Janis Ruksans selection, again compact but with creamy white flowers.

The flowers of **ssp.** *incisa* are pale purple and held in dense racemes above deeply divided bracts and finely dissected foliage. A strong-growing form, reaching a height of 15cm (6in) and showing early in the year, it is a Balkan plant and grows well in cultivation, having scent as an extra attraction.

## Group 2

In areas with low summer rainfall, this next group could probably be grown in raised beds without any protection. And it is always worthwhile experimenting by planting seedlings outside in the best open ground conditions you can provide. This group will need a rest period in summer when the tubers can be just dry (or barely moist), a condition that can only be guaranteed under glass. Most growers have the tubers in a fast-draining soil-based compost. The tubers are planted while dormant in late summer and then watered once, after which time they are kept just moist until leaf growth is visible in late winter. Even better is a raised bed under glass, where the tubers can be planted in plastic pond baskets, for lifting when dormant, and where for much of the year the glass is removed to allow full light and natural rainfall. If the weather is very wet or snowy the glass can be simply slid back into place, as it will need to be in summer to ensure a cool dryish rest. Any of the species from group 1 will also grow well in these conditions, with the addition of extra moisture.

### C. darwasica

This early flowering plant from Central Asia is very distinct in every respect. The foliage is a glaucous lime-green and the raceme has up to thirteen creamy white flowers suffused with pink. It is a species that needs full light, or the compact flowerhead will stretch and lose its charm. Height 10cm (4in).

### C. ledebouriana

The flowers of this species vary greatly so it is best to buy it in flower to ensure satisfaction. They can be purple through pink to white, with paler spurs which are upward pointing. They are not large but some plants produce many racemes and look very attractive planted *en masse*. The glaucous leaves are divided into quite large rounded lobes and can emerge from more than one growing point on the tuber. This plant has a large corky tuber, like many of the corydalis from Central Asia, but is very willing to grow in the slightly damper conditions of this grouping. Height 15cm (6in).

### C. shanginii

This beautiful species deserves a choice position in full light in a bulb frame. Early in the year the large tubers send up tall racemes bearing large, 4cm (1½in) long flowers of pink with a darker tip and a long white spur. Height 15cm (6in).

The flowers of **ssp.** *ainae* have a bright yellow nose and a white or pink spur. This was discovered just over twenty years ago in Kazakhstan.

## Group 3

There are just a few hardy corydalis that need that extra dryness in summer to grow well in warm temperate climates. Even these must not be dried too much, but as soon as the foliage dies down in summer they will require a cool dry rest. They all seem to have less dense racemes with larger flowers than the species found further to the west. The list below includes those that are most easily obtained from specialist nurseries.

### C. afghanica

A beautiful species bearing a raceme of few, but large white or pink flowers, with thin curved spurs and grey-green leaves, divided into many lobes. Native to a very arid sandy area in Afghanistan. Height: 20cm (8in).

### C. aitchisonii

This stunning plant has bright yellow flowers with upturned spurs, on lax stems. It will need maximum light to stop the plant stretching. The foliage is sparse and the bracts large and oval. From Afghanistan and neighbouring countries. Height: 15cm (6in).

### C. chionophila

The flowers are white with purple tips to the petals and up to 3cm (1¼in) long. The sparse foliage is grey-green. The large corky tuber grows at a considerable depth to avoid the high summer temperatures found in its native Iran and Afghanistan. Height: 15cm (6in).

### C. firouzii

A species that is well-established in cultivation. Allied to *C. chionophila*, it is more compact and has with yellow flowers that turn purple with age. The leaves are grey and rather sparse. Height: 10cm (4in).

### C. macrocentra

This species remains compact in cultivation, with yellow flowers that age to orange. The tubers are up to 10cm (4in) in diameter. Found on sandy screes in Afghanistan and Tadzhikistan. Height: up to 10cm (4in).

### C. popovii

This plant is one regularly found in collections of corydalis, as it is easily grown and long lived. The large flowers are pale pink to purple with white spurs with a sharp curve at the end. They are fragrant and can reach 4.5cm (1¾in) in length in cultivation. The tuber is large, often with a number of growing points. The leaves are close to the ground. From Central Asia where it grows in screes. Height: up to 25cm (10in).

## CROCUS

### Iridaceae

One of the best-known bulbs and one that can be identified by nearly everyone, whether a gardener or not. Over eighty species have been defined with numerous subspecies, named cultivars, but few hybrids. They flower from late summer through to nearly late spring but here only the winter and spring crocuses will be mentioned.

Most require a well-drained sunny site and, depending on their size and vigour, this can be provided by naturalizing in grass, planting in raised beds or bulb frames, or pot cultivation.

The little goblet-shaped flowers, from 2–8cm (¾–3¼in) long, have just three stamens. At flowering the styles and anthers are very useful to help distinguish between plants, unlike the colour and markings of the flowers, which can vary greatly in a wild colony. The divide between autumn- and winter-flowering crocuses is difficult to define as some species like *Crocus laevigatus* have forms that flower in mid-autumn and others that continue until early spring. The leaves of most winter and spring crocuses begin to grow before or as the flowers emerge and continue growing well after flowering; all are narrow with a white centre line. Identification is also often helped by inspecting the corm tunic, which is husk-like and split in patterns. *Crocus* range in height from 5cm (2in) to 15cm (6in).

### C. abantensis

A striking blue-flowered species with a contrasting yellow throat from NW Turkey, with many narrow leaves to each corm. Although hardy, it is best grown in a bulb frame or in a pot under glass.

### C. alatavicus

The flower petals have a white background overlaid with a fine stippling of deep silver-grey and a yellow throat, with numerous leaves. This plant comes from Central Asia and is best grown under the protection of glass.

### C. ancyrensis 'Golden Bunch' (see picture plate VII, 12)

The form most usually seen, this easily grown crocus produces a succession of pale yellow flowers in late winter that are rather like some autumnal colchicums.

### C. angustifolius ♔

Sometimes known as the 'cloth of gold' crocus, this has flowers that are an intense orange-yellow, with the outside of the three outer segments and the bases of the inner segments prominently marked with mahogany stripes. It thrives in a well-drained position and although quite small, it is an eye-catching sight in late winter.

### C. baytopiorum

A relatively recent introduction from SW Turkey, with pale blue flowers with darker blue veining and without extra colour in the throat. Grown at first under glass, it is now proving growable outside in a well-drained spot.

### C. biflorus

This variable species with many subspecies and named selections, has also been hybridized with *C. chrysanthus* to give a range of garden crocuses (see *C chrysanthus*).

Here are some of the best *C biflorus* selections. The flowers of **ssp.** *adami* are lilac with purple stripes and a yellow throat. A robust and long-lived crocus, **ssp.** *alexandri* has a whitish background with a deep purple

*The mauve and yellow flowers of* Crocus sieberi *ssp.* sublimis *push their way through the stony surface of a raised bed early in the season, in midwinter.*

outside and a white throat. Known as the Scotch crocus, **ssp.** *biflorus* is sometimes available as *C.* 'Parkinsonii'. It has whitish segments with purple or brown external stripes and a yellow throat. The flowers of **ssp.** *pulchricolor* are plain blue and, as it is found in damp meadowland in NW Turkey, it requires a damper site to succeed in cultivation. One of the finest forms, **ssp.** *weldenii* has white flowers, often with pale blue outer segments and uniquely, no yellow throat, but white instead.

# PLATE VII *Crocus*

2 *Crocus tommasinianus* var. *pictus*

1 *Crocus tommasinianus* var. *roseus*

4 *Crocus tommasinianus* 'Ruby Giant'

3 *Crocus tommasinianus* 'Eric Smith'

5 *Crocus tommasinianus* 'Claret'

*All plants shown approximately actual size*

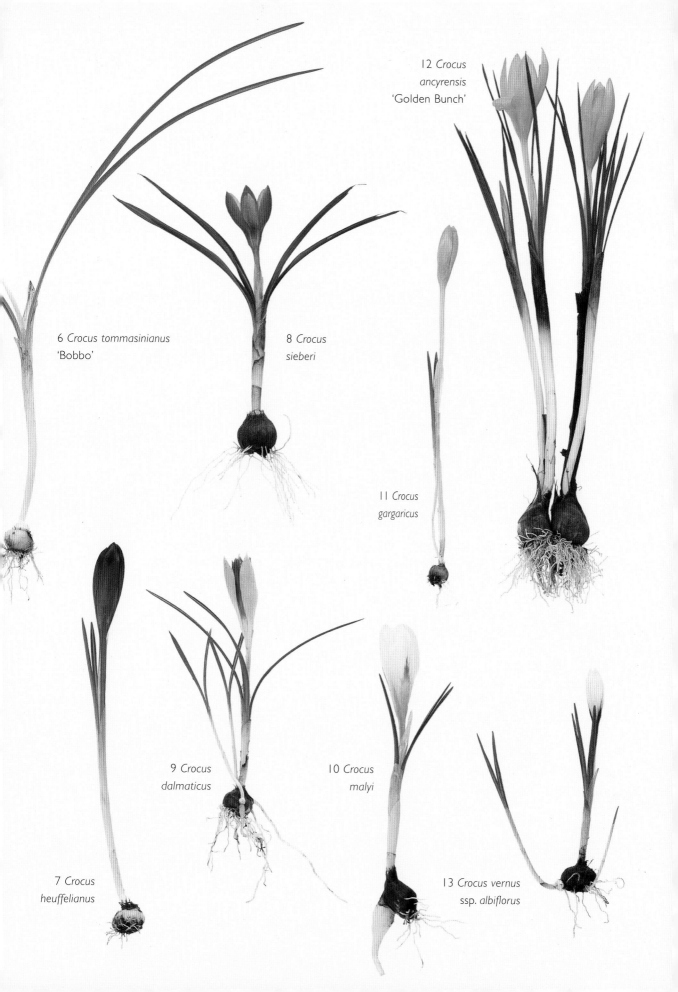

6 *Crocus tommasinianus* 'Bobbo'

8 *Crocus sieberi*

12 *Crocus ancyrensis* 'Golden Bunch'

11 *Crocus gargaricus*

9 *Crocus dalmaticus*

10 *Crocus malyi*

7 *Crocus heuffelianus*

13 *Crocus vernus* ssp. *albiflorus*

## *C. chrysanthus*

This species has given rise to a large range of seedlings of which many have been named. The blue and white forms are probably hybrids with *C. biflorus*. In the wild, in the Balkans through to Turkey, various shades of yellow, some with stripes, can be found. All the named forms are long-lived plants and, as long as they receive some sun, are tolerant of many different garden sites.

'Advance' has flowers with striking violet-streaked outer segments and yellow inner ones. 'Blue Bird' has large rounded white segments with dark purplish blue outer markings. 'Blue Pearl' ♈ is a pale blue variety with a large orange base to the segments and conspicuous orange stigmata. 'Cream Beauty' ♈ has pale creamy yellow flowers with a small purple patch at the base of the outer segment. In 'E.P. Bowles' the outer segments are lemon yellow with a dull purple blotch at the base, which continues as light feathering towards the tip. 'Gipsy Girl' has bright yellow outer segments, striped with chocolate, forming large rounded flowers. 'Goldilocks' has bright yellow segments with a purplish brown blotch that covers most of outer three segments.

'Ladykiller' ♈ has white flowers with purple markings, fading towards the tips of the outer segments but still with a white margin. 'Miss Vain' is a delicate white, with a hint of grey – an unusual but very attractive crocus needing a well-drained site to grow well. 'Moonlight' has large sulphur-yellow flowers which fade with age and have, at the base, a purplish brown mark that extends halfway up the segments. 'Prins Claus' is a large rounded variety with white flowers with an even plum-coloured blotch on the outer segments.

'Saturnus' is bright yellow with five plum feathered stripes and narrow segments that make a star shape when open. 'Snow Bunting' ♈, the one E.A. Bowles selection from 1925 that is still widely available, has flowers that are white edged, changing to cream in the centre and with a feathering of dark lilac, reminiscent of the wings of the actual snow bunting. 'Spring Pearl' has flowers with a cream background with a flush of brown on the exterior, above a purplish brown blotch. 'Warley', sometimes found as 'Warley White', has a plum-purple blotch on the outer segments that fades into cream and eventually white, around the edges. 'White Triumphator' is a strong growing cultivar with white flowers with just a few blue basal stripes. 'Zwanenburg Bronze' ♈ has orange segments which are heavily suffused with deep purplish mahogany.

## *C. corsicus* ♈

This small species, only found on Corsica, is one of the later crocuses to flower. In early spring the pale lilac or buff-coloured segments, heavily feathered with deep purple, are a beautiful sight. The throat is white to pale lilac on the inside and yellow outside, and adding to the contrast, is the orange style.

## *C. dalmaticus* (see picture plate VII, 9)

This crocus is quite large with lilac or buff-silvered outer segments and a yellow throat. Found wild in the Adriatic coastal region of Yugoslavia and N Albania, it is easily grown in cultivation.

## *C. etruscus* ♈

This is an easy species to grow, with flowers with a lilac background and some buff colouring, and mauve feathering on the outer segments. It is from W Italy where it grows in deciduous woodland.

## *C. flavus*

From the Balkans and W Turkey comes this pure yellow species. It is somewhat overshadowed by its larger and far more vigorous hybrid, *C.* 'Dutch Yellow', a plant that is is very popular for naturalizing in grass and for bedding schemes, having brilliant orange globes on strong stems.

## *C. fleischeri*

The white flowers of this species sometimes have a little purple striping towards the base of the rather narrow segments. Its striking feature is the stigma, which is orange-scarlet and finely divided, making a good contrast with the white background. It is a small plant that requires some protection at flowering.

## *C. gargaricus* (see picture plate VII, 11)

This diminutive bright yellow crocus from Turkey will light up a dark border quite early in the year. It needs a moist humus-rich bed, that does not dry out in summer. It will spread by stolons when growing well, with clusters of naked flowers just above the soil level. The leaves follow immediately the flowers have faded.

## *C. heuffelianus* (see picture plate VII, 7)

An easy garden plant with dark purple tips to the purple segments. It does not need a dry summer rest and so is ideal for gardens in temperate regions.

## *C. hyemalis*

A white-flowered species with black anthers that flowers in early winter. It is from the E Mediterranean and requires a well-drained and protected site to flower well.

## *C. imperati* ♈

A stunning crocus from W Italy, this begins to flower very early in the new year. The flowers are a rich violet on the inside with a pale buff exterior. It will grow well outside in a raised bed or in a frame with some protection from wind and rain.

### C. korolkowii

Found growing wild in the very harsh environment of N Afghanistan, where it flowers in midwinter, this crocus blooms in late winter in cultivation. It flowers with the leaves and has long segments of deep yellow, which have many different markings on the outside. These featherings, stipplings and lines have, rather like *C. chrysanthus*, led to an increasing number of selections being named. All seem very vigorous.

### C. laevigatus ♔

As mentioned earlier, the different forms of this crocus flower from mid-autumn through to early spring. The segments are lilac-purple with purple feathering on the outside – inside are the white anthers and orange stigma. It is scented and will grow well in a sunny spot. It is one of the very best crocuses for the winter garden.

One selection in particular, 'Fontenayi' (see picture p.30) is worth acquiring; in Britain it flowers around the shortest day, December 21st.

### C. × luteus 'Stellaris'

A crocus of unknown origin, this is quietly attractive, with yellow segments lined with blackish veins. It is sterile and long lived but slow to increase, so is rather scarce.

### C. malyi ♔ (see picture plate VII, 10)

From the limestone Velebit Mountains of Yugoslavia, this species is proving to be robust and easy to grow in a well-drained sunny position. The large white flowers open horizontally and flat showing a yellow throat.

### C. minimus

Although not as small as the name suggests, this species is best grown under glass where its fine markings can be appreciated. The outer segments are beautifully feathered and marked with dark purple over a buff background. It comes from Corsica and Sardinia but at lower levels than *C. corsicus*, to which it is similar but a little smaller.

### C. olivieri

The leaves are very broad, up to 5mm (¼in), in this Balkan and Turkish plant, making this an obvious feature to help recognition.

Like the species, the flowers of **ssp.** *olivieri* are uniformly bright golden yellow; in **ssp.** *balansae* they have some brown or purple suffusion on the segments.

### C. pestalozzae

This species has tight bunches of white flowers with a yellow throat. This crocus is unique in having a black spot at the base of each filament (the stem of the anther) which helps in identification. Although small it is a superb crocus for pot culture.

The purple form, **var.** *caeruleus* is a very effective and long-lasting plant.

### C. sieberi ♔ (see picture plate VII, 8)

This is a very useful garden species in all its forms and although very variable, all the cultivars and varieties have a yellow throat in common.

From the Greek mainland, **ssp.** *atticus* has deep mauve flowers, whereas **ssp.** **sublimis** (**var.** *tricolor*), from the N Peloponnese, has a distinct white band separating the mauve from the yellow throat. From Crete comes **ssp.** *sieberi*, with pure white flowers striped with violet on the outer three segments. E.A. Bowles found a pure white form with an almost golden throat in his garden, which was then named 'Bowles' White' and is now known as 'Albus' ♔ (see picture p.13); it is of an easy disposition and does well in the open garden. 'Cedric Morris' is very early flowering with large blue-mauve segments and a conspicuous orangey yellow throat. 'Hubert

*Crocus sieberi* 'Cedric Morris' can be in flower by Christmas if the winter is mild.

An interesting selection, *Crocus tommasinianus* 'Eric Smith' has eight-petalled flowers.

**Edelsten'** ♔ is an old selection with pale mauve flowers banded with dark purple and white. **'Violet Queen'** has rounded violet-blue flowers and great vigour.

### C. tommasinianus

Once this species has been introduced it will spread quickly by seed and by division of corms, particularly on light soils. It is a very useful and effective crocus in the right place. Areas like a shrubbery or mixed border are ideal, where the 'tommies' can be left to colonize and where if a few are inadvertently dug up it is of no consequence. The species comes from SE Europe where it is found in light woodland.

Some of the named selections (see pictures plate VII) are very choice and need careful siting if they are to be admired more closely. Some of the great gardeners like E.A. Bowles and O.E.P. Wyatt named several selections of this species. The flowers of **f. *albus*** have the faintest dark flecking on a pure white background. **'Bobbo'** has lavender flowers with a white tip to each segment. **'Claret'** is the nearest colour to red, being a rich deep rosy purple. **'Eric Smith'** is white with purple flecking and occasionally it has eight outer segments, making it very distinct. The flowers of **var. *pictus*** are lilac with a purple band and with a small white tip to the segments. When the flowers of **var. *roseus*** are half open the pink inner segments are revealed, contrasting well with the silvery grey outer. **'Ruby Giant'** is a dark form. **'Taplow**

Ruby' is reddish purple and becoming scarce, whereas **'Whitewell Purple'** is still widely available.

Once a colony of this plant is established you may find inferior seedlings crop up in the named forms. The gardener has to act while the plant is flowering and lift the clump, removing the offending corms. It is almost impossible to mark the plant to be removed, as come summer you can find even more corms beneath the surface than there were flowers. In practise, it is good to tease the whole group apart and replant and so extend or make further colonies elsewhere.

The contrasting petals of *Crocus tommasinianus* var. *roseus* are particularly noticeable when the flowers are half open.

### C. veluchensis

A Balkan crocus, this resembles *C. sieberi* but without the yellow throat. The flowers vary between pale to dark purple, sometimes with dark tips to the segments. It will grow well in ordinary garden conditions and thrives in quite moist situations.

### C. vernus (see picture p.47)

As the snow melts in the mountains of Europe, huge drifts of these crocuses spring from the sodden turf, some with purple flowers, others with white. Gardeners have long tried to emulate this spectacle, unfortunately without success. However, the many wild forms, particularly ssp. *vernus*, have give rise to a large group of garden hybrids, often referred to as the *Dutch* hybrids. These

selections date back over several centuries and only a few of those more easily obtained will be described. They are vigorous and adaptable and are suited for planting in grass, in large mixed borders or the wild garden, usually in drifts of the same colour, although of course plantings can be mixed.

'**Jeanne d'Arc**' has large pure white flowers with a purple base, and those of '**Pickwick**' are rounded with a violet striping. '**Purpureus Grandiflorus**' has cup-shaped violet blooms with a purple base. '**Queen of the Blues**' is pale blue with paler edges and a dark base. '**Remembrance**' has large rich purple flowers with a silver gloss. '**Vanguard**' blooms early with soft lilac flowers that have a silvery sheen.

If they are planted in grass, the first mowing must not be until the leaves have turned yellow. The grass clippings are best not gathered up if self-sown seedlings are looked for, as the seed capsules would also be collected with the clippings. These bulbs are also often grown in bowls for short-term decoration indoors. When planted they must be grown in a cool greenhouse and not forced or they will abort. When the buds show colour they can be brought into the house, kept moist and if grown in good light will flower well. When they fade the mass of soil and roots can be planted directly into the garden.

### C. versicolor

The white to pale lilac-grey flowers have a prominent feathering of purple on the outer segments. Although coming from the Maritime Alps it is an easy garden plant and is often found in catalogues as *C. v.* 'Picturatus'.

### C. vitellinus

This species has small bright orange flowers, sometimes with external brown veins. Internally the yellow orange anthers and style make identification an easy task. Native to S Turkey through to Lebanon, it does need the protection of a bulb frame or greenhouse.

## CYCLAMEN

### Primulaceae

A must for any garden and really you can never have enough of these beautiful tuberous plants. It is possible to find cyclamen in flower every month of the year, but just those that bloom in winter and early spring will be described here. The flowers are composed of five strongly reflexed, often twisted petals, joined at the base to form a

Planting *Cyclamen coum* in an attractive container is an ideal way of bringing a spot of colour to any site in midwinter.

tube. The leaves are fleshy and often kidney- or heart-shaped, with or without silvery markings.

Those species described here are either hardy or tender in warm temperate climates, such as that of Britain. The hardy varieties will provide a marvellous shot of bright purplish magenta to the winter garden, a colour possibly more welcome at this time of the year than at any other season. The tender forms are best grown in a frost-free greenhouse.

### C. balearicum

This slightly tender species is best grown in shade in a greenhouse or frame. The flowers are white with very pale pink veins and very fragrant. Although not produced in great numbers they look very attractive over the toothed heart-shaped leaves, which are heavily washed with silver. The plant is found in the Balearic Islands and coastal areas of S France. Height: 10–15cm (4–6in).

### C. coum ♕ (see pictures pp.6, 39, 84–85 and plate VIII)

This very variable hardy species is found from Bulgaria through Turkey to the Caucasus and Iran. The flowers have short broad petals and a wide throat to the mouth of the corolla and look almost square. They all have a purple-magenta marking round the throat and vary from dark carmine, through pink to white. They flower on short stalks and are unaffected by frost or snow. As in all cyclamen the leaves are nearly as attractive as the flowers; they are rounded or cordate, some marbled or unmarbled, vary from dark green to a pewter-grey above, and include every conceivable mix of these two greens, with crimson beneath. To be effective, C. coum should be planted in bold groups in sun or part shade, in an area without competition. They will self-sow freely and although quite expensive, just a few will soon develop into a colony. It is very rewarding to grow cyclamen from seed, as you see the diversity of leaf in the first year with the flower a bonus in the second or third. Height: 8–13cm (3¼–5¼in).

An Iranian form of the species, **ssp.** *elegans*, is a little tender and needs greenhouse protection. It has slightly larger pinkish lilac flowers with a large carmine blotch around the mouth and its leaves have slight scalloped edges. There is a white-flowered cultivar, **f.** *coum* 'Maurice Dryden', that has green-edged leaves with a pewter-coloured centre, which although seed-raised, seems to stay fairly consistent.

### C. creticum

Native only to Crete, this delicate beauty is tender and needs frost-free conditions. In summer, when resting, it must not get too hot and so is best plunged under the staging in a greenhouse to rest in the warm shade. In Crete it will always be found under shrubs or in the shade of rocks, out of direct sunlight. The petals are quite long and narrow, white to pink, with a slight wave and quite fragrant. The broadly toothed, heart-shaped leaves are deep green, slightly marked with silver splashes, and crimson beneath. Height: 10–15cm (4–6in).

### C. libanoticum ♕

One of the most beautiful of all the cyclamen, this species seems to vary little in flower or leaf, unlike most cyclamen. The large pale pink flowers have a small red mark near the base, with oval quite large flat petals, which are said to smell of pepper. The leaves develop long before the flowers and are cordate, deep green with pale marbling and quite thick and rubbery. It is usually grown in the frost-free greenhouse but is possible in a sheltered position facing west. The first colony I saw that grew with great vigour and flowered every spring in Britain, was under the western overhang of a thatched roof. Siting this plant tight under a wall or fence would probably have the same effect. Native to the Lebanon. Height: 10–15cm (4–6in).

### C. parviflorum

One of the smallest cyclamen, it flowers as the snow melts in a habitat of pine and rhododendron forest in the Pontus Mountains of Turkey. This gives us some clue to its cultural requirements. Firstly, as it is so small it is best grown in a pot or a trough with a mix that includes more peat or leaf mould than usual and which is always kept moist and cool. It is hardy but as it produces leaves in autumn and then flowers in the spring it can look a little battered if left outside all winter. The flowers vary from pale purple to pink with a purple blotch at the base and it looks similar to a small C. coum, with plain green leaves. Height: 3–12cm (1¼–4¾in).

### C. persicum

This variable species has given rise to the ever-popular florists' cyclamen. The wild plants have a grace and beauty that has, in some part, been lost in the florists' forms. The tubers of the species are long lived in cultivation but tender, needing frost-free conditions in winter, although they can be plunged in a shady outside frame during the summer. Not actually found in Persia (Iran), the species is native to Cyprus, some Greek islands, Palestine and N Africa. The stalk of the seed capsule stays straight, unlike all the other species, which coil up when fertilized. The leaves are extremely variable in their silvery markings and shape and the flowers vary from white through to carmine, but rarely red in the wild. They are sweetly scented and do need a dry summer without being desiccated. Height: 15–30cm (6–12in).

The development of the florists' cyclamen has changed the plant so radically that unless the name *C. persicum* was applied, you would never suspect the connection. Victorian nurseries began making selections of the species and it was not long before some larger flowered forms were

The delicate flowers of the white form of *Cyclamen repandum* lighten a shady spot in early spring.

available. In this century, development has moved on in leaps and bounds with plant breeding done on a grand scale. Today, grown in computer-controlled conditions, a cyclamen can be ready for marketing in ten months from sowing the seed. The plants then cope with poor growing conditions in homes and offices, where they give a lengthy display. However continuing that display into another year is harder to achieve as nursery conditions are so exacting that most amateurs can not replicate it. They must have a period of rest and if possible this should coincide with summer, although this may be difficult as they are dispatched all year from the nurseries.

# PLATE VIII
## *Cyclamen*

2 *Cyclamen coum*
(showing tuber)

1 *Cyclamen coum*
ssp. *elegans*

3 *Cyclamen coum*
(pale form)

4 *Cyclamen coum*
(magenta form)

5 *Cyclamen coum* ssp.
*caucasicum*

8 *Cyclamen coum*
(plain leafed form)

6 *Cyclamen coum*
(white form)

9 *Cyclamen*
*trochopternthum*

7 *Cyclamen coum*
'Maurice Dryden'

10 *Cyclamen*
*trochopternthum* var.
*album*

*All plants shown approximately actual size*

For the amateur grower of these florists' cyclamen the annual cycle of cultivation is quite straightforward and will be described beneath. The tricky part is trying to get your superbly flowering plant to slow down and fit this regime. When the flowering begins to wane it is safe to assume that most of the pot's nutrients will be exhausted, so repotting is the first priority. They will probably be in soil-less compost, which needs to be gently teased and washed away from the roots and then repotted in a soil-based potting mix (ideally John Innes No 2). Keep the top of the tuber just above the soil surface and water well. Keep the plant in bright light conditions, but not in full sunlight in summer, at between 13–16°C (55–60°F) and never near a direct source of heat such as a radiator. To maintain moisture around the plant, plunge the pots in a saucer of gravel or similar, which is kept damp. When the plants are in growth water around the edges of the tuber making sure water does not lie in the tight mass of emerging leaves and buds. Every two to three weeks add the usual liquid feed to the water (that is, one low in nitrogen, such as a tomato feed).

When the flowers being to fade always remove them from the tuber to avoid rotting and reduce the frequency of watering. When growth stops keep them completely dry for two to three months. Do not leave them in full sun in a greenhouse or they will become too dry. After this period, start with repotting and restarting the growth cycle. In common with most of the genus, *C. persicum* can be very long-lived plants and give increasing displays year by year.

### *C. pseudibericum* ♈

This species is really spectacular when mature, after many years of growing. It does not form large tubers but gradually builds a circular tuber with perennial roots, which grow from the base. The violet-scented flowers are quite large and vary from crimson to magenta with a dark magenta basal blotch and a pale pink or white mouth to the corolla. The broad cordate leaves are dark green, broadly toothed around the edge, marked on the upper surface with light yellowish green and crimson beneath. These leaves are produced in the autumn and can form such a dense umbrella that the emerging flower stems may need a little help to get above them. It is proving to be hardy under cold glass. Native to S Turkey where it is found in forest leaf litter, it may succeed in the garden if a place can be found that is dry in the summer. Height: 10–25cm (4–10in).

### *C. repandum* (see pictures p.32 and p.87)

This S European species is found from Italy eastward to the Peloponnese and the Greek islands. Often called the ivy-leaved cyclamen, it increases slowly but surely in the open garden. The ideal site is sheltered with a little shade and when establishing a colony, plant the tubers 8–9cm

Best grown in a pot, *Cyclamen trochopteranthum* var. *album* also makes an attractive plant for a cold greenhouse.

(3¼–3½in) deep – seedlings will find their own depth. It begins to flower in early spring, continuing well into spring and displaying the typical pink flowers well above the foliage. The scented flowers are pink, crimson or white and in the pink forms the colour darkens towards the nose. Height: 10–20cm (4–8in).

Most of the plants growing in the open garden are **ssp. repandum**; **ssp. peloponnesiacum** ♔ and **ssp. rhodense** are more tender and are usually grown in the greenhouse or frame. These latter two have beautiful speckled silvery white foliage and pale pink flowers with darker noses.

### C. trochopteranthum (see picture plate VIII, 9)

This distinctive small cyclamen usually flowers so profusely, it hides the small ground-hugging leaves. There seems to be almost two different height forms in cultivation, one short and with a profusion of flowers and small leaves and the other taller with fewer but larger flowers and leaves. Although known for over one hundred years this species was not formally named until 1975. It is characterized by the masses of whirligig flowers, with pink to carmine petals with a magenta blotch at the nose, which are held almost horizontally. All have leaves similar to *C. coum* but smaller, with very variable amounts of marbling, some of which are very attractive. The tuber can become flat and almost concave with age, with many growing points on the surface. To avoid any rotting, pot cultivation is recommended, where watering can be carefully directed round the edge of the pot or only given by plunging the pot in bowl of water until moist. Height: 7–12cm (2¾–4¾in).

The form **var.** *album* seems to come true from seed but it is best described as off-white.

## CYRTANTHUS

### Amaryllidaceae

A purely African genus which although essentially tender in temperate climates, is proving possible to grow in conditions that are only just frost-free. The majority are summer flowering, but a few do bloom in spring. The name *Cyrtanthus* means curved flower and describes the flowerheads, which hang down from the top of the stalk. The individual flowers are tubular with the opening a little wider than the rest of the tube. These spring-flowering bulbs should be planted in autumn in a rich but well-drained soil mix (John Innes No 3 with additional grit) and kept just moist throughout the winter, in frost-free conditions. Once in growth they will require regular liquid feeding and good light conditions.

### C. brachyscyphus

The flowers are bright red and about 2–3cm (¾–1¼in) long. Plant the bulbs with the necks at soil level, from which will emerge almost succulent 25cm (10in) long and 5mm (¼in) wide leaves. Native to S Natal and E Cape Province. Height: 30cm (12in).

### C. falcatus (see picture p.26)

This Natal native is proving to be slightly frost resistant. In 1998, as the result of a heating failure in my greenhouse, a large pot of the bulbs was subjected to −6°C (21°F) for three consecutive nights; they survived, probably because it was barely moist, and flowered well next spring. The bulb is quite large, up to 8cm (3¼in) in diameter, and produces large strap-shaped leaves 25cm (10in) long and 3cm (1¼in) wide. The leaves grow as the stem lengthens until it is topped with six to fifteen pendulous flowers. These are 6cm (2½in) long and pink to brick-red with a hint of cream-green on the outside of the tube. In the wild it grows in the crevices of cliffs, often close to waterfalls, where the decaying foliage forms a protective mulch. Height: up to 45cm (18in).

### C. obliquus

Grown for over two hundred years, this is the largest cyrtanthus, found in Natal and down towards the Cape. The leaves are 45cm (18in) long and only 1cm (⅜in) wide and there is a short stout stem with up to twelve large nodding tubular flowers, some 8cm (3¼in) long. They are yellow at the base, flushed orange to red with green tips to the segments. It can flower over a long period (early to late spring) depending on when watering commences in winter. Height: 30cm (12in).

## ERANTHIS

### Ranunculaceae

*Eranthis*, or winter aconite, is a small genus of tuberous plants with bright yellow cup-shaped flowers, appearing in early spring, that are renowned for their ability to naturalize under deciduous trees. Once established they seed around profusely, but if the gardener wishes to collect the seed they must be very vigilant as seed is shed while the capsule is still green.

When it is collected, the seed needs to be sown immediately, as once dried it soon loses viability. In sparse grass under deciduous trees where aconites thrive, colonies have been extended by using a strimmer. The flail cuts down the ripe seed heads and rather explosively spreads the seed far and wide. The common aconite is native to S Europe, but has escaped to naturalize many parts of the

Even on a dull day, *Eranthis hyemalis* (the common aconite), brightens up the garden.

world, including Britain. They reach a height of 10–15cm (4–6in). A few double aconites, like *E.* 'Noel Ayres', are becoming available but do need searching for at flowering time, as they are never likely to be sold as dry tubers.

**E. hyemalis** ♔ (see picture also p.35)

The common aconite, this has bright 2.5cm (1in) wide lemon-gold flowers with a ruff, or involucre, surrounding the flower. At flowering time it is stalkless but eventually lengthens to 10cm (4in) when the seed is ripe.

There is a scarce bright orange form called **'Auranti-aca'**. The **Cilicica Group** (syn. *E. cilicica*) flowers a little later than the species and is a little taller, with a very dis-

sected leaf-like bract behind the shiny golden-yellow flower. It is less easy to please than other members of the genus and it seems to need a sunnier site or even pot culture to do well.

The **Tubergenii Group** (syn. *E.* × *tubergenii*) are sterile and have to be propagated by division. After flowering is the time to take courage and lift and divide these special aconites. The tubers are knobbly and can be snapped into smaller plants and immediately replanted, so they do not dry out. A little fungicide powder applied to the wounded surfaces is a good insurance against rotting. The cultivar **'Guinea Gold'** has a very divided involucre with a bronze hue. The bronze does fade to green but for a week the contrast of bright orange and bronze is quite stunning. It is a little later than the others but grows well in shady parts of the garden.

### E. pinnatifida

This is the odd one out as it has white flowers and is native to Japan. It needs good drainage and does grow successfully in a raised bed in the shade, but is more often grown in a pot under glass. Like many eastern woodland plants it is extremely attractive with a pale flush of blue on the reverse.

## ERYTHRONIUM

### Liliaceae

An aristocratic genus of mostly American bulbs that flower in early spring, these plants would grace any bed with dappled shade. Their pendent flowers, with their reflexed segments, look like small Turk's cap lilies and their two ground-level leaves are often beautifully marbled or blotched. These seemingly frail plants are totally hardy. In N America, the western species are the most

beautiful, but unfortunately these include some that are very hard to grow away from the fast snow-melt and powerful sunshine of their native home. Luckily there are many available that are more amenable to cultivation, but all need a little care especially when transplanting. The bulbs have no tunic or protective membrane and so are very susceptible to being dried to the point where they die, unless packed in barely moist moss or peat and then replanted very quickly.

The only European *Erythronium* is *E. dens-canis*, the name referring to the dog's tooth-shape of the bulb, a shape shared by all the species. The conditions found in a partly shaded raised bed that is full of humus but dries out a little in summer suits them very well. They do not want the wet conditions that might be found in a bog garden. When growing well, seed is regularly set and is very easy and convenient to collect, as the capsule is held well clear of the dying foliage, holding for some weeks the small but easily handled circular seeds. It will be some three to four years before these seeds flower, but it is the surest way to form a colony.

Seen from above, the pale, delicately marked, reflexed petals of *Erythronium oregonum* 'White Beauty' are set against the mottled leaves.

### E. americanum

A small woodland species with rich yellow flowers, flushed with a dull red on the back and only slightly reflexed. The glaucous leaves are mottled with green and a liver colour. It is stoloniferous and soon forms a dense group, unfortunately not always flowering in cultivation. Occasionally, conditions are right as at Savill Gardens, west of London, where they flower well in very sandy soil. From S Canada to Florida. Height: 10cm (4in).

### E. californicum ♇

This easy plant has creamy white flowers with orangey central markings, white anthers and a three lobed stigma. It has up to three flowers with very reflexed tips. The leaves are mottled green and brown. As the name suggests, it is native to California. Height: 30cm (12in).

### E. caucasicum

Related to *E. dens-canis* this species flowers the earliest, often in midwinter. It has yellow pollen – not blue as in *E. dens-canis* – and large pure creamy white flowers above beautiful mottled foliage. Height: 30cm (12in).

### E. citrinum (see picture plate IV, 4)

This is similar to *E. californicum* in many respects and is best identified by its stigma which are entire. Found in N California and S Oregon. Height: 20cm (8in).

### E. dens-canis ♇

Often referred to as the dog's tooth violet, this has an unusually wide distribution, stretching from Europe through Asia as far as Japan. The typical European form has heavily marbled bluish green and brown leaves and flowers that show a great range of colour from white through cream to almost purple. Height: 10cm (4in).

Among the named cultivars available are: 'Album', with white flowers; 'Charmer', pale lilac with a greenish centre; 'Frans Hals', violet-purple with a yellow ring around the throat; 'Lilac Wonder', lavender to rich purple; var. *niveum*, creamy white and very early flowering; 'Pink Perfection', an early large-flowered clear pale pink variety, and 'White Splendour', early white flowers with a dark centre.

### E. grandiflorum

This is a challenge to grow, as it is a snow-melt plant from the mountains of W America, where it is known as the glacier lily. It has large bright golden-yellow flowers and plain leaves – a most clean and refined beauty. In cultivation it must be in a cool position where growth in

*The pale but interesting flowers of Erythronium howellei are held on slender stems above patterned leaves.*

spring is late and then hopefully quick, so the plant does not flower at ground level but quickly stretches to be in character. It can be a martyr to slug damage, so needs protection from these pests. Height: 20cm (8in).

### E. hendersonii

A robust and beautiful erythronium that, given a well-drained position in partial shade, will multiply year by year and give an early boost to any garden. The pale lilac flowers have dark purple markings at the base. The mottled leaves are distinct with light green lines dividing the darker patches. This species comes from the lower hills of S Oregon and N California. Height: 30cm (12in).

### E. howellii

From S Oregan woodlands, at fairly low altitude, this is an easy plant for a shady humus-rich bed. White flowers age to pale pink around a yellow throat. The slim leaves are beautifully marbled. Height: 20cm (8in).

### E. japonicum

This species has the largest flowers of deep violet with a dark centre, above light and dark green, mottled leaves. This plant seems to attract slugs more than most and needs protecting. Height: 20cm (8in).

### E. multiscapoideum

In this species any branching of the stem occurs at or just above ground level, distinguishing it from the very similar *E. californicum*. It is also very free with its offsets. Height: 30cm (12in).

### E. oregonum

Although similar to *E. californicum*, this species differs in having white flowers with yellow centres and anthers. Very easy in the garden it is found along the west coast of N America. Height: 30cm (12in).

The dark mottled leaves of ssp. *leucandrum* (see picture p.96) are really stunning, and worth growing on their own account. Still available, although not as widely, is 'White Beauty' (see picture p.93), a vigorous plant which has also been connected to *E. californicum*. Whatever its origin, it is a first-class plant with large white flowers that recurve at the tips with prominent orange-brown markings at the base and heavily mottled leaves.

### E. revolutum ♇

This plant is considered by some to be the pink-flowered equivalent of *E. oregonum*. The large plain pink flowers do vary in shade It is a very good garden plant and regularly sets seed. Height: 30cm (12in).

The selected variety **Johnsonii Group** seems to be no more than a good pink that could result from any batch of seed-raised stock.

*Erythronium oregonum* ssp. *leucandrum* has stunningly mottled leaves, although the markings fade as the flowers open.

### *E. tuolumnense* ♔

This may be confused with *E. grandiflorum*, but *E. tuolumnense* has an entire stigma and is easy to grow in the garden. It has plain, rather yellowy green leaves and all yellow flowers. It is a little shy with the number of its flowers but bulks up well by offsets. Height: 30cm (12in).

'Kondo' and 'Pagoda' ♔ (see picture also pp.8–9) have larger yellow flowers, slightly mottled leaves and great vigour. Even more stunning is a more recent cross, 'Sundisk', with bronze leaves and large yellow horizontally held flowers, with a red ring in the throat.

## FRITILLARIA

### Liliaceae

A bulbous genus of over one hundred species, the name comes from the Latin, *fritillus*, or dice box, and probably refers to the shape of the seed capsule or to the traditional chequered pattern found on these boxes, which is similar to the tessellated patterns on some *Fritillaria* segments. They are found only in the Northern Hemisphere, in temperate regions, particularly around the Mediterranean Basin and eastward into Central Asia and parts of China. There is a separate development of the genus in western N America. They have adapted to live in very different habitats within these regions, from high mountain screes where they are true snow-melt plants, to coastal areas that are never frosted, wet in winter, but dry in summer. As with most plants, you are more likely to be successful with cultivation if you have at least some knowledge of growing conditions in the wild. But that said, it is very rewarding to experiment with growing plants in garden situations that tradition dictates will fail. For instance, *F. meleagris* is found in wet meadowland that has not been improved and will naturally grow well in similar positions in the garden. However, it is very adaptable, doing very well in semi-shade beneath shrubs and even sunny areas topped with gravel.

To grow a range of these attractive and subtle plants, gardeners need to expand their growing conditions to include raised beds, bulb frames or pots and, if some of the western N American species are to be cultivated, frost-free conditions are necessary. In Britain, with the milder winters we have had more recently, these American fritillaries have succeeded under cold glass. If, however, the temperature remains below freezing for days on end and the nights freely radiate warmth, the frost will penetrate the whole pot. Even this may not damage the bulb if it is in barely moist, free-draining compost, but if they have just been watered then the chance of cells being damaged by expansion increases. Another aspect of cultivation that needs careful administration is when to water after a period of severe frost. Quite often plants will actually suffer from drought as the expansion and contraction of water within the compost will allow air to penetrate to the roots. Seeking out a long-range weather forecast will often answer the question of when to water and when to leave alone.

A choice selection, *Erythronium tuolumnense* 'Sundisk' has elegantly recurved flowers.

*Erythronium tuolumnense* 'Pagoda' is a reliable performer for any gardener who has not grown this genus before.

Fritillary flowers have six segments, are bell-shaped or occasionally conic or saucer shaped, are arranged in two whorls and are usually pendulous and tessellated. The flowers, 1–10cm (⅜–4in) long, are borne on leafy stems, some just a few centimetres high with white, yellow, orange and brown, to pink, purple and green. These colours are often mixed by striping and tessellation. They flower from late winter through to mid-spring, depending on the species and the weather. On a sunny day, the bulb frames containing fritillaries will draw queen wasps, attracted by the density of the planting, which fertilize the plants; this can be slightly disconcerting, but they are so intent on the job in hand they ignore a human presence. These insects seem to be the main pollinators of the early fritillaries and although they pass from one species to another, hybrids are very rare. The seed ripens in a three-chambered capsule, which contains six columns of seed. Each seed is flat, brown with a darker embryo in the centre and quite large, making it an easy task to gather the seed in high summer as soon as the capsule turns brown.

The bulbs of *Fritillaria* vary greatly, but most are composed of two fleshy scales joined at the base by the basal plate. The flowering stem grows from the basal plate and emerges between these scales, which protect it in the early stages of growth. Some American and Asian species have bulbs comprised of many scales, rather like some lilies, with a further group producing 'rice grains', or bulblets, around the parent bulb. These bulblets provide an easy, but slow method of propagation. The plants described here are in two separate sections; the first, the American species, are grouped together because they are so different from the second group of European and Asian species.

## AMERICAN SPECIES

### F. affinis
The flowers, up to fifteen in a raceme, are pendulous with distinct shoulders and claw-like segments. They vary from lime-green to purple and are usually tessellated. The leaves are in whorls up to three in number each with as many as five leaves, but usually less. The parent bulb sports plenty of 'rice grains' when growing well, so do experiment with a few outside in a sunny well-drained position. This is a very widespread plant found from Alaska, south to California. They do quite well in my garden, which has an annual rainfall of just 54cm (22in), flowering each year but not increasing. The variation in height within the species is vast, ranging from forms over 1m (3ft) tall to little ones, not exceeding 15cm (6in).

In **var.** *tristulis* the flowers are especially dark and covered with a glaucous hue. It is under 20cm (8in) tall.

### F. atropurpurea
This again is a species widespread in western N America and found in open woodland and scrub up to 3000m (9840ft), where it is a snow-melt plant. This plant has narrow leaves, scattered all the way up the stems. The flowers are quite wide and broad shouldered, usually mottled purple and yellow, but there are variations, all in a scattered raceme. If the plant flowers very well with up to eight blooms, it often takes a few years to build up strength to flower again – this is a quite common feature of American fritillaries. The purple bulb spawns masses of bulblets, which can be grown on to flower in four to five years. Height: up to 50cm (20in).

### F. biflora
An easily grown species appears very early in the year. Consequently, the foliage needs protecting from frost or the shiny, mainly basal leaves can be burned and soon look unsightly. The plant is a lusty grower, with shiny, dark chocolate, hanging bells, maybe as many as six in a scattered raceme. Some fritillaries do not produce 'albino' offspring, but instead have yellow sports; *F. biflora* is one of the exceptions as it quite often has whitish flowers which make a dramatic contrast with the normal dark chocolate forms. The bulbs are quite large and without bulblets, so it needs a large pot to flower to its potential. Native to coastal California, so a slight tenderness must be expected. Height: up to 50cm (20in).

'**Martha Roderick**' has exceptionally stout stems to 20cm (8in) and broad flowers of dark brown with a whitish patch.

### F. camschatcensis
This stunning species is unique among fritillaries in being found wild around the Pacific rim, in both N America and in E Asia. The bulb is composed of many scales, which need careful handling when dormant. It may also grow stolons as a means of propagation. It further rebels in preferring a damp site in partial shade. It bears up to eight pendent dark purple bells, which in some forms are almost black. There are yellow and double forms available, but none are quite as spectacular as a well-grown type species. Height: up to 60cm (24in).

### F. eastwoodiae
This plant seems to be intermediate between *F. recurva* and *F. micrantha*, with flowers that vary from greenish yellow, through orange to red. It is from N California where it grows in light shade on acidic rocks. There are fewer flowers in the raceme, which are narrowly bell-shaped with recurved tips, and the grey-green leaves are mostly basal with only a scattering on the stem. This plant requires frame or pot culture. Height: 20–60cm (8–24in).

### F. glauca
The leaves of this fritillary are amongst the most attractive of the genus. An even pale grey, they are covered with a bloom, and this needs protection from rainfall or high wind if it is to remain perfect. The flowers are composed of pendent broad yellow bells, which have varying amounts of brown flecking on the inside. This plant comes from screes in NW California and Oregon, found up to 2500m (8200ft) and needs a well-drained compost that is kept dry, but not baked in summer. Height: 10–20cm (4–8in).

The form **'Goldilocks'** seems to fall within the range you might expect from seed-grown stock.

### F. grayana

For many years this plant was known as *F. roderickii*, a Californian species that grows in heavy clay near the coast. It is not necessary to dig clay for cultivation purposes; just the usual well-drained compost will suffice. The plant is rather like a shorter *F. biflora* with reddish brown flower segments with a conspicuous white patch. The tips do not flare out like *F. biflora* and are straight sided. Height: 20–50cm (8–20in).

### F. liliacea

This is another plant from coastal California, this time with white, widely conical flowers on a bare stem. The basal leaves grow outward at an angle of thirty degrees and are a shiny green. The bulb can become very long with age, reaching some 8cm (3¼in) but only 2cm (¾in) wide. When they reach this length it is very easy to be unsure which is the top when it is being repotted, so carefully lay the bulbs in a line to avoid any disasters. The bulb size is best accommodated in a 'long tom' pot, to give adequate space for root growth and support for the stem. If the temperature fluctuates greatly when the plant is in bud or just opened the stem is inclined to bend as if seeking light, so if possible grow the plant in as cool a place as possible, but with good light. The obvious place is outside but frost and high wind would do even greater harm, so a north-facing frame is a good compromise. Height: 15–35cm (6–14in).

### F. micrantha

A small-flowered species, with a loose raceme of up to twenty bell-shaped flowers, which vary from greenish yellow to a browny purple and are usually tessellated. It grows in dry open woodland in California but in countries like Britain, needs a bulb frame or pot culture. The bulb produces plenty of 'rice grains', taking a number of years to build up the size to flower. Height: 30–100cm (1–3ft).

### F. pluriflora

Along with *F. recurva*, this is the most sought after American fritillary and one of the harder to flower successfully. The plant is found in open fields in N California, growing in heavy soil that dries out in summer. The flowers are usually a stunning mid-pink, conical but quite open and outward facing. The grey-green waxy leaves are mostly basal and slightly twisted, growing from a bulb composed of a few long fleshy scales and just the occasional bulblet. The plant is best grown in a 'long tom' pot, with frost protection. Height: 40cm (16in).

### F. pudica

This is usually a snow-melt species and is fully hardy, found over a wide area of N America, from New Mexico to British Columbia. It has the appropriate nickname of 'Johnny-jump-up', as it is often the first American fritillary to flower very early in the new year. The flowers, an intense yellow which age to become orange, are held as pendent bells, above two to seven quite narrow dark green leaves. The bulb is flat and circular with a distinct cone; this plate produces many 'rice-grain' bulblets every year. If the plant is grown from seed there are quite large variations in size and flower colour, some of which are far inferior to many in cultivation. This plant is well suited to frame or cold-greenhouse treatment, where full light is essential to keep the stems from etiolating. The plant will also grow in a scree or sink as long as there is good winter light. Height: 15cm (6in).

The sterile form **'Richard Britten'** (see picture p.41) is larger in flower and when well-established will produce double heads on a single stem.

### F. purdyi

A very distinct compact plant with up to seven, often outward-facing, bell-shaped flowers with a whitish background, spotted and streaked with purple. The foliage is basal, in a whorl and often twisted, with a greyish bloom. The bulb is composed of three or four thick scales and is best grown in a frame or pot in a greenhouse. A Californian, where it can be found growing in the Inner Coast Range to 2000m (6560ft), it should be hardy, but it does need a dry summer rest. Height: 10–40cm (4–16in).

### F. recurva

The most eye-catching of all the fritillaries, with bell-shaped orange-scarlet flowers, which are tessellated and held in a neat raceme. The glaucous leaves are in whorls. The bulb produces many bulblets and after flowering takes some years before it repeats the feat. It seems best in a bulb frame or pot, but has been known to flower in an open border in the Suffolk garden of the late Sir Cedric Morris, where the soil was very well drained and sloped to the south west. In the wild it is found in California and S Oregon, growing in light woodland up to 2000m (6560ft). Height: up to 1m (3ft).

## EUROPEAN AND ASIAN SPECIES

### F. acmopetala ♔

This is a very good open border plant with large green pendent bell-shaped flowers which have a variable reddish brown stain on the inner segments. The flowers are usually single, more rarely two or three. The number of flowers will never match the number of bulbs the gardener finds beneath the ground and I suspect the bulbs have years of building up before flowering again. This hardly matters as the colony soon grows naturally to produce a good annual show and the blind bulbs are not missed. The bulb is 3cm (1¼in) in diameter and produces a few bulblets each year. The leaves are grey-green, quite narrow and spaced alternately up the stem. Native to SW Turkey, Cyprus and the Lebanon, where it is found on limestone from sea level up to 2000m (6560ft). Height: 40–50cm (16–20in).

From S Turkey, ssp. *wendelboi* is just as easily grown. It has squarer shoulders to its flowers and is usually a shorter plant.

### F. alburyana

An attractive snow-melt plant from NE Turkey, this flowers late in the year in the wild. In cultivation it often appears early in the year only to flower at ground level. This can happen in winters with mild periods that induce growth when the light is poor, so the shoot does not lengthen as it should. If the winter is cold and the spring warm, then this beautiful pink cup-shaped fritillary will flower in character. The flowers, one or two to the stem, are lightly tessellated and up to 5cm (2in) across with a few thin grey leaves. One solution might be to have an old but working refrigerator set at 4°C (39°F), where these snow-melt bulbs could be kept until spring was well underway and light and temperature could more nearly match the needs of these plants. When in growth, they will need copious water, but not of a stagnant nature. Height: 5–10cm (2–4in).

### F. alfredae ssp. glaucoviridis

This is the form of the species most often encountered by gardeners. It is quite robust with two or three, narrow bell-shaped green flowers with yellow tips. some 3cm (1¼in) long, It has grey-green leaves, including a whorl of three just behind the flower stem. From S Turkey, where it grows above limestone in heavy clay soil. It grows well in a pot or bulb frame, frequently setting seed. Height: 15–30cm (6–12in).

### F. ariana

The first of a small and distinct section of fritillaries from the Rhinopetalum group, so called on account of a bump housing the nectaries at the base of each segment. The flowers, generally six in number, are a dark untessellated pink and face outward. The leaves include a pair of bract leaves at the base of each pedicel. The plant grows in mobile sandy soils in Iran and Afghanistan. It is quite tricky to grow in cultivation and must have a warm dry summer rest. Height: 10–20cm (4–8in).

### F. armena

In Turkey there are a number of small 'purple' fritillaries, all reasonably easy to grow in a bulb frame or pot. This is a short species with one to three, dark plum-coloured narrow bell-shaped flowers, covered with an attractive bloom. From E Turkey, this is a snow-melt plant that takes to cultivation very well. Height: up to 15cm (6in).

### F. assyriaca

A slender species with narrow bell-shaped flowers, slightly recurved at the tips and with a grey exterior and greenish or yellowish inside. The leaves are alternate, grey-green and often caniculate, which gave rise to the old name of *F. canaliculata*. From Turkey and Iran where it grows in a wide variety of conditions, which probably accounts for its amenability in cultivation. Height: up to 20cm (8in).

### F. aurea

A container full of these Turkish fritillaries is a stunning sight. They have large yellow flowers tessellated with brown, held on short stems that lengthen after flowering. The leaves are grey and few in number and as each stem has only one flower, a few are needed to create an effect. However they do produce bulblets, so a good pan full can be achieved in a few years. Early into flower, often seen in late winter, they are totally hardy and suited to the bulb frame. Height: 5–10cm (2–4in).

### F. bithynica

This plant is from W Turkey and the adjacent Aegean islands, growing in stony soils amongst scrub. The flowers are narrow yellowish green bells and can have a glossy sheen, especially on the inside. The lower leaves are usually a pair and the upper are set in a whorl of three, all grey-green. Best grown in a bulb frame or in a pot. Height: up to 20cm (8in).

### F. bucharica

The white flowers are borne in a fairly dense raceme and are more cup-shaped than the rest of the group. The lower grey-green leaves are in pairs, with the rest alternate, with two bract leaves at the base of each flower stem. One of the Rhinopetalum group and the largest, it is native to Afghanistan and Central Asia, where it is found in mountains up to 1800m (5900ft), growing in heavy soil that dries out in summer. An easy plant growing very well in an unheated frame or greenhouse. Height: 20–35cm (8–14in).

## *F. carica* (see picture plate IV, 5)

A charming plant for the greenhouse or frame, but probably best enjoyed in a pot as it is quite small, but totally hardy. The yellow flowers are bell shaped and the grey-green leaves are all alternate. There is a very distinctive form with reflexed outer segments, which increases very well from freely produced bulblets. From SW Turkey where it is found in low hills, growing over limestone. Height: 10–15cm (4–6in).

The shorter **ssp.** *serpenticola* has broader leaves and more widely open yellow flowers. It is from the same area but found on acidic rocks.

## *F. caucasica*

This is one of the Turkish 'purple' group, but with larger flowers than *F. armena*, and which are often greenish on the inside. In Turkey natural hybrids between the two

The subtle, muted flowers of *Fritillaria elwesii*, an easily grown fritillary.

species are commonly found. It is an early species to flower, often in full bloom by late winter. Fully hardy but best in a pot or frame to protect it from heavy rain or damaging wind. Height: 10–20cm (4–8in).

## *F. chitralensis*

This is, in essence, a shorter *F. imperialis* and so far, is very rare in cultivation. It has yellowy green hanging bells. It will definitely be hardy, as its habitat is the rocks and cliffs of NE Afghanistan. Height: 40cm (16in).

## *F. chlorantha*

A stocky green-flowered species from Iran, where it grows in the stony mountain steppe at high altitude. The sparse shiny green leaves are alternate and mask the emerging flower stem until the moment the narrowly bell-shaped flowers open. All the forms in cultivation seem to be constant in colour, but forms with purple striping have been noted in Iran. Height: 10cm (4in).

## *F. cirrhosa*

One of the few Himalayan and Chinese fritillaries commonly found in cultivation, these plants seem to require a cool position, which never dries out, and remains just moist in summer when the bulbs are dormant. Cultivation is quite simple and successful, but growth to the flowering stage is slow. If grown in a pot, they are totally hardy and thrive in a north-facing frame, growing in a humus rich, but well-drained compost. They are amongst the later fritillaries to flower. The flowers vary in colour but are often a greenish yellow with a light tessellation of brown. In China the range of colour is much greater and these forms perhaps will acquire new names. The bulbs are naturally small and send up slender stems with thin pointed leaves in whorls, with the upper ones having tendrils for grasping shrubs for support. In the mountains the plants are often found around shrubs, which have given them some protection from the local wild and domestic herbivores. Height: 50cm (20in).

## *F. collina*

This plant is similar to *F. aurea*, but from the Caucasus. Its flowers are yellow with brown tessellations, its leaves are slender and grey-green. The flowers are not as chunky as *F. aurea* and seem to be slower to reach flowering from seed. They do need strong light to encourage the bud to open just clear of the enclosing leaves, or the beauty is spoilt. Height: 10cm (4in).

## *F. conica* (see picture plate IV, 3)

A perfect little yellow species from the SW Peloponnese, where it grows in heavy soil over limestone at quite low levels. In spite of its provenance it is quite hardy in an unheated frame or greenhouse, simply needing a dry rest period in summer. If this can be arranged in a raised bed, it will do well in the open garden. As the name suggests the plain yellow flowers are cone shaped and are held singly above shiny green leaves. Height: 20cm (8in).

### F. crassifolia ssp. crassifolia

This and ssp. *kurdica* are the most commonly encountered forms of this Turkish species. There are usually only four fairly broad leaves and a stem with one or two pendent bells, greenish to yellowish and tessellated with brown. The long nectary is very obvious under each segment, running down the length towards the apex. This plant is very easy in a frame or cold greenhouse. Height: 10cm (4in).

The leaves of **ssp.** *kurdica* are narrower, up to seven and often a glaucous grey. The plant is widespread in E Turkey and Iran and is consequentially very variable, with varying amounts of tessellation on the flowers over green to purple backgrounds.

### F. davisii (see picture plate IV, 2)

This little fritillary is only found in the Peloponnese, where it was first recorded by Dr P.H. Davis during World War II and eventually brought into cultivation by Brian Mathew in 1966. In the wild it flowers very early in the year and has often set seed by early spring. It has purplish segments, which are yellowish green inside with faint purple tessellations and shiny, quite lush leaves. An early flowering little species, it is hardy in a pot and can be grown in a raised sunny bed as long as the snails are kept at bay. Height: 15cm (6in).

### F. drenovskyi

A Balkan plant with narrow bell-shaped flowers of reddish purple with a bloom. Inside the flowers are yellowish with a purple tessellation. There is a yellow-flowered variant called *F. rixii*, which is found on the island of Euboea, off E Greece. Height: up to 30cm (12in).

### F. eduardii

This is a plant that has affinities with *F. imperialis*, but it is immediately recognisable by the pendent flaring segments of orange. The large bulbs begin to root very early in summer so should be amongst the first to be repotted, to avoid root damage. They are totally hardy but do require a dry rest in early summer, so a large pot suits them very well. They may be possible outside, but it would be safer to experiment with the next generation when grown from the seed that is regularly set. If grown from seed you may check that it is a true *F. eduardii* by pinching a leaf; if the scent is 'foxy' you have *F. imperialis*,

but if it is a bland smell you have the correct plant. It comes from Central Asia in the Pamir-Altai mountains growing in soil pockets amongst rock to 2000m (6560ft). Height: 30–50cm (12–20in).

### F. ehrhartii

The reddish purple conical flowers have a grey bloom and a yellow dot at the tip of each segment which helps in identification. The shiny green leaves are opposite at the base, then alternate. From the Greek islands, most notably Euboea, where this little dwarf fritillary grows on acidic rocks in light scrub at low altitude. Height: up to 15cm (6in).

### F. elwesii (see pictures p. 101 and plate IV, 1)

This is a larger fritillary that will grow very well in an open sunny position, even in an open border. Here, it proliferates quickly and although only a few bulbs flower each year, the massed short leaves around the tall flowering spikes are very unusual and attractive. The surrounding leaves have a glaucous hue, while the flower stems and its leaves are a dark purple-brown. The flowers are narrow bells of dark purple with a stripe of green. It is from coastal S Turkey. In cultivation it rarely sets seed, but makes up for this by multiplying very rapidly vegetatively. Height: 30cm (12in).

### F. epirotica

This dwarf species is instantly recognisable by the twin grey-green twisted bract leaves, which stand up above the flower. The flowers are predominately purple with some yellowish tessellation and a brown interior. In Britain, it flowers in early spring, under pot cultivation. Its home is at high altitudes in NW Greece, on acidic rocks. Height: 10cm (4in).

### F. euboeica

This species has yellowy green segments, the green being provided by veins which are, unusually, similar on both faces. An attractive plant for pot culture in full light, but under cold glass. As the name implies, it comes from Euboea, in E Greece, where this dwarf plant is found growing in limestone screes to quite high altitudes. Height: 10cm (4in).

### F. forbesii

The single pendent flowers are yellow, suffused with green, and with a dark nectary at the base of the segments. The stem and leaves are a mid-green colour and quite slender. It grows early in the year and requires some protection from the worst of winter's weather. Native to a small area in SW Turkey, growing quite close to the sea. Height: 25cm (10in).

### F. gibbosa

One of the most beautiful of the Rhinopetalum group, this is a challenging plant to grow well, although it can be achieved, as is regularly seen at Alpine Garden Societies' shows in early spring. In the wild, the flowers vary from pale pink to a deep brick red, but in cultivation most are a mid-pink. The flowers are held facing outward, with up to five on a stem, above the grey leaves, which can have undulate margins. The plant is native to Iran and neighbouring areas, where it grows in dry hills and steppe between 1000m (3280ft) and 2000m (6560ft). Height: 20cm (8in).

### F. graeca

The flowers of this species are a brownish purple and strongly tessellated with green. Down each segment is a prominent green stripe. Up to four flowers are held on a stem. There is considerable variation, but all are worth trying in a raised bed or bulb frame. Native to S Greece. Height: 20cm (8in).

From N Greece and adjoining countries, **ssp.** *thessala* is taller and stronger – a good plant for the garden. This plant is soon identified by its whorled tuft of three bract leaves behind the the greenish, only lightly tessellated flower bells, which are some 4cm (1½in) long. This is often given species status and so can also be found under the name *F. thessala*. In the wild it grows in scrub and screes to 2000m (6560ft). In the garden it is easy in the frame and does quite well in a sunny raised bed.

### F. gussichiae

The leaves of this plant are amongst the most glaucous grey of any fritillary and because they are relatively broad and clasping, they are a prominent feature. The flowers are predominately green with reddish brown shading that is glimpsed as they open in good light. There are as many as six in a flowers in a good specimen. It is a woodland and pasture grower from NE Greece, Bulgaria and Yugoslavia and if it ever becomes widely available it may do well in a sunny position. At present, I grow the plant in a cold frame in full sun, and a small stock planted out some years ago has persisted but not increased. Height: 30cm (12in).

### F. hermonis ssp. amana (see picture plate IV, 6)

This subspecies is grown more frequently and is more easily available than the species. It has lightly tessellated green and reddish purple flowers that are also marked with a prominent green stripe. There are many forms available with the purple nearly absent, while in others the green is replaced with yellow. The plant is native to S

*Fritillaria imperialis* 'Lutea', clearly showing the 'pineapple tuft' of leaves above the flowers.

Turkey, Lebanon and Syria in screes, rocky places and abandoned fields at 1500–2200m (4920–7220ft). This plant is vigorous enough to grow in a sunny raised bed. Height: 35cm (14in).

### F. imperialis

The crown imperial is by far the largest fritillary, with tall stout stems bearing many outward-hanging bells of red, orange or yellow. If the bells are examined closely from underneath the large nectaries will be seen to contain ample transparent nectar, beloved by wasps and bees. The crown imperial is said to be the flower associated with the legend of Calvary; it was the one flower that would not bow its head as Jesus passed and so ever since has bowed its head in repentance. This bulb has been grown in gardens for hundreds of years and figures in many of the oldest gardening books. It is a truly perennial plant that slowly produces offsets, next to the bulb, that can be as large as a tennis ball, and regularly sets seed. When the bulbs and young foliage are handled there is a strong smell of fox, but this does not detract from their desirability as garden plants. They grow most strongly in loam and clay, with poorer results on sandy soils. When growing well they will need lifting every few years when dormant and replanting 20cm (8in) deep with extra fertilizer added to the soil. After this move they usually take a year to settle down again, before flowering with renewed vigour. They are quite gross feeders and need an annual feed of a fertilizer which is high in potash. The plant is found from S Turkey eastwards through Iran and Afghanistan to Pakistan, growing on rocky hillsides. Height: 1m (3ft).

Naturally there are variations, which enabled Dutch growers, in particular, to select and name over thirty forms in the heyday of bulb collecting in the seventeenth and eighteenth centuries, of which only a few are available today. **'Argenteovariegata'** has red flowers and whitish variegated leaves. **'Aureomarginata'** is one of the old clones with a creamy yellow edge to the leaves and red flowers. **'Aurora'**, a vigorous plant with deep reddish orange flowers, is widely available. **'Lutea'** (see picture p.103) is a clear yellow cultivar with faint purple veins. **'Maxima Lutea'** ♈ is a taller and larger flowered form of 'Lutea'. **'Prolifera'** is sometimes known as 'crown-on-crown' – the pale orange flowers have one crown of flowers sheathed within another.

**'Rubra'** (see picture also p.50) is a strong growing form with dark orange flowers with faint purple veins. **'Rubra Maxima'** has been grown for over 300 years and is a rich burnt orange shaded with red and still showing great vigour. The Dutch variety, **'Slagzwaard'**, might be a candidate for Bowles' 'lunatic asylum', with its brown-red flowers and fasciated stems – definitely an acquired taste! **'Sulpherino'** is a very unusual form with tangerine-orange flowers with faint purple veins and a yellow margin. The reverse is flushed purple-black. **'The Premier'** is a reliable cultivar with soft tangerine-orange, purple veined flowers.

### F. involucrata

This species has flowers that are essentially green with purple markings and only a slight tessellation. They are variable but all have an attractive 'bloom'. The leaves are slim and the basal pair opposite, then becoming alternate and, finally, there is a tuft of three behind the flower. Native to SE France and NW Italy, where it grows in scrub and woodland to 1000m (3280ft), it does well in the garden, where increase is by seed rather than bulb multiplication. Height: 30cm (12in).

### F. japonica

A rare Japanese fritillary which is found in light wood-

land and seems to need frost-free humus-rich conditions in cultivation. It appears delicate and small, with narrow leaves, with a whorl of three above the flower. The broadly bell-shaped whitish flowers are marked with brown. Height: 10cm (4in).

### F. kittaniae

A newly described species that is proving to be easily grown under cold glass in standard well-drained soil mix. The solitary nodding untessellated flowers have pale purple outer segments and yellow-green inner ones. The stem and alternate leaves are glabrous. It is from SW Anatolia in Turkey where it grows over limestone in thin coniferous forests, at 1500m (4920ft). Height: 15cm (6in).

### F. kotschyana

A very robust, almost top-heavy-looking plant, this fritillary has broad bell-shaped brown-purple flowers, which are heavily tessellated and often have a green stripe. It has a few alternate glossy green leaves and is best grown under cold glass, to ensure a summer rest. It is from high levels in the Elburz Mountains of Iran, where it grows in rich seams of soil amongst the rocky outcrops. Height: 20cm (8in).

### F. latakiensis

This species is similar to *F. elwesii* and is just as good a garden plant. It has broader and more tubular flowers but it still has the same 'bloom' over the stem and foliage. Native to S Turkey, Lebanon and Syria, growing in scrub and open pine forest to 1000m (3280ft). Height: 40–50cm (16–20in).

### F. latifolia

A snow-melt species from the Caucasus and NE Turkey, this has flowers that are very large, with square shoulders caused by the prominent nectaries and typically purple segments, which curve in at the mouth. There is some tessellation, which is more noticeable on the inner faces. It has shiny green leaves with the lowest pair far wider than the rest. This plant does not need drying in summer and seems best in a north-facing frame when resting in summer. Height: 15cm (6in).

The form known to gardeners as **var.** *nobilis,* flowers just above ground level and has large chunky blooms that eventually etiolate to 10cm (4in).

### F. lusitanica

The flowers of this species vary from dark chocolate brown to green with varying amounts of tessellation. The thin leaves are all alternate and do not form a tuft above the flowers. This is useful in separating it from similar species like *F. involucrata* and *F. messanensis*. From the

Iberian peninsular, found from sea level to 3000m (9840ft) in the Sierra Nevada. The high mountain forms are short and are best grown in the bulb frame or pot, whereas the taller lowland forms are good garden bulbs. Height: 10–50cm (4–20in).

The prominent nectaries of *Fritillaria imperialis* 'Rubra' are popular with queen wasps during spring.

***F. meleagris*** ♔ (see pictures p. 32 and plate IV, 7)

Often referred to as the snake's head fritillary, this European native grows in damp meadowland and light woodland, in peaty as well as chalky soils. The flowers are often, but not always, solitary, broadly bell-shaped, purplish to pink with tessellation, or white veined with green. There are four to six alternate thin leaves. There are some named forms, but if you start a colony from a

mixture of colours and then grow from seed exchanges, you will soon have many variations of your own. In some gardens the white forms seem recessive and do need replacing every few years, but the general colonies will go from strength to strength. Height: 30cm (12in).

The three forms regularly offered for sale are: 'Aphrodite', with large white flowers, with some green veining; 'Jupiter', a red clone, with chequering, and 'Mars', a deep purple form.

### F. messanensis

A widespread variable species, found in Crete, Greece, the Balkans and Sicily. The single flowers are quite broad and are tessellated chocolate or purplish brown, with a pale green stripe down the centre of each segment. The leaves are narrow, with the lowest usually opposite and a whorl of three behind the flower. It is an easy garden plant that builds into a good stand quite quickly, often in semi-shade which is unusual considering its native habitat. Height: 40cm (16in).

The flowers of ssp. *atlantica* are very dark and the foliage wider. This plant is found in the Atlas Mountains in Morocco and is easily grown in a bulb frame or pot. It may well be as amenable to the open garden, so it's worth a try if you grow from seed and have enough young bulbs with which to experiment.

From Yugoslavia and Albania, where it grows in rocky places in open woods over limestone, ssp. *gracilis* grows well in a sheltered place in the open garden. The leaves do not form a tuft above the flowers, which are without any tessellation.

### F. michailovskyi ♀

This species has very quickly changed from being a very rare sought-after bulb, to being available in netted bags behind colour photographs on hooks in most garden suppliers. This transformation is due to amazing propagation facilities used by the Dutch nurseries. Luckily it is an easy fritillary to grow, suited to a raised bed or deep trough. It is also a very attractive plant with bicoloured flowers of purple and yellow. The yellow is around the mouth of the bell and can vary, if the plant is seed grown. Native to NE Turkey where it is found in pastures near the snow line. Height: 30cm (12in).

### F. minuta

This species has an unusual coloured flower; reddish brown to a brick-red with pendent, slightly flared bells, which is quite enclosed by a tuft of bright green lanceolate leaves. A slow plant to build up from seed, it is well worth the wait. From SE Turkey, where it is found in

rocky and stony slopes to 3500m (11,480ft). Height: 10–20cm (4–8in).

### F. montana

An easily grown species, for the sunny or part-shaded border. In strong specimens there are three flowers to a stem, with green bells that are heavily tessellated with blackish purple. This species has many linear green leaves, including a small tuft of three behind the flowers. Found in hills to 1600m (5250ft) along the northern shores of the Mediterranean Sea, this is a plant of limestone pavements, where the bulbs and roots are protected from great temperature extremes. Height: 40–50cm (16–20in).

### F. obliqua

This beautiful plant has a very restricted habitat in the suburbs of Athens and is unfortunately in danger of extinction in the wild. The species has quite rounded black segments with a glaucous hue, without any tessellation. Unusually for fritillaries there is an attractive scent of vanilla, not the usual musty smell found in most. The foliage is glaucous, slightly twisted and comparatively broad, and is alternately arranged around a stem which bears just one or two pendent flowers. An easy plant in cultivation, whether in a frame or in a sunny raised bed. Height: 20cm (8in).

### F. olgae

There can be as many as eight, broadly bell-shaped, greenish flowers, shaded with reddish brown, on this slim plant. The leaves are in pairs or whorls and the uppermost are narrow, ending in tendrils. This species is gaining ground in cultivation, from seed collections and second-generation cultivated stock. It is from Central Asia, where it grows in rocky terrain amongst scattered trees, up to 3500m (11,480ft). Height: 30cm (12in).

### F. olivieri

The broad flower bells of this species have a slightly upturned tip and are green and brown with only slight tessellation. The leaves are alternate and a shiny green, with a quite stout stem. It does need a rest in summer, but should not be dried too much. This Iranian fritillary grows in damp upland meadows in the Zagros Mountains. Height: 40cm (16in).

### F. orientalis

For many years this plant was often referred to as *F. tenella* or *F. montana*. Now, however, *F. montana* is a plant in its own right and *F. tenella* is merely a synonym of the

*Fritillaria messanensis* is an excellent fritillary for naturalizing under shrubs.

species *F. orientalis*. This species is a good garden plant that will thrive in semi-shaded positions in the open ground, where it usually sets seed. The flowers are bell-shaped and a heavily tessellated purple, and the leaves linear, often opposite with an upper whorl of three. Height: 15–20cm (6–8in).

### *F. pallidiflora*

A plant with great presence in the open garden, where the primrose-yellow flowers, each some 4.5cm (1¾in) long, are seen to perfection above the broad glaucous grey foliage. This species settles best in a semi-shaded bed in humus-rich soil that does not dry out in summer. As the seasons progress, these fritillaries will need lifting and splitting as the large bulbs can become very congested and fail to flower. They regularly set seed, which is held in handsome winged capsules which make interesting decorations in their own right. The plant is from NW China and further west where it grows in subalpine meadows. It seems likely there are tessellated forms or new species that are similar to *F. pallidiflora* in China, that have yet to be tried in garden cultivation. Many fritillaries are grown in China for their pharmaceutical properties. Height: 80cm (32in).

### *F. persica*

The stems of this fritillary are clad with quite narrow, slightly twisted grey-green leaves that grow all the way up the stem, just leaving the panicle of flowers clear at the top. This panicle is made up of up to twenty-five small conical flowers that show great variation in colour, from a pale straw to a plum purple. The plant does need a hot position such as at the base of a south-facing wall to flower well. Wherever the plant is sited, it will start into growth very early in the season, often as early as midwinter. Initially this is not a problem, but as the stems lengthen they do get bent in hard frosts and can be damaged during gales. So siting in a sheltered niche is very worthwhile, as the frost does not kill this handsome plant, but leaves it bent and unsightly. From Turkey and eastward to Iraq and Iran, where it grows on rocky slopes, in scrub and at the edge of cornfields. Height: up to 1m (3ft).

From Turkey comes the form 'Adiyaman' ♛, with dark plum flowers, which is always a regular flowering plant. From Iran there are some paler flowered forms that do not have the garden impact of those with dark flowers.

*Fritillaria pallidiflora* and *Trillium albidum* are caught by the low slanting sunlight of springtime.

### F. pinardii

Typically, this plant has up to four narrow bells of purple, slightly reflexed at the tips, with a grey bloom outside and yellowish green or orange on the inside. The leaves are quite broad, alternate and glaucous. The bulb often produces bulblets. It is an easy pot-grown plant for the cold greenhouse or frame. A widespread and variable species from NW Turkey, Armenia, W Iran and the Lebanon. Height: 20cm (8in).

### F. pontica

A rather under-rated fritillary that is easy to grow in a semi-shaded garden position. The quite large flowers are essentially green, but with some brownish purple which is more prominent on the inner segments, especially when the flower is fully open. The flower is untessellated and topped by a large tuft of three bract leaves. A Balkan plant, which extends into NE Turkey, growing in wood-land up to 1000m (3280ft). Height: 30cm (12in).

The **ssp.** *substipelata*, from the island of Lesbos, is a very worthwhile addition to the garden. It is not as common as the species, but has a quite broad reddish purple tip to the outer segments, which although coloured on the inner surface, shows through to the outer which is a noticeable feature of this easily grown bulb.

### F. pyreniaca ♈ (see also picture p.1)

This should be one of the first fritillaries in a collection, easily grown, attractive and clump forming in just a few years. In the Pyrenees, it flowers in meadows and woods at quite low levels, but enjoys a sunnier spot in the open border, or raised bed. The flowers are broad tessellated bells of dark brown-purple, with shiny yellow inside. There are some selections in shades of yellow; some are pure yellow with faint lines down the segments and others a tessellated yellow. These very beautiful plants unfortunately do not breed true from seed. However, the progeny are often much paler than usual and just as attractive. Height: 30cm (12in).

'Cedric Morris' frequently bears two heads per stem, with very dark bells, which rarely set seed. It is stouter and reaches a height of 45cm (18in).

### F. raddeana

This belongs to the *F. imperialis* group, but is a smaller, earlier flowering plant with a panicle of pale yellow bells that can number twenty in a well-grown plant. A raised bed suits the cultural requirements, possibly a cold one to make it flower a little later in the capricious springs of temperate climates. Early growth can be damaged by frost and every slug and snail about early in the year finds

the foliage irresistible. The charm of this plant makes a little protection well worthwhile. From N Iran and adjoining countries, where it grows in cliffs and screes up to 1500m (4920ft). Height: 80cm (32in).

### F. reuteri

Like a tall *F. michailovskyi*, this has quite open bicoloured yellow and purple bells, that have two small bract leaves at the base of each pedicel. It is very early into growth, but doesn't flower until mid-spring, so does need the protection of a cold greenhouse or frame. Even when the flower first opens, you do not appreciate its full beauty for a few days until the segments fully expand to reveal the contrasting colours. Another of the damp-growing fritillaries from Iran, it is quite easy in cultivation as long as there is a wet spring and a cool rest during summer. Height: 20cm (8in).

### F. rhodocanakis

Growing in vineyards and only from the small Greek island of Hydra, just east of the Peloponnese, this species has purple untessellated flowers, with yellowish tips to the segments. It is early into growth, and has scattered green lanceolate leaves. Height: 15cm (6in).

### F. rhodia

A species from the island of Rhodes, similar to *F. bithyn-ica*, but taller and more slender, with alternate green leaves that seem to spiral up the stem. The flowers are narrowly bell-shaped and a yellowish green, with a flared mouth. Inside is more yellow, with a small green nectary at the base. Found in scrub and open pine woods up to 500m (1640ft), it is best grown in a pot or frame. Height: 30cm (12in).

### F. roylei

Often said to be a more robust form of *F. cirrhosa*, to the gardener this is very different in many respects. This robust species is from high level meadows in the foothills of the W Himalayas. The broad-shouldered flowers can be as many as four and can have gaps between the seg-ments. They vary from yellowish green to a reddish pur-ple, with some streaking of a darker shade. It has whorls of pointed leaves without any tendrils. A good plant for a shady humusy border where it is long lived but rarely multiplies, except by setting seed. Height: 60cm (24in).

### F. ruthenica

One of the features of this species are its leaf tendrils, which separate it from *F. orientalis* and *F. montana*. The

*Fritillaria pyreniaca* is a good fritillary to start a collection as it is easily grown in a number of situations.

outer segments of the flowers are very dark purple with some tessellation, which contrasts well with a yellowish interior. There are up to five flowers. An easily grown garden plant from S Russia and the Ukraine, where its lowland habitat is often in oak and willow woodland. Height: 50cm (20in).

### F. sibthorpiana

A very distinctive fritillary, this has a solitary, narrow bright yellow bell, over 2cm (¾in) long. The foliage is sparse, just two or three quite broadly lanceolate leaves, with the largest at the base. It is from SW Turkey, where it grows in open pine forest to 1450m (4750ft). An easy plant for frame or pot cultivation. Height: 25cm (10in).

### F. stenanthera

One of the most commonly cultivated of the Rhinopetalum group of fritillaries, it has a raceme of up to eight, pink outward-facing flowers, very early in the new year. It grows well in a cold frame in a clay pot that is protected from excessive rainfall but open to the wind and temperature changes. A native of the mountains of Central Asia, like the Tien Shan and Pamir-Altai, but not found above 2000m (6560ft). Height: 15–20cm (6–8in).

### F. straussi

An Iranian and Turkish species, with quite large leaves and flowers that give the plant a presence, when grown in a frame or pot. The shiny broad lanceolate and twisted leaves are in whorls, surrounding one or two dark purple and green tessellated bells, with a long thin nectary along the segments. It inhabits earth pockets in oak scrub between 1800–2400m (5900–7870ft). Height: 15–20cm (6–8in).

### F. stribrnyi

This species has flowers that can be purple externally, with green inside, or green with purple markings, all overlaid with a bloom and without any tessellation. The stem is clothed in many alternate leaves and it also has the tuft of three bract leaves behind the flower. A lowland plant from fields and light woodland, it is found wild in Bulgaria and the small area of Turkey north-west of the Bosporos. Height: 20cm (8in).

### F. thunbergii

This very good garden fritillary is often confused with F. verticillata, a less common plant in cultivation. F. thunbergii frequently forms large free-flowering patches in the open border, where they can be left for many seasons before

*Fritillaria thunbergii has tendrils that help keep the plants upright and together in all weathers.*

there is any need to split up the bulbs. Only when flowering begins to lessen, is there any need dig deeply, to release the bulbs. The flowers are in a raceme of up to six, cup-shaped cream bells, about 2–3cm (¾–1¼in) across. They are tessellated with some green and occasionally crimson flecking. Seed is only rarely produced in temperate countries, but there is prolific vegetative multiplication. The foliage is very distinctive in whorls, with the bract leaves coiled as tendrils for clasping shrubs for support. In the garden they grasp each other and remain a very stable in any gale. It is native to E China, where it is grown extensively for the pharmaceutical trade. Height: 60cm (24in).

### F. tubiformis

This is a most attractive plant with large, square-shouldered purple flowers, heavily tessellated and covered in a bloom of greyish white. The five to seven leaves are grey-green and held alternately. The short varieties are best under glass, as the flowers open at ground level and can be spoilt by splashes of water. A species from SE France and NW Italy where it grows in high summer pasture between 1500-2000m (4920–6560ft), always over limestone. Height: 10–25 cm (4–10in).

The flowers of **ssp.** *moggridgei* are yellow with brown chequering. It is found in the Maritime Alps.

### F. tuntasia

This species had up to six purple-black glaucous and bell-shaped flowers and many alternate leaves, which are twisted like a propeller. It will grow very well in a sunny well-drained border or in a pot under cold glass and like F. obliqua has sweetly scented flowers. This species is found only on the islands of Kythnos and Serifos just south-east of Athens, where they grow over acidic rocks in low scrub. Height: 30cm (12in).

### F. uva-vulpis

This species is still confused with F. assyriaca. It has solitary flowers without any recurving at the tips of the segments. They are narrowly bell-shaped, with a glaucous hue overlaying the browny purple and yellow tips of the segments. They grow easily in the garden, but are prone to wind damage, needing a sheltered niche or an airy bulb frame. The shiny alternate leaves are quite erect. Bulblets are freely produced in this Turkish and Iranian plant which is found in fields in the high plateaus. Height: 30cm (12in).

### F. verticillata

This species is from the Altai Mountains of Mongolia and NW China, with foliage similar to F. thunbergii, but with pure white, square-shouldered and more bell-shaped flowers that are faintly tessellated. It is a most beautiful fritillary, which is proving to be quite easy to cultivate in a bulb frame. When stocks allow, this will be worth trying outside in a sunny position in the open garden. Height: 50–60cm (20–24in).

### F. walujewii

This is another species from the Central Asian mountains of the Pamir-Altai and the Tien Shan. The tessellated flowers are pinkish with green suffusions and quite long bells to 4cm (1½in) with pointed segment tips. The foliage is very narrow with the upper leaves having tendrils. It seems to grow well with more shade-loving bulbs, like *Erythronium*, in places where it does not dry out in summer. Height: 30cm (12in).

### F. whittallii

This looks rather like a green-tessellated, brown snake's head fritillary, but it is from SW Turkey where it grows in cedar forests over limestone, to 2000m (6560ft). It will grow in a well-drained position in the garden, but is strongest in a bulb frame. Height: 20cm (8in).

### F. zagrica

This species has a dark purple flower, but differs from similar plants in having small yellow tips to the segments. It has four to six quite erectly held alternate green leaves. A snow-melt plant from the Zagros Mountains of SE Turkey and neighbouring Iran. Height: 10cm (4in).

## GAGEA

### Liliaceae

A large genus of bulbs, all from temperate Eurasia, of which relatively few are in cultivation. They are all quite small plants with yellow starry flowers, which often have green or brown markings. There is just one exception; *Gagea graeca* has white flowers which are bell-shaped. They are a spring-flowering genus and are well worth the effort of introduction as they seem hardy and quietly attractive, always repaying a close inspection of the subtle mix of yellow and green. It pays to first build up a stock in a pot before risking them out in the garden. In a pot they soon multiply and the small bulbs can be transferred to a sunny raised bed or even the front of an ordinary border. They flower from what seems like tiny bulbs, which will need occasional splitting, since the old bulb tunics tend to smother new bulb development, allowing the production of leaves but not flowers.

### G. fibrosa

This short plant has a few yellow flowers up to 4cm (1½in) across which are green in bud and held on downy pedicels. The leaves are narrow, appear basally, but spread to become prostrate. A widespread species from the Mediterranean basin eastward to Central Asia, it is found growing in limestone areas and also sand dunes. Height: 6cm (2½in).

### G. fistulosa

A very early flowering species, often out in midwinter if grown in a frame, this is quite a tall *Gagea*. It has up to six starry yellow flowers, to 3cm (1¼in) in diameter, on hairy pedicels. The one or two bright green leaves are hollow in section and reach 20cm (8in). This is again a widespread plant from the mountains of S Europe eastwards to Iran, where it grows in damp meadows and in snow-melt zones. Height: 15cm (6in).

### G. graeca

This plant has as many as five flowers in a small panicle that are pendent and white with a purple stripe. When open, they remain bell-shaped and are about 1cm (⅜in) across and 1cm (⅜in) long. There are a few stem leaves as well as the narrow basal variety. The bulbs are very small and regularly split to build up a colony, which because of their size, are probably best grown in a pot. From Greece, Crete and Turkey, where it grows in grassland that is dry and rocky. Height: 10cm (4in).

### G. lutea

This plant has yellow flowers, 3cm (1¼in) across and up to ten in an umbel; when a number are grown together they form an attractive feature. There is just one leaf per bulb, over 15cm (6in) long and over 1cm (⅜in) wide, which is quite glabrous. It is best in the open garden in a cool position, as it is native to European woods, where it is quite widespread. Height: 15cm (6in).

## GALANTHUS

### Amaryllidaceae

Snowdrops must be among those flowers that people most closely associate with early spring and the genus has attracted many colloquial names such as Candlemas bells and February fairmaids. Whether or not they are truly native in the British Isles is debatable but whatever their origin, these dainty white beauties have successfully colonized many stunning locations.

These wild colonizers are usually *Galanthus nivalis* but some other species are beginning to spread beyond the confines of the garden, hybridizing as they do so, and giving rise to many of the hundreds of selections grown today. The undisturbed sites that give snowdrops the

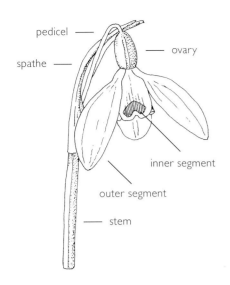

pedicel

spathe

ovary

inner segment

outer segment

stem

A typical snowdrop flower – *Galanthus* 'Straffan'

chance to thrive are often found around churches and the neighbouring clerics' houses where cutting the grass is often the only maintenance undertaken. Large drifts of apparently wild snowdrops are spread by the work of earthworms, moles and other animals. In some localities, honey bees will become active on a sunny day in early winter and make short flights to the pendent flowers, resulting in an abundance of seed. Nearby hives are another ideal for snowdrops as those that are not visited by bees have very little seed set. Gravity can also play a part in the distribution of bulbs on a steep slope. However, gardeners can not afford to let only nature maintain and propagate their bulb collection, especially if selected and named varieties are grown. It is sound practise to split the groups of bulbs every three years and then divide them into two or more groups, so if disaster strikes, by way of disease or hungry wildlife, you will not lose everything. It always seems that if you have just one rare bulb that is the one that attracts the grub or is excavated by a short-tailed vole.

The flowers have three small inner segments and three larger outer ones, and can be up to 4cm (1½in) long. Markings on the flowers, generally a 'V', 'X' or 'Y' shape, can help identify the different species and varieties. Snowdrops are usually 10–25cm (4–10in) in height. The following selection is based on the leaf and flower formation, but as so many hybrids have occurred, they are described under the heading that fits most closely their variable nature. It is not meant to be a full list of those available, that might total some seven hundred, but is instead a list of those which with care and luck, can give great pleasure on many a grey day, from late autumn through to early spring.

**G. allenii** (see picture plate IX, 9)

This is a mid-season snowdrop with wide slightly glaucous dull green leaves. The outer segments of the flowers are quite globose and the inner are marked with a single basal 'V'. The flowers appear with only half-grown foliage which extends markedly later. The bulbs are quite large and take a number of years to divide often preferring to simply enlarge. It seems to prefer a damp site, easily achieved in winter, but harder to provide in summer. It is possibly a wild hybrid as no plant has yet been found to match it and is named after James Allen, who selected so many choice snowdrops.

**G. caucasicus 'John Tomlinson'**

This strong-growing grey-leaved form has distinctive green lines on the outer segments of the flowers. It blooms in mid- and late winter.

*Galanthus caucasicus* 'John Tomlinson' is a choice snowdrop selection, named by Christopher Brickell.

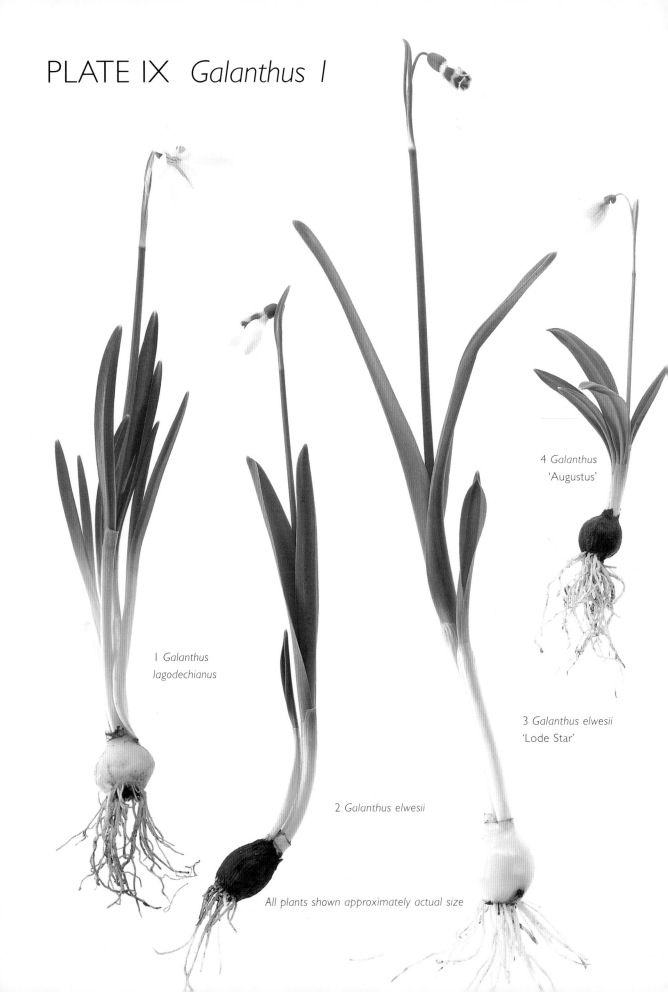

PLATE IX *Galanthus I*

1 *Galanthus lagodechianus*

2 *Galanthus elwesii*

3 *Galanthus elwesii* 'Lode Star'

4 *Galanthus* 'Augustus'

*All plants shown approximately actual size*

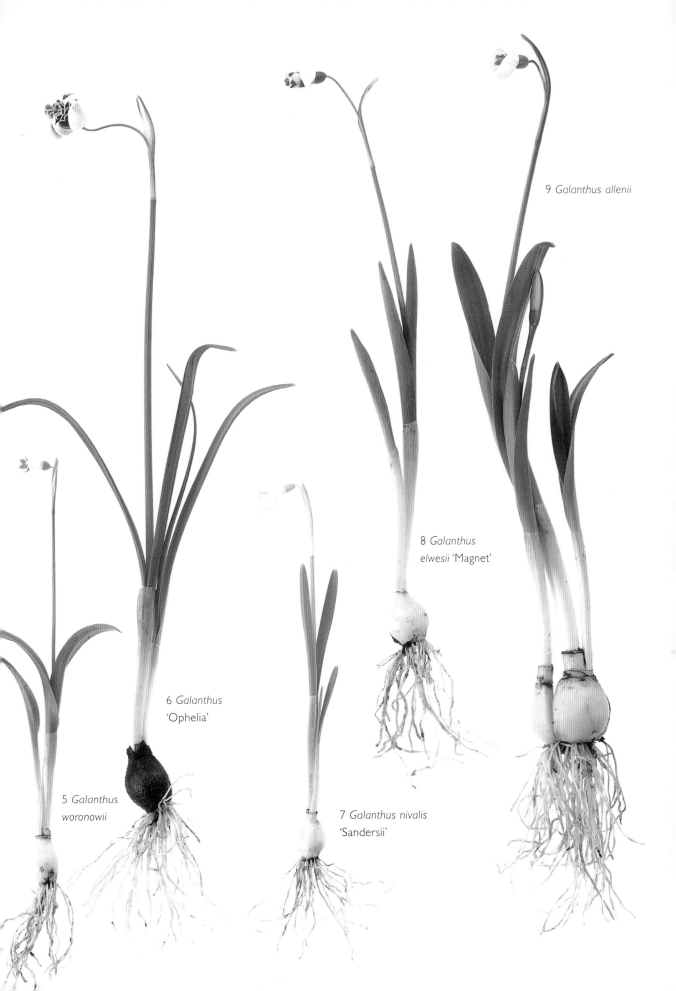

9 *Galanthus allenii*

8 *Galanthus*
*elwesii* 'Magnet'

6 *Galanthus*
'Ophelia'

5 *Galanthus*
*woronowii*

7 *Galanthus nivalis*
'Sandersii'

'Earliest of All' is a similar selection but with slightly less globose flowers.

### G. elwesii ♔ (see pictures also plate IX)

In this very variable plant, the inner segments of the flowers sometimes have both basal and upper green markings, whereas others, which are often referred to as *G. caucasicus*, only have a basal 'V'. Indeed in some selections the green becomes a solid block in the segment. The leaves are glaucous and convolute. These bulbs have been imported from Turkey in millions, so it is to be expected that there will be many variations available.

'Caroline Elwes' is a beautiful yellow-marked variant. 'Lode Star' (see picture also p.120) has the typical markings on the inner segments and great vigour. 'Magnet' is a slow-growing form with a very long pedicel and glaucous foliage. The inner segment has an inverted 'Y' which turns up at the ends rather like in a caricature of a Victorian gentleman's moustache and is connected to the basal blotch by the stem of the 'Y'.

### G. fosteri

This species grows in S Turkey and the Lebanon, where

*Galanthus elwesii* 'Caroline Elwes' is a unique yellow form of the species.

it experiences a much drier summer than many snowdrops. It will need a good summer ripening to induce flowering instead of bulb multiplication and so is one of the few snowdrops that takes to pot culture and is treated like a fritillary with a fairly dry summer rest. Alternatively a south-west aspect in the roots of a deep rooting tree might suit. The leaves are deep apple-green and the flowers have one broad basal mark on the inner segments. Some growers are finding *G. fosteri* to be quite adaptable to cultivation.

### G. gracilis (see picture plate X, 5)

A very distinct snowdrop because of its narrow glaucous twisted leaves and the basal green marking on the inner segments, which separates it from *G. nivalis*. It is very variable in size, but usually flowers just after the turn of the year, thriving in a sunny position. Hybrids between *G. elwesii* and *G. gracilis* have occurred even in W Turkey and N Greece, where the two species overlap, but they can usually be identified by the wider leaf which may still be twisted with a little hooked tip.

### G. ikariae ssp. ikariae

The flowers of this subspecies do not have any basal green marking on the inner segment, and the outer segments are half as long as broad. The convolute leaves are quite a dark green. This is one of the shorter snowdrops with a late season of flowering. Found only on a few Aegean islands.

An earlier, smaller-flowered form, **ssp.** *latifolius* is found across a widespread distribution from Turkey to N Iran. It proliferates quickly and will grow well in quite dark and dry conditions.

### G. lagodechianus (see picture plate IX, 1)

The flowers of this snowdrop have outer and inner segments that are both quite long and pointed. The inner segment can have a pale inverted 'V' marking, but it is inconsistent, sometimes merely being represented by two spots, or even being absent altogether. The leaves are dark green and shiny. This snowdrop can be seen in profusion at Anglesey Abbey in Cambridgeshire, where it grew so well that it received the name *G.* 'Anglesey Abbey'. However, it should be referred to as *G. lagodechianus*. Native to the Caucasus region.

### G. 'Magnet' ♔ (see picture plate X, 3)

This tall variety has a particularly long pedicel, which arches out letting the flower hang well away from the stem. The outer segments lift up to be very nearly horizontal and sway in any breeze. It can be confused with *G. nivalis* 'Galatea', which is of a similar height and

When left to their own devices, colonies of *Galanthus elwesii* can seed profusely, forming bold features in the garden.

demeanour, but which has a pedicel that has a right angle bend just above the ovary. They both seem to flower from very small bulbs. This James Allen selection has maintained its vigour for over one hundred years. Height: 20cm (8in).

**G. nivalis** 🏆 (see picture plate X, 6)

The common English snowdrop, this has single, and occasionally double, pendulous flowers with six white segments of two sorts. The outer three segments are largest, oval and often described as 'petals', whereas the three inner segments are half the size of the outer with a notch at the end, forming a tube. In the species there is a green marking at the end of these segments, sometimes in the shape of a horseshoe. *G. nivalis* is readily distinguished by the two emerging leaves which are pressed flat against each other, this is the applanate leaf structure. The leaves are linear, greyish green and quite flat, usually less than 1cm (³⁄₈in) wide.

Many varieties which have affinities with *G. nivalis* have been selected, of which the following are amongst the most robust or are particularly special. **'Flore Pleno'** 🏆 is the double-flowered form where the inner segments have multiplied, forming a dense rosette. In some of the better selections the rosette is neat and even, rather like a double primrose. It is vigorous and is just as good at colonizing large areas as the single species. There is a yellow marked double, **'Lady Elphinstone'** which after planting can revert to green and then in the following year revert to all yellow again. The flowers of **Poculiformis Group** have inner and outer segments that are white, but just occasionally there appear tiny spots where the inner 'V' marking is usually situated. The name 'poculiformis' means 'cup-shaped', which is a strange epithet as the outer segments are not at all unusual in this respect. The selection **'Sandhill Gate'** is said to be stable and always white, without any faint green markings.

In **'Sandersii'** (see picture plate IX, 7) both the ovary and the 'V' marking on the inner segment are yellow. There are various clones, none of which have the consti-

*Galanthus elwesii* 'Lode Star', a large selection from Anglesey Abbey in Cambridgeshire.

tution of *G. nivalis*, its green counterpart, but it is well worth the effort to find a sheltered humus-rich spot for this delightful plant. Its origins seem to lie in some Northumbrian woods where the colonies of *G. nivalis* contain some yellow variants. Unlike some double 'yellow' snowdrops they do not revert to green when transplanted. 'Scharlokii' is a late-flowering form found in Central Europe, by Julius Scharlok. It has a very distinctive divided spathe, likened to the ears of an ass, and substantial green markings at the ends of the outer segments. An easily grown selection, it increases well.

'Virescens' is a late-flowering selection where the inner segments are almost entirely green and the outer ones are shaded green. It is slow growing and is best in a position that receives strong winter light to encourage the outer segments to lift up, otherwise they look rather dull. In 'Greenish', another similar single 'green', the flowers come a little earlier and although less intense in markings, it is proving to be an easier plant to manage. 'Viridapicis' is larger than 'Scharlokii' but has similarly

marked flowers consisting of green lines on quite claw-like outer segments. The spathe is large and is like a hood bending over the flower.

### G. plicatus ♛

This must be one of the most prolific of garden plants, since it has been in cultivation since the Crimean War, when some were brought back to Britain from Turkey by returning soldiers. It has quite large flowers with a prominent, but variable green mark at the base of the inner segment and broad, glaucous leaves with the margins folded back.

The flowers of **ssp.** *byzantinus* (see picture p.48) have green markings at the base and at the tip of the inner segment. From NW Turkey, this plant shows great variation in size and time of flowering. One of the most attractive selections of this subspecies is **'Three Ships'** (see picture p.31), found by John Morley beneath a cork oak tree in the garden of Henham Hall in Suffolk.

Many selections of the species have been made with **'Warham'** being the most famous, named after a garden in Norfolk, and receiving the highest plant award, the First Class Certificate of the RHS, in 1937. There is a painting of this snowdrop by E.A. Bowles in the Lindley library which is of particular use in trying to be sure of the authenticity of this beautiful plant. **'Wendy's Gold'** was found in Cambridgeshire in the 1980s and has a yellow ovary and inner segment marking.

### G. reginae-olgae ssp. vernalis (see picture plate X, 4)

The autumn-flowering species *G. reginae-olgae* has finished flowering by early winter but ssp. *vernalis* starts to flower in midwinter. The flowers are the typical *G. nivalis* form. The leaves have the intense silver centre line of the species and enjoy a far sunnier position than most, where they often set seed.

### G. rizehensis

This species has neat rounded flowers, with a single dark green 'V' at the tip of the inner segment, that are seen early in the snowdrop season. The leaves are unusually narrow, deep green, not glaucous and are recurving after flowering. It has a restricted distribution from the Black Sea coast around Trabzon in Turkey, where it grows in light woodland in heavy soils. Despite growing wild in a mild climate, it seems unaffected by low temperatures.

### G. woronowii (picture plate IX, 5))

A small easily grown species from the Black Sea coast of Turkey that produces many offsets. The flowers have only a basal green bridge marking on the inner segments. The green leaves have no trace of bloom and are short.

## SELECTED HYBRIDS WHERE THE PARENTAGE IS UNSURE OR MIXED

### G. 'Atkinsii' ♆ (see picture also p.33)

A Victorian selection which has excellent vigour and is ideal for setting in drifts, as it is large and robust. It does not always have the most perfect form, as occasionally it has aberrant segments, but these are lost in a group effect. The outer segments are large and pointed with a well defined and rounded 'V' on the inner ones. The leaves are easily recognized, with only one edge rolled back, glaucous and with a silver centre line.

### G. 'Benhall Beauty'

A tall, slim plant with thin flat glaucous leaves, held well above the ground. The flower is below a long ovary and with an upper and lower mark. The lower mark is an inverted 'V', with the two arms widening. The inner mark is another 'V' but with narrowing arms. The plant came from John Gray's garden at Benhall in Suffolk and was named by E.A. Bowles.

### G. 'Clare Blakeway-Phillips'

This has flowers that are of good substance with a lime-green inner marking – a broad X – which fades towards the base. The ovary is also lime-green and adds to the unique colour contrast of this cultivar. It has very glaucous leaves, which are plicate and extend to become an attractive feature.

### G. 'Colesbourne'

A plant found by Henry Elwes (of *G. elwesii* fame), this has glaucous convolute leaves. The inner segments and connecting ovary of the flowers are very slim and long. The inner segments have an all-green marking with a noticeable white edge. It is slow and quite late flowering, but very distinct.

*Galanthus* 'Atkinsii' growing among the young foliage of fennel makes an attractive combination.

*Galanthus* 'Galatea', showing its defining right-angled kink in the pedicel.

**G. 'Galatea'** (see picture also p.12)

James Allen's paper to the RHS in 1891, mentioned his seedling 'Galatea' as being 'one of the giants of the family as to size of flower, but not in stature. I have never been able to decide whether this or 'Charmer' is the more perfect flower.' Today we have a tall snowdrop with obvious affinities with *G. nivalis*, that has quite large well-proportioned flowers. The distinguishing feature is the right-angled bend in the pedicel, just above the ovary, which separates it from G. 'Magnet'. Unfortunately G. 'Charmer' has been lost and the comparison Allen was making is no longer possible. Height: 20cm (8in).

**G. 'John Gray'**

Another of the few snowdrops to be awarded the First Class Certificate by the RHS, this plant was selected from a snowdrop labelled XXX, found in Gray's Suffolk garden and named by E.B. Anderson. It proved to be outstanding, with exceptionally early large flowers above very glaucous grey foliage. The inner segment has a large 'X' mark, which fades towards the base. It is not always easy to cultivate, but does thrive in a raised bed of good loam in full sun, that is kept just moist in summer.

**G. 'Ketton'**

A strong grower with a large single flower, the inner segments have a thin triangular mark at their end and two faint spots below, close to the ovary. From Ketton in Leicestershire and first introduced by E.A. Bowles.

**G. 'Merlin'**

Another fine selection from James Allen, this snowdrop has all-green inner segments with a distinct waist and large clean white outer segments.

**G. 'Mighty Atom'**

On the same occasion that G. 'John Gray' was selected by E.B. Anderson another special selection was found – this was named 'Mighty Atom'. It is a later large-flowering *Galanthus*, with a substantial single dark green inverted 'V' beneath large pure white segments with a distinct claw at the tip. The flower is held close to the stem on a short pedicel, above leaves which have a uniform grey bloom, with edges that are just rolled back and taper slightly towards the base and apex. There are many spurious 'Mighty Atoms' around, so to be sure, do acquire it while in flower.

**G. 'Robin Hood'** (see picture plate X, 2)

This variety has flowers held in an almost military fashion, tightly against the scape, with an upright spathe. The flowers have a green 'X' that is barely joined in he middle, with the outer end darker than the base. The thin glaucous leaves, fold in the same way as *G. plicatus*. Another Allen selection, it is still very vigorous and an excellent garden plant, liking full sun in a good loam.

**G. 'S. Arnott'** ♆ (see picture pp.14–15)

This is another snowdrop that has the constitution to colonize large areas and indeed an unexpected colony was part of the inspiration for Col. and Mrs Mathias to begin The Giant Snowdrop Company in the early 1950s. This snowdrop is highly perfumed. Its large perfectly formed flowers have a very deep green heart-shaped mark on the inner segment and are borne on stout stalks.

**G. 'Straffan'**

This is one of the aristocrats of snowdrops, with some of the purest white single flowers. It has an extended season as the bulb sends up a second flower as the first is fading. One of the last to bloom, it often still looks pristine in early spring. This is probably a hybrid between *G. nivalis* and *G. plicatus* and was from stock collected in the Crimea and grown in Ireland, where from just two plants a colony was established.

**G. 'The Pearl'** (see picture plate X, 7)
This very elegant plant has a long pedicel and large flowers, which sway very noticeably in any breeze. The inner segments are filled with a large mid-green 'X'. It is slow to increase and seems to need a well-drained and sunny site to succeed. It has even plicate leaves. This selection was probably made by F.C. Stern, the author of the only monograph on *Galanthus*, written over forty years ago.

**G. 'Trym'**
A small snowdrop with quite extraordinary flowers. The inner and outer segments have green markings and a notch at the end of each. All segments flare and the outer ones are not as large as usual and also have a green inverted heart shape that covers half of the segment. It has slim plicate leaves. It regularly sets viable seed in some gardens and produces many similar but slightly different progeny.

*Galanthus* 'Blewberry Tart' has outward-facing double flowers that show the loose green inner segments.

## DOUBLE-FLOWERED SNOWDROPS

There are very few neat double snowdrops available that remain constant. Many of those offered come from crosses done by Mr H. Greatorex, who took the pollen from *G. nivalis* 'Flore Pleno' and fertilized some strong single forms of *G. plicatus*. The resulting cultivars were generally given the names of women in Shakespeare. These selections have proved to be strong-growing doubles, some of which have neat inner rosettes, with outer segments that are often slightly pinched at the tip. **G. 'Jacquenetta'** and **G. 'Ophelia'** are widely available.

Another double *G. plicatus*-cross came from Ireland; **G. 'Hill Poë'** has a very neat inner rosette with five outer segments, which when mature looks very fine and not at all peculiar. **G. 'Blewberry Tart'** is a more recent selection with outward-facing flowers, marked with green. Recently, the hybrids that are the result of years of naturalizing snowdrops at Anglesey Abbey, have produced some doubles. The first of these has been named **G. 'Richard Ayres'** after the head gardener. This is probably

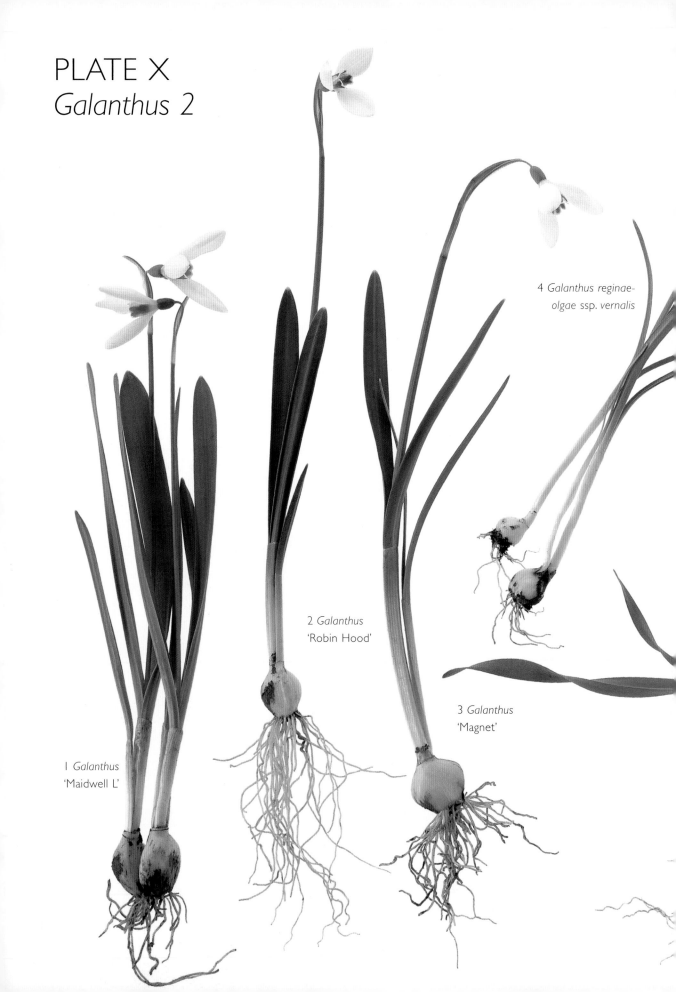

PLATE X
*Galanthus 2*

4 *Galanthus reginae-
olgae* ssp. *vernalis*

2 *Galanthus*
'Robin Hood'

3 *Galanthus*
'Magnet'

I *Galanthus*
'Maidwell L'

6 *Galanthus nivalis*

8 *Galanthus* 'Oliver Wyatt's Giant'

5 *Galanthus gracilis*

7 *Galanthus* 'The Pearl'

*All plants shown approximately actual size*

A new, rare snowdrop, *Galanthus* 'Ailwyn' has very neat and even inner segments.

a cross between *G. nivalis* 'Flore Pleno' and *G elwesii* and it has a very tight double inner rosette with the inverted 'V' becoming a 'Y' and joined to a paler green base blotch. Like *G.* 'Hill Poë' there are five outer segments. The second discovery was **G. 'Ailwyn'**, an extremely neat double that exhibits great vigour and which has a small green bridge on the inner segments.

## HAEMANTHUS
### Amaryllidaceae

This South African genus has a multitude of common names, all alluding to its peculiar construction. 'Paint-brush' seems to be one of the most appropriate, as the flowers are produced in a dense umbel, with many pro-truding stamens, giving it the appearance of a stubby paintbrush. There are no petals and the colour is pro-vided by the long cylindrical perianth segments, joined in a tube around the prominent yellow stamens, which are surrounded by broad bracts, that can be white to red, depending on the species. They can become large bulbs, with long roots and do need to grow in large containers or in a greenhouse border. They are tender and need a minimum of 5°C (41°F) in winter.

There are species that flower throughout the year depending in their habitat; here only the late autumn- and winter-flowering plants will be described, which come from coastal SE South Africa.

### H. albiflos

Flower spikes emerge during autumn and slowly rise to bloom through late autumn into winter on this, the most commonly cultivated species. They have whitish to green bracts around the conspicuously yellow pollened stamens. Often after flowering the head bears very deco-rative red berries. The evergreen leaves, usually two, are very broad, strap-shaped and dark green with ciliate edges. It needs some shade in summer, but full light in autumn and winter. The potting compost should have extra grit added to aid drainage, in order to replicate the sandy soils of their home, but still be quite fertile, so a John Innes No 3 is a good base. Although this plant is evergreen it should have a drier period in late summer. Height: 45cm (18in).

### H. deformis

This is a much shorter plant, with white bracts and paler yellow pollen on the prominent stamens. Also evergreen, it requires similar cultural treatment to *H. albiflos* if it is to flower in late autumn. Height: 10cm (4in).

## HERBERTIA
### Iridaceae

Although from temperate regions of S America, these plants are best treated as tender and given winter protec-tion. If the minimum temperature is never lower than −5°C (23°F) then it might be worth trying to grow them outside with a covering of straw or similar to pro-tect from the occasional slight frost.

A succession of single iris-like flowers that last just for a day are borne on wiry stems in spring. The colours are usually blue or purple on three large flat segments sur-rounding three smaller central ones. The leaves are nar-row and erect and pleated lengthways. Once the leaves begin to fade in spring the pots need a dryish rest period without being baked. The bulbs are covered with black or dark brown tunics and are winter growers; they can be potted and started into growth in autumn. Seed is regularly produced and if sown fresh can be brought to flowering in two years. There are also offsets, which can be separated during dormancy.

### H. lahue

Found wild in Argentina, Chile and Uruguay, and with a far-flung subspecies in Texas, this species produces 3–5cm (1¼–2in) diameter violet-blue flowers with green spathes, over a long flowering period. Height: up to 20cm (8in).

### H. pulchella

The most commonly encountered species, this is found wild in S Brazil and Chile. The flower segments are about 5cm (2in) across and are pale blue with a white blotch at the base. The inner petals are flecked with a dark violet-blue. It is usually grown as a cool greenhouse plant. Height: 30cm (12in).

## HERMODACTYLUS

### Iridaceae

There is just one member of this genus, which was once included in *Iris*, but it is distinct in only having a one-celled ovary (irises have three). This is usually noticed when extracting seed.

### *H. tuberosa* (see picture p.128)

This is commonly called the snake's head iris or widow iris, because of its sombre, but subtly coloured flowers, which are well worth close inspection. The rush-like leaves begin to grow in autumn and, in the right position, become quite dense. The iris-like flowers appear amongst these leaves in late winter and early spring. As in irises, the flowers have 'falls', the three, drooping outer petals, which are yellowish green with a velvety black-brown tip and about 5cm (2in) across. The 'standards', the three inner petals, vary from green to yellowish and have led to a few selections being named. The flowers are scented and can make attractive cut flowers in a cool room. In wet regions it might be best to grow them under glass, preferably in a border rather than a pot as they soon exhaust the nutrients and become pot-bound. After flowering the fertilized flowerheads hang down and the peppercorn sized seed is easy to collect.

The rootstock creeps, gradually colonizing new ground. From the root's tip a shoot is produced and then the finger-shaped tubers (*dactylos* means finger) produce a second root that will grow away as next year's shoot. The plant is from the Mediterranean basin and has been in cultivation for 400 years, growing well in sunny positions that dry out in summer. Height: 40cm (16in).

## HYACINTHELLA

### Hyacinthaceae

A small genus from SE Europe, Israel and Turkey, where they grow on rocky hillsides that are rather hot and dry in summer. These plants will grow in a sunny raised bed with good drainage, as long as the climate provides a warm summer. Otherwise, a bulb frame or pot culture will ensure success for these hardy little bulbous plants.

The flowers have segments that are joined to form a bell-shaped tube, with six lobes. They are held in small racemes 3–5cm (1¼–2in) long and look a little like miniature hyacinths. They vary in colour from pale to deep blue and violet and all have dark violet-blue anthers. There are one to three basal leaves that are prominently veined. They are not spectacular bulbs but do make a very attractive group if a good number are grown together. So, when repotting pack the bulbs more closely than normal, or simply take the congested group and do not loosen them before replanting in a larger pot.

### *H. atcheyi*

Narrow deep blue bell-shaped flowers are produced in late winter on this Greek plant. The erect leaves are 1cm (⅜in) wide and 15cm (6in) long. Height: 15cm (6in).

### *H. campanulata*

In spring, this species has pale blue flowers on a raceme held within two wide glaucous leaves. A Turkish plant found in limestone areas up to 1300m (4265ft) in spring. Height: 10cm (4in).

### *H. glabrescens*

This has spring flowers that are violet blue and narrowly bell-shaped on longer pedicels. The glaucous grey-green leaves are 15cm (6in) long and 2cm (¾in) wide. Found wild in the Taurus Mountains in S Turkey. Height: 10–15cm (4–6in).

### *H. heldreichii*

Similar to *H. glabrescens*, this has darker flowers on shorter pedicels and narrower leaves, to 15cm (6in) long. Native to SW Turkey in deciduous woods and gravel areas. Height: 10–15cm (4–6in).

### *H. hispida*

The leaves of this species are sometimes twisted and undulate and are covered with long white hair, which changes to purple spotting near the base. The flowers are dark violet-blue in loose racemes on long pedicels. A Turkish native growing on scree to 1100m (3600ft). Height: 10–12cm (4–4¾in).

### *H. leucophaea*

A taller species, this has upright leaves and up to twenty very pale blue flowers on dark purple stems. This is native to E Europe. Height: 25cm (10in).

### *H. lineata*

This species can have as many as twenty-five flowers to a stem, but usually fewer, and they are deep to violet-blue. The leaves have long hairs on the edges giving them a grey appearance. It is from S Turkey, found in stony areas up to 2000m (6560ft). Height: 10–15cm (4–6in).

### *H. nervosa*

A compact raceme bears ten to twenty-five pale blue flowers up to 8mm (⅓in) long. The leaves tend to undu-

late and twist and can reach 15cm (6in) in length. This plant has a wide distribution from Turkey to Iraq, Jordan and Israel, where it is found in many rocky situations up to 1200m (3940ft). Height: 10–15cm (4–6in).

### H. pallens

This plant is often sold as *H. dalmatica* and indeed it does come from the Dalmatian coast, reaching only some 400m (1320ft) into the limestone hills. It has pale blue flowers held in a dense raceme. Height: 10cm (4in).

## HYACINTHOIDES

### Hyacinthaceae

This genus is more generally known as the bluebell, that common wild bulb of woods and hedgerows, and popular colonizer of gardens. The flowers can have a beautiful fragrance that will fill a wood with perfume on a still spring day. All the bluebells have bell-shaped flowers, about 2cm (¾in) wide, but some are slightly more tubular than others. And they are not always blue; *Hyacinthoides non-scripta* and *H. hispanica* have hybridized and selected colours have been named. They all have strap-shaped or linear leaves.

The bulbs are almost solid and non-scaly and are renewed annually. They do well in humus-rich soil under the canopy of deciduous trees, where they can find the neutral or slightly acidic soils that they seem to prefer. They will grow in nearly any shady position and do spread by seed and bulb multiplication very quickly, so it is best to keep them away from less vigorous plants that might well be overwhelmed. The bulbs will pull themselves down to a considerable depth and once established are hard to control.

These plants may still be known by the old name *Endymion*, but this has been superseded by what is in fact the older name, *Hyacinthoides*.

### H. hispanica

Commonly known as the Spanish bluebell, this quickly forms clumps of erect strap-shaped dark green leaves, up to 60cm (24in) long. In spring they produce many unscented blue flowers, that flare outwards or face upwards. It grows wild in the Iberian Peninsular and in N Africa. Height: 30cm (12in).

There are many different coloured hybrids that grow just as strongly; '**Danube**' has many dark blue flowers, '**Excelsior**' has violet-blue flowers with a paler blue

*Hermodactylus tuberosus*, planted *en masse*, makes an attractive sight in late winter.

stripe, '**La Grandesse**' has nodding pure white flowers, '**Mount Everest**' has a broad spike of white flowers and '**Rosabella**' has a raceme of violet-pink blooms.

### H. italica

Unlike the other two species here, the Italian bluebell has more open and starry flowers that are mid-blue, held in a dense conical raceme. The leaves are dark green and rather dull. Height: 20–30cm (8–12in).

### H. non-scripta

The English bluebell is a vigorous clump-forming bulb which produces flowering stems with six to twelve scented pendent bells of a mid-blue shade. The leaves are glossy and strap shaped. A pure white form with cream anthers, and occasionally a pink one, can be found. Height: 50cm (20in).

## HYACINTHUS

### Hyacinthaceae

Actually quite a small genus, so many selections of just one species have been made that it has become one of the most well known of bulbs. Upright spikes of outward-facing bell-shaped flowers with reflexed petals appear in mid-spring. They are usually well-perfumed and come in a variety of colours. All the members of this genus originally come from W and Central Asia.

### H. litwinowii

A plant for the bulb frame or pot culture, this species needs fast drainage and a period of rest in summer. It is not common but it is a well-proportioned attractive plant. The unscented flowers have very reflexed petal lobes of pale blue with a dark blue line down each segment. The leaves are fewer in number than the common hyacinth and are also broader to 5cm (2in) across. It comes from high altitudes and in rocky places in E Iran. Height: 20cm (8in).

### H. orientalis ssp. orientalis (see picture p.130)

The truly wild species has a longer flower spike than *H. litwinowii* with some four to six narrow channelled bright green leaves, 15cm (6in) long and 5mm (¼in) wide. The flowers vary from pale to deep violet blue, pale to deep pink and white to cream. Found in S Turkey, Syria and the Lebanon on limestone. Height: 15–20cm (6–8in).

The flower lobes of *H. o. ssp. chionophilus* are more deeply incised and the leaves are wider. Mention of several varieties of *H. orientalis* can be found in a Dutch catalogue as early as 1600. By 1629 six were shown in Parkinson's *Paradisi in sole paradisus terrestri*, including a white semi-double form with green stripes. By the middle of the next century George Voorhelm of Haarlem was growing 150 double blues and purples and half that number of singles, together with reds and whites which again were predominately double. Sometime late in the 1700s, the first yellow hyacinth was offered, again by the same Dutch Nursery. The double form is now quite a rarity in catalogues, but the breeding of new varieties is still undertaken in Holland.

Every year many hyacinths are specially treated so that with care they will flower very early in winter, even over the Christmas period. These bulbs are lifted in the green and then heated as dry bulbs to set temperature levels, which gradually diminish week by week, until they are ready for planting in bowls or water containers in early autumn. Other stock is not warmed and flowers naturally

*The wild species, Hyacinthus orientalis, has a grace that is missing in the modern selections.*

later in the spring, in containers or in the open garden. There are two forms of *H. orientalis* available. Firstly and by far the most numerous are the large single-spiked hybrids, which provide the 'forced' bulbs as well as most of the bedding plants. Second is the Multiflora group, producing several slender stems to a plant, with individual blooms more loosely spaced; often used for outdoor bedding, they can do well in bowls for a spring show. The Royal General Bulbgrowers' Association of Holland still lists nearly 200 different cultivars of *H. orientalis*. Of these only a handful are double. Fickle fashion plays a large part in the demand for plants, and hyacinths are no exception to this.

Among the best cultivars are: **'Anna Marie'** ♛, also sometimes known as 'Christmas Joy', which is pale pink; **'Blue Jacket'** ♛ has large dark blue, purple-striped flowers and is useful for forcing; **'Blue Orchid'** (see picture p.49) is a modern semi-double variety with vibrant

blue flowers with a darker vein; **'City of Haarlem'** ♔, an old cultivar with soft primrose-yellow flowers is good for late forcing; **'Delft Blue'** ♔ has soft lilac-blue blooms and can be used for early forcing; **'Gipsy Queen'** ♔ has dark salmon and apricot flowers; **'Holly-hock'** is widely available with a double flower of crimson red; **'King Codro'** is a dark violet double; **'L'Innocence'** ♔, over one hundred years old, has single ivory white flowers; **'Ostara'** ♔, has single flowers that are a pansy violet and pale purple blue, and **'Pink Pearl'** ♔ has flowers of fuchsia purple with a pale edge.

## IPHEION

### Alliaceae

This is a small genus from S America, of which one species is proving very amenable to general garden cultivation in the Northern Hemisphere, while a few others are best grown under cold glass. These plants have quite narrow, but long linear leaves and six-lobed flowers on a short stem. The leaves grow throughout the winter with the main flowering period being in mid-spring, but precocious flowers often appear much earlier. The whitish bulbs are prolific with their offsets. They are best planted in a well-drained position and in times of prolonged frost may need some protection.

### I. sellowianum (see picture p.27)

The yellow flowers have a thin purple stripe on the outside of each segment and resemble a large half-opened crocus, about 2cm (¾in) across. Under cold glass they are proving to be easy and free flowering. They begin to leaf in autumn, with narrow dark green quite rigid leaves, up to 20cm (8in) long, and which have an oniony smell. The plant comes from S Brazil, Uruguay and Argentina. Height: 5cm (2in).

### I. uniflorum

This is the most commonly cultivated species, with many named cultivars. The pale blue flowers are usually solitary and about 3cm (1¼in) across on erect stems. The narrow glaucous leaves are fleshy and up to 25cm (10in) long. They are wild in Argentina and Uruguay in hilly areas. Height: 15cm (6in).

'Album' was an early white selection which has been superseded by the larger strong-growing cultivar, 'Alberto Castillo' which was found in an abandoned Buenos Aires garden in the 1980s. It is a little taller than the other selections, with perfect flowers of pure white and is proving to be a very attractive bulb for a raised bed in full sun. 'Charlotte Bishop' seems to flower very

early and has a hint of red in the flower. **'Froyle Mill'** ♔ is a prolific variety with deep violet-blue flowers. **'Rolf Fiedler'** ♔ is very different from the others and may be a selection from another species. It needs cold glass cultivation to grow well, but the sky-blue flowers with a white throat are worth the pot and bench space. The leaves are wider, just as glaucous and a fine background to the beautiful flowers. **'Wisley Blue'** ♔ has great vigour and proliferates freely. It is a pale lilac blue.

## IRIS

### Iridaceae

With some of the most beautiful and unusual flowers of the plant kingdom, this is an intriguing genus of bulbous and rhizomatous perennials. Just one small flower can exhibit a huge range of subtle colours. The flowers have six segments; the larger and lower three segments are called the falls, looking like a landing pad for insects, and often with patches of colour on crests and ridges. The inner three segments, called the standards, are much smaller, often upright or spreading and occasionally reduced to not much more than a claw. In between the standards are three winged and often segment-like style arms, each one sheltering a stamen.

Only bulbous varieties are considered here as the others flower late in spring and into summer. The genus is usually divided into groups; those that concern us here are the Reticulata Irises, from W Asia, and the Juno Irises, harder to grow successfully, but well worth the effort. They flower in late winter and early spring.

## RETICULATA IRISES

These dwarf early flowering bulbs are quite hardy; they can be grown in a raised bed, a bulb frame or pot in a cold greenhouse. They are tough sturdy plants with two or three, usually square-sectioned leaves, which are short at flowering time but lengthen later. The flowers, about 6cm (2½in) across, are borne on short stems and are large in comparison to the size of the bulb. In the species, *I. reticulata*, the flowers come in an array of colours thanks to many varieties being selected. One of the early selections still available is *I.* 'Cantab', selected in 1914 by E.A. Bowles. The bulbs are covered in a reticulate or net-like coat of a creamy brown colour. Many of the species produce bulblets, which are found clustered around the basal plate and at repotting time it is a simple task to separate them, and repot or plant out in a raised bed. The bulbs can suffer from ink disease, a fungal disease easily recog-

*Iris* 'Cantab' was a selection made by E.A. Bowles and is still one of the most beautiful.

nized by the black blotches on the outside of the bulbs. If a patch of plants is loosing vigour or has yellow marks on the leaves, lift the bulbs immediately; if infected they must be discarded or burnt, to avoid any further infection. If the bulbs are pot grown, the summer inspection can give you early warning of any trouble. If the marks are very small a systemic fungicide may curtail the disease, or at the very least protect the other bulbs. Unless given otherwise, the plants included here reach a height of 10–15cm (4–6in).

### I. bakeriana

This plant is easily recognized by its unique leaf section; instead of the usual four sides this has eight ribs, giving the leaf an almost circular appearance. The flowers have a

very conspicuous deep violet spot on the falls and on a warm day it smells of violets. It is shorter and more slender than *I. reticulata* and not quite as strong, so perhaps is best under cold glass. It is found in Iraq, SE Turkey and W Iran on dry hillsides.

### I. danfordiae

In this bright yellow iris, the standards are reduced to mere bristles, but the falls are lemon-yellow with some orange marking in the centre. A very compact and early plant, often flowering as early as midwinter, it usually splits into non-flowering bulbs after the first year. The bulbs are very cheap and are often are treated as annuals with fresh stock bought each year. Some success in inducing flowering has been achieved by planting the bulbs 10–15cm (4–6in) deep and feeding with a high potash fertilizer in spring, after flowering. It is a Turkish plant from the snow-melt zone.

### I. histrio

This plant flowers as early as *I. danfordiae*, but is a beautiful pale-blue with darker blue blotches and yellow marks on the falls. The flowers are large and are best under cold glass, as although this is hardy, they can be spoilt by inclement weather. It is from a more southern location, found in S Turkey and the Lebanon.

The falls of **var. *aintabensis*** are far smaller but of a similar colour. It is tougher and does well in a sunny well-drained spot.

### I. histrioides

This is the strongest garden iris of the Reticulata group, with royal-blue flowers produced year after year. They are large, up to 8cm (3¼in) across, with the falls having a yellow ridge surrounded by a paler blue zone. They are very weather resistant and lighten up any winter garden, with the leaf-less solid flowers. The leaves soon push through and can reach 30cm (12in) or more in length. it is found only in N Turkey.

There are some excellent cultivars that include: 'George', which has plum-purple standards and darker falls with a yellow blotch on a white background; 'Lady Beatrix Stanley', an old but vigorous cultivar, with mid-blue falls and the usual yellow and white markings, and 'Major' ♆, which used to be the best known, but has now died out in some gardens and is becoming scarce. The flowers of **var. *sophenensis*** are narrower, a deep violet-blue and with less spotting on the falls.

### I. hyrcana

This has small, very clear pale blue flowers, with hardly any spotting or veining on the falls. The bulbs are nearly spherical. It is best grown under glass. Found only south and west of the Caspian Sea area.

### I. 'Katharine Hodgkin'

This hybrid, although stated by its raiser E.B. Anderson to be a crossing of *I. histrioides* and *I. danfordiae*, seems far more likely to have been *I. histrioides* with *I. winogradowii*; this is supported by the resulting progeny, for when the same cross has been repeated, the plants are very similar. They have yellowish falls, veined with blue and a pale blue suffusion, and the stature of *I. histrioides*.

### I. kolpakowskiana

This iris has three to four, thinner channelled leaves, rather like crocus. It is smaller than many, with flowers 3–4cm (1¼–1½in) across, with red-purple falls and an orange-yellow ridge. The leaves are just emerging at flowering time and never become very long. It is tricky to grow and seems to need frame or pot cultivation and a long summer rest. Found in the Tien Shan Mountains, making it the most easterly of this group.

### I. pamphylica

This species has flowers that are very mixed in colour, with falls a deep brownish purple with a yellow blotch which merges into a greenish veined purple end. The standards and style branches are pale blue. It requires a deep pot to grow well or unrestricted root space in a bulb frame. The leaves grow to 55cm (22in). It is a large recently discovered Reticulata iris from S Turkey, where it was found at the edges of forests in rocky places. Height: 20cm (8in).

### I. reticulata ♛

The actual species is rarely found in cultivation, but selections and hybrids with *I. histrioides* and *I. bakeriana* are among the very best early bulbs. If seed can be obtained from the true species, then natural variations will be found in the resulting flowers with an extra delicacy not found in the hybrids. In the wild, the colour varies from purple to blue. The wild plant is found in a wide area from E Turkey, through the Caucasus and Iraq into Iran, and in a wide variety of locations from mountainsides to cultivated fields. This diversity suggests, correctly, that it is an adaptable plant to cultivation and as long as it has good light and drainage it will persist for many years. The problem of ink disease is the most likely cause of its demise.

### Reticulata cultivars

Selections of the species *I. reticulata* are widely available and relatively cheap. The early namings came from English gardeners, like E.A. Bowles, and the later ones from Dutch nurseries, although even here, no new forms have been registered in the last twenty-five years. These bulbs are ideal for pot cultivation and are often used in semi-permanent plantings, mixed in decorative containers with other plants.

They are very perennial in bulb frames and will often last for many years in a raised bed in full sun. In this situation, I think they appreciate an occasional thinning when dormant, to remove the accumulation of old tunics and so allow young bulbs a chance to grow unimpeded in freshly fertilized soil.

They have thin four-ribbed leaves that are short at flowering time but will continue to grow until they reach 30cm (12in) or more at maturity. This list of cultivars does include some selections not always found at every garden supplier but it does give an idea of the range available to the gardener.

*Iris 'Katharine Hodgkin' is a sturdy plant that looks ideal planted at the edge of a border or in the rock garden.*

*I.* 'Cantab' (see p.132), a selection by E.A. Bowles is quite small, with Cambridge-blue flowers that have a yellow-orange crest. There is a scarce selection 'Cantab Alba', which is the palest of blues. Although very beautiful it is, unfortunately, without much vigour. *I.* 'Clairette' is an *I. bakeriana* cross with sky-blue flowers that have white-striped falls. The blooms of *I.* 'Gordon' are light blue with violet falls and with an orange blotch surrounded with white.

*I.* 'Harmony' is a strong selection, the result of a cross with *I. histrioides* 'Major'. It has flowers of a deep sky blue with prominent gold markings on a white-streaked background. *I.* 'Hercules' has velvety purple flowers with an orange blotch on their falls. *I.* 'J.S. Dijt' is a strong reddish purple selection named after the raiser. *I.* 'Jeannine' is a sweetly scented and has deep violet flowers with an orange blotch. *I.* 'Joyce' is a result as the same cross as *I.* 'Harmony' and is similar except that the blotch is streaked with a greyish brown.

*I.* 'Natascha' has an ivory white flower, with the falls veined green and a golden yellow blotch. It is a very beautiful selection. *I.* 'Pauline' has standards that are violet and falls that are purple with a large white blotch that is variegated with blue. *I.* 'Purple Gem' is an *I. bakeriana* seedling. The flowers are violet with purple falls, blotched with purple and white.

*I.* 'Royal Blue' has deep blue flowers with a velvety gloss and yellow-blotched falls. *I.* 'Springtime' has mid-blue standards with its violet falls being tipped with white. The ridge is yellow with purple spots. *I.* 'Violet Beauty' is an *I. histrioides* 'Major' crossing of some substance. Its flowers are of a uniform purple with an orange centre to the falls. *I.* 'Wentworth', a selection from the last century, has disappeared from nursery lists, but hopefully still exists in collections.

### I. 'Sheila Ann Germaney'

Another cross of *I. histrioides* and *I. danfordiae* which has very pronounced blue veining. The amount of veining on all these hybrids varies year by year and the possible causes are debated. It may be a virus or hopefully, just temperature and moisture-induced seasonal variations, which as long as the leaves remain healthy need not cause too much alarm.

### I. vartanii

This rare species from Israel and Jordan is probably tender, requiring at least cold greenhouse cultivation, with a summer rest. The flowers vary from whitish to a slate blue with a cream crest on the falls.

### I. winogradowii ♀

A most attractive species, this is found in only one location in alpine meadows in the Caucasus. It resembles a primrose-yellow *I. histrioides* with some green spots on the falls. It has become widely grown, but unfortunately still remains quite expensive. This plant does not require growing in a bulb frame, but it does need a position in the garden that does not dry out in summer. A raised bed, which has been humus-enriched, in part shade, seems to suit it best. It regularly sets seed, which should be sown as soon as ripe; this is a particularly effective way of increasing your stock.

## JUNO IRISES

This second bulbous group includes some of the most beautiful flowers found anywhere. Unfortunately most, but not all, are tricky to grow, needing precise conditions and a little luck. They have thick fleshy storage roots at the base of the bulbs, and these must not be snapped off during handling or transplanting. In growth, the normal feeding roots grow out from the basal plate around these semi-permanent roots. The leaves of this group are distinct in being deeply channelled with the base folded around the stem, like a leek. The flowers have a much reduced standard, which usually grows out horizontally or hangs down.

The Juno irises are found in the wild from Turkey eastwards to Central Russia and Asia and southward to Jordan, with one solitary European, *I. planifolia* from SW Europe and N Africa. The plants all have hot dry summers and cold winters with snow cover, so unless this is your garden's climate, they must nearly all be grown in airy frames or greenhouses, either in deep pots or planted directly in well-drained beds within these structures. Whatever happens watering must be very carefully applied – water must not be trapped in the channelled leaves or they may rot.

To describe cultivation techniques it is simpler to further divide this group into two: group 1 includes those that will grow out in the garden, group 2 includes those that need cultivation under glass.

### Group 1

For those few that grow well in a sunny well-drained garden site, it is good practice to dig in some coarse grit and slow-release fertilizer like bone meal. They are quite gross feeders and will refuse to flower unless there is adequate nutrient. When growing well they will set seed.

*Iris* 'Natascha' is a stunning new selection that is best grown in a container.

Sown fresh, the seed will germinate in the following spring and give you fresh infection-free stock to flower in four to five years. If any of the leaves ever show any signs of striping with cream or yellow remove them immediately, to avoid the virus spreading, which it will surely do if left unchecked.

### I. aucheri ♛

A plant with three to six flowers, which are blue or rarely white, with a central yellow ridge to the falls, and reaching up to 8cm (3¼in) across. The leaves, to 25cm (10in), completely conceal the stem until fruiting. The native plants are from the area centred around SE Turkey and Syria. The commercial strain is reasonably hardy and is quite perennial in a sheltered spot. Height: 40cm (16in).

### I. bucharica ♛ (see picture p.136)

The easiest Juno to grow, it has up to seven flowers that are creamy white, 5–6cm (2–2½in) across with a con-spicuous wide, deep yellow blade to the falls. The shiny mid-green channelled leaves are up to 40cm (16in) tall. There is also an all-yellow form in cultivation, sometimes erroneously found as *I. orchioides*. *I. bucharica* is found in Central Asia in stony places and field edges. Height: 40cm (16in).

### I. cycloglossa

This species from Afghanistan is unusual in being found in wet places, consequently it will grow well in a sunny spot in Britain and other similar temperate climates. The flowers are few in number but quite large, a bluish violet with a yellow blotch on the falls and they stand well clear of the leaves. The foliage is sparser than many of the Junos, but with the usual clasping channelled leaves. It seems to set seed regularly in gardens and is an easy species to bring to flowering quite quickly. Height: up to 50cm (20in).

### I. graeberiana

In the drier east of Britain, where I garden, this species is an excellent plant for a sunny well-drained position.

Elsewhere, some protection from summer rain is advisable. It is a tall Juno, but starts to flower at about 20cm (8in) and then as the flowers are fading it reaches 40cm (16in). The leaves are already formed at flowering; initially they appear tightly spaced but they spread out along the stem as it reaches its full height. The flowers are 5–7cm (2–2¾in) across and are mainly blue with some purple veining, and a white centre to the falls with blue veins. Found in rocky regions in Turkestan. Height: 20cm (8in).

### I. magnifica ♛

This is one of the tallest and easiest of the Junos seen in cultivation. It has up to seven pale lilac flowers, with a yellow area in the centre of the falls. They are 8cm (3¼in) across and live up to the species name. There is a white form, which still has the yellow blotch on the falls. The shiny leaves are scattered along the stem. This is found in mountains around Samarkand in Central Asia. Height: 60cm (24in).

*Iris cycloglossa* is an attractive Juno iris that will thrive in a well-drained sunny border.

### I. 'Warlsind'

This is a hybrid between *I. aucheri* and *I. warleyensis*. It is later flowering than the parents and taller, with blue falls that are edged yellow and deep blue standards. Height: 40cm (16in).

### Group 2

The remaining Junos require growing conditions where they can get the summer ripening and deep root run they need. The airflow needs to be buoyant to avoid any fungal attacks. The most successful method of growing Juno irises has been pioneered at the Royal Botanic Gardens at Kew, in west London. Here, waist-high raised beds with brick walls, are filled with a sand plunge and covered by a greenhouse without walls, so air movement is very free. The irises are grown in deep clay pots, which are watered when necessary in winter and spring. All that is missing is the snow protection of winter and occasionally in hard winters a searing wind may damage the foliage. Most amateurs cannot afford this sort of structure but tall frames with sliding side vents and removable glass roofs do work very well, especially if they can be placed

on a brick or concrete base. This base needs to be 60cm (24in) or more high to afford good drainage for the deep plunge medium and help with the free movement of air. The irises need a very free draining mix with at least fifty per cent sharp grit in the potting compost. During summer they can be repotted; in fact they must not become too congested or botrytis may affect the plant, which can be fatal. These irises are only available from specialist nurseries, enthusiasts and through societies like the Alpine Garden Society, which have shows country-wide where these plants can be seen in peak condition. Although tricky to grow, their unique colouring and structures makes every effort in cultivation worthwhile.

### I. caucasica

The flowers, 5cm (2in) across, are a greenish yellow with a yellow ridge on the falls. The light green leaves surround the plant at flowering, reaching some 15cm (6in) in height. In this plant the tuberous roots are thinner and need careful handling. This species is found in E Turkey and in adjacent countries in high mountain screes up to 3000m (9840ft). In spite of this range it has proved to be quite growable in lowland Britain. Height: 15cm (6in).

### I. fosteriana

This species is very distinctive with creamy yellow falls which contrast starkly with the bright mauve standards. It is a short plant, with the stem almost hidden by the rather narrow leaves. Again, it has thinner storage roots than is usual. It grows on dry hills reaching 2000m (6560ft) in E Iran and Afghanistan. Height: 25cm (10in).

### I. kuschakewiczii

Despite the tongue twisting name this species is eminently growable in a deep pot or frame. The flowers are pale lilac with many streaks and dots of purple and with a white crest on the falls. The leaves are very handsome, dark green with a contrasting white edge, and reaching up to 15cm (6in) in height. Found in the Tien Shan mountains of Central Asia on north-facing rocky slopes. Height: 15cm (6in).

### I. persica

A beautiful diminutive Juno, with variable flowers, from grey-green to a silver-grey, with purple or purple-brown falls and about 5cm (2in) across. It has slim storage roots and a few narrow leaves, greyish beneath with a pale edge. This plant is often available but is a challenge to grow, although well worth the effort. It is not from Iran as the name would suggest, but is from quite low altitudes in S Turkey, N Syria and Iraq. Height: 10cm (4in).

### I. planifolia

The only European Juno, this species is native to the Iberian peninsula, N Africa, and larger islands in the Central Mediterranean, where it can be in flower at Christmas. Even in Britain it starts into growth very early and does need protection to grow well. This protection must balance the need for good ventilation to keep the plant free from botrytis. The flowers are quite large, up to 7cm (2¾in) across, and lilac to blue-violet, with a gold ridge down the centre of the falls; it makes a stunning pot plant in very early spring. The plant has very large storage roots, which need a deep pot to grow freely. Height: 15cm (6in).

### I. × sindpers

This is a strong-growing hybrid between I. aucheri and I. persica with flowers that are usually blue with yellow on the falls. This is an easy plant and ideally suited as a starter for pot cultivation. Height: 15cm (6in).

### I. vicaria

This is similar to I. magnifica but on a smaller scale. It may take to a sunny position but at present is best grown in a frame. It is pale lilac with a yellow blotch in the centre of the falls, which narrow more to their base than in I. magnifica. It is quite widespread in Central Asia in rocky slopes to 1500m (4920ft). Height: 20–30cm (8–12in).

### I. warleyensis

This Juno will do quite well in a sunny sheltered site, but for most growers it is safest in the frame. It has up to five flowers which are purple-blue or deep to pale lilac, with a prominent deep violet patch on the blade which is edged with a narrow band of white. There is a bright yellow crest, which is toothed and ruffled. A plant of rocky slopes in Central Asia. Height: 25–45cm (10–18in).

### I. willmottiana

This robust plant is available commercially and flowers when the glossy green leaves are only just emerging. They are four to six in number, 7cm (2¾in) across, and deep lavender to light blue with a large whitish blotch on the falls, surrounded by violet lines and streaks. Height: 25cm (10in).

## KOROLKOWIA

### Liliaceae

A genus of just one species, which is closely related to *Fritillaria*, this has bell-shaped flowers that resemble some lilies more that many fritillaries.

### K. sewerzowii (see picture p.138)

This plant erupts from the soil in mid- or late winter.

An attractive bloom covers the leaves of
*Korolkowia sewerzowii.*

The leaves and stem are a glaucous greeny bronze colour
and the pendulous flowers are green or purplish brown.
Although hardy under cold glass, this plant would be
unlikely to thrive in the open garden, so the growing
conditions in a deep pot or a bulb frame are ideal. A tall
plant, it needs the space of a large container. It also needs
very good light to remain compact and even then may
bend towards the south, so an occasional turn will help
to keep it upright. The bulb is large, up to 8cm (3¼in) in
diameter, and composed of large scales. The roots, which
are large and brittle, begin to grow in late summer, so
these plants should be amongst the earliest to be repotted or lifted. The seeds are flat and long, about 1cm
(⅜in), and are best sown as soon as ripe by inserting
them end on into a seed mix. They should germinate
at the turn of the year, when they need bringing in to
protect them from the worst of the winter. Found in
Central Asia and NW China. Height: 30cm (12in).

## LACHENALIA
### Hyacinthaceae

This exclusively South African genus of bulbous plants
has rather waxy bell-shaped or tubular flowers over
slightly succulent foliage, which is often attractively mottled with dark blotches over paler backgrounds. After
*Gladiolus*, they are the next most popular bulb grown by
South Africans, with over one hundred species to chose
from. They are just frost tender, but they also dislike great
heat, often beginning to flower in late winter; they grow
and flower best where temperatures range from 13–18°C
(55–65°F). I have seen plants survive and flower very
well in an large unheated greenhouse, doing well enough
in fact, to need dividing each year. However, this is not
usually recommend unless you live in areas with little or
no frost. Elsewhere, you need a suitably heated greenhouse. In late summer the bulbs need repotting with all
the old root debris removed and then planting in a half
pan in a well-drained mix of John Innes No 3 plus added
grit. Only plant the bulbs just below the surface and then
water sparingly until new growth appears; that is when
the watering needs increasing. The bulbs need full light
and a dilute feed during the spring. Once it is summer,
they need a cool rest without water and then an annual
repot, when the numerous offsets can be removed.

### L. aloides var. aurea 🏆
This is just one variety of a widespread species, named
after its resemblance to the aloe. It has pendent tubular
flowers, which in this variety are a striking golden yellow. Height: 25cm (10in).

The flowers of **var. luteola** are yellowish green and
there are often a number of orangey red sterile flowers
at the top of the inflorescence. This is usually the last
to flower. The flowers of **var. quadricolor** 🏆 have a reddish orange base to the outer segments, which shade to
yellow and terminate in green. The inner segments are
yellow with maroon tips, making it altogether a most
stunning plant. The outer segments of **var. vanzyliae** are
pale blue at the base shading to white with green tips.

### L. bulbifera
This very reliable plant often begins to flower at Christmas. Its pendent red flowers, with slightly protruding
inner segments and green tips surrounded by purple, are
held over dark spotted leaves. As the name suggests, it
produces bulbils at the base of the leaves. Height: up to
40cm (16in).

### L. contaminata
A strange name for such an attractive plant, this species

has bell-shaped, horizontally aligned flowers of white that have a maroon dot at the apex and white inner segments with have a maroon central stripe. The foliage is grass-like and very different from the other varieties. Height: 20cm (8in).

### L. glaucina

The fragrant flowers are pale blue to purple and composed of slightly upward facing segments; the inner ones open wide at the tips and are twice as long as the outer. The leaves are usually spotted and striated, 2cm (¾in) wide and 25cm (10in) long. Height: 30cm (12in).

### L. multablis

This tall species is long lasting with colourful flowers. The tip of the inflorescence is composed of sterile, tightly closed, electric-blue flowers, above urn-shaped flowers of pale blue shading to white with dark brown tips. The protruding inner segments are yellow with brown tips and the yellow is more noticeable as the flower matures. As the flower ages the lower flowers turn a brownish red colour. Height: 30cm (12in).

### L. pustulata

The unattractive name of this plant refers to the warty features found on the fleshy all-green leaves. The plant is really rather attractive with bell-shaped flowers of cream or straw-yellow, with green tips to the outer segments. The inner segments are green with dark pink marks at the tips. Height: 30cm (12in).

### L. rubida

A very early flowering plant, this often begins in late autumn. The pendent tubular flowers are a ruby colour. The leaves are spotted green or dark purple and are often quite immature at flowering time. Height: 20cm (8in).

## LEDEBOURIA

### Hyacinthaceae

Previously included in *Scilla*, this genus from South Africa is grown just as much for its attractive foliage, as its starry bell-shaped or open cup-shaped flowers. They can be grown in a cold greenhouse, or better still in a cool greenhouse, or even on the kitchen windowsill. The plants included here reach a height of 10cm (4in).

### L. cooperi

Also known as *L. adlamii*, this is a commonly cultivated plant with succulent green linear to lanceolate leaves with stripes of purple-brown. The purple flowers are held in a short raceme and the bulbs are stoloniferous. This species is deciduous and has survived for many years without protection in a sunny scree bed.

### L. socialis

The silvery lance-shaped leaves have dark blotches on the upper surface and a pinky purple under the surface. The raceme bears many pale purple and green flowers.

## LEUCOJUM

### Amaryllidaceae

Often known as snowflakes, this small genus is allied to *Galanthus*. All six segments of the flowers are of equal length, unlike *Galanthus*, which has three small inner segments and three larger outer ones.

### L. longifolium

A delicate-looking spring-flowering snowflake from Corsica, it needs the dry rest in summer that a frame or greenhouse can provide. It seems to require excellent drainage with a great deal of sharp sand added to the compost to induce a good show of the clusters of two to four white flowers. Height: 15cm (6in).

### L. nicaeense ♀

Known as the French snowflake, this compact plant has small white flowers in early spring. Although usually grown under glass this bulb is flowering regularly in a raised bed that has no winter protection. It has no foibles and sets seed and multiplies well in cultivation. Found growing wild in the Maritime Alps and surrounding area. Height: 10cm (4in).

### L. trichophyllum

Early in the year this delightful small *Leucojum* produces white or pink flowers. It has up to four flowers per stem, which is usually surrounded by three slender, filiform leaves. It is native to sandy soils in the Iberian peninsular and N Africa, so is best planted deeply in a pot of sandy compost and kept dry in summer. Height: 20cm (8in).

### L. vernum ♀

The spring snowflake is a robust garden plant that comes from the damp meadows and woods of S and E Europe, and it appreciates the same damp habitat in the garden. The white bell-shaped flowers are the largest of the genus and are produced in late winter or early spring. The tall stem usually bears one to two flowers which generally have green tips to the segments. The broad strap-shaped leaves are deep green and the fleshy bulbs have a thin brown tunic. There is a small form of the species with narrower and darker leaves and a stem of only 20cm (8in) tall. Like snowdrops, they can be divided and moved 'in the green' after flowering. Height: up to 30cm (12in).

In **var. carpathicum** the tips of the segments are yellow.

A very robust form from Hungary, **var.** *vagneri* has two flowers to the scape.

## MASSONIA

### Hyacinthaceae

This genus is from South Africa, where it is found in areas with dry hot summers, like the SW Cape, growing in poor soils. The flowers are held in umbels on a non-existent or short stem, from which the prominent stamens provide the attraction to the gardener. They have a pair of broad flat leaves that grow out horizontally from the bulb, just above the ground. These are often covered with bumps and bristles called, very unattractively, 'pustules'. In Britain, they are winter growers and need a cool greenhouse and exposure to all the brightest light available to stop them growing out of character. The compost used can also help; it should contain plenty of sand or grit and have little fertilizer added, so that growth is short and in keeping. They look best if grown singly, as the leaves need space to mature evenly without competition. Their flowering height is just above ground level.

### M. depressa

This species has smooth, large, near circular leaves to 15cm (6in), one of the largest of the family. In the sandy flats of the Great Karoo in the N Cape it flowers after the rain. The bulbs are reported to be edible. The flower cluster is white, pink or red, with yellow stamens.

### M. echinata

The prickly massonia, this has flowers which are yellow or white fading to pink. It has prostrate, obviously veined leaves, covered in little bumps or prickles.

### M. jasminiflora

The flowers of this species are white or pink and fragrant, with varying coloured anthers and it has ovate fleshy leaves, 8cm (3¼in) long. From the Orange Free State, Cape Province and Lesotho.

### M. pustulata

The leaves of this species are more oblong than most, up to 8cm (3¼in) long and 2cm (¾in) wide, and are covered with pustules, as if blistered. The inflorescence is densely packed with flowers of creamy pink, white or yellow. This plant is mostly found in Namaqualand. Height: 5cm (2in).

## MELASPHAERULA

### Iridaceae

There is one species in this South African genus, where it is found in dampish areas in the SW Cape and Namaqualand. It is frost tender and winter growing, so is best potted and watered in autumn and grown in good light in a cool greenhouse, where it will flower in late winter or early spring. Easily grown, it regularly produces new papery corms and sets seed, which germinates in the most unexpected places, often preferring the neighbouring pot or a crack in the greenhouse paving. When the leaves turn brown in summer, the pot can be kept quite dry until autumn, when repotting is carried out.

### M. ramosa

This species is often found under the now invalid name of *M. graminea*. It has narrow iris-like foliage, which is heavily veined and conceals the stem for much of its length. The panicle of small creamy flowers contains many delicate-looking, but long-lasting blooms. Each of the flowers has six pointed segments, which are rather irregular in shape and are sometimes suffused with purple. Height: 30cm (12in).

## MERENDERA

### Colchicaceae

This small genus is closely related to *Colchicum*, but differs in that the flower does not have a complete tube. Some look open at the base of the segments and they tend to fall apart more as the flower matures. The genus is well spread from Spain eastwards to Afghanistan and south to Ethiopia, with autumn- as well as spring-flowering plants. They are best grown in a bulb frame or pot to protect them from winter storms, and particularly heavy rain, which can easily damage the flowers. Most corms look like typical small *Colchicum* corms and are happy in any soil. *M. sobolifera*, however, has horizontal rhizome-like corms that prefer a sandy compost.

### M. attica

A late-autumn species from S Greece and W Turkey, this produces a succession of rather spidery pale pink flowers. They are 3–4cm (1¼–1½in) in diameter and have dark brown or deep violet anthers. The narrow leaves appear at the time of flowering and then continue to grow, reaching 12–15cm (4¾–6in) by spring. It is found in open stony places and sparse grass to 1000m (3280ft). Height: 4cm (1½in).

### M. filifolia

The flowers appear in late autumn and the leaves in winter and spring; they are very narrow and up to ten in number. This species may be a little tender, as it comes from S France, Algeria and the Balearic Islands, where it grows in low-level sandy and stony places in scrub and beneath pines. It requires a well-drained sandy soil in a raised bed or bulb frame that is also quite sheltered from the coldest weather. Height: 4cm (1½in).

### M. hissarica

A very hardy winter-flowering species from Central Asia, where it is found in stony places to 4000m (13,120ft) in the Pamir-Altai and Tien Shan Mountains. The few leaves expand after the pale pink rounded flower appears. It needs pot culture or bulb-frame treatment with a dry rest in summer. Height: 4–5cm (1½–2in).

### M. kurdica

The large bright pink flowers of this species have have wide segments and can be 6cm (2½in) in diameter, giving a very pleasing show. The leaves grow on after flowering and are also broad, reaching 4cm (1½in) in mature specimens. Some seed of this plant is regularly available and should be quickly ordered as demand always outstrips supply. A very attractive and scarce corm from SE Turkey where it grows on mountains at high altitude. In Britain it is prone to botrytis, so an airy siting in a frame is essential, as is the removal of the dead flower segments as soon as they darken. Height: 5cm (2in).

### M. robusta

This is unusual in having up to eight erect leaves, which are just visible at flowering in early spring. The segments are rather thin and can be pale pink or white, with green anthers. It is from southern parts of Central Asia. Height: 4cm (1½in).

### M. sobolifera

This is the species with horizontal corms that prefers a sandy, but well-fertilized growing medium. Here it will send up many quite small white or pinkish flowers, which are soon surrounded by thin upright leaves. Found from Bulgaria eastwards to Afghanistan in damp spring pasture. Height: 3cm (1¼in).

### M. trigyna

This widespread species is very variable, so it is worthwhile selecting only those with good colour and wide segments for display. The leaves, usually three in number sheath the pinkish flowers, which can be more globose than many other forms of *Merendera*. It is found in Turkey, Iran and in the Caucasus, with the more eastern forms having greater substance. Height: 5cm (2in).

## MUSCARI

### Hyacinthaceae

Often referred to as grape hyacinths, these bulbous plants consist of a large number of species, many of which are very similar in the eyes of a gardener. However, there are some very attractive *Muscari* which are distinct and do not spread too quickly, a trait of many of the species. The flowers are held on leafless stems in dense or loose racemes, composed of many small bells with varying constriction at the mouth. The narrow, often channelled leaves begin to grow in autumn. There are one or two with broader and gradually tapering leaves, again with channels. The 'true' bulbs are globose and fleshy, with a thin papery tunic, which is often dark in colour. Some of the species spawn numerous bulblets at the base of the bulb and and it is these that can become rather too invasive in an intensively gardened bed, although they have their place in a wilder setting.

All grow best in full sun and most will thrive in the ordinary border, where planting in drifts amongst spring-flowering shrubs can give a very easily achieved dramatic effect. There are just a few, which will be highlighted, that need a little extra care and placing to grow well and not suffer damage from late winter weather.

### M. armeniacum ♔

This very easy and robust species is found in woods and meadows from Yugoslavia eastward to the Caucasus. The flowers are held in dense racemes on short stout stalks and are bright blue with a very narrow white edge to the mouth. The leaves are long, channelled and greyish above; after a few years they can choke the flowers, so these plants do need regular splitting when dormant. Height: 25cm (10in).

'Blue Spike' is a Dutch selection with a dense double blue head. 'Cantab' is a later flowering, bright Cambridge blue and of shorter habit. An old British selection, 'Heavenly Blue' (see plate III, 2) is still one of the best.

### M. aucheri ♔

This species has a raceme with cobalt-blue fertile flowers around the base and paler blue infertile ones at the top of the cluster. The pale green, glaucous-faced leaves have an incurved tip. *M. tubergenianum* is probably a selection of this species, or maybe a hybrid with *M. armeniacum*. A Turkish species, this plant is slower in multiplying, but just as easy to grow. Height: 10cm (4in).

### M. azureum ♔ (see pictures pp. 20–21, 56–57, plate I, 1)

This species will self-sow very quickly, but creates a patch of such a bright sky blue in very early spring, that its spreading habit is very welcome. It is one of the *Muscari* which has little constriction to the flowers. The two or three glaucous green leaves are compact, with an incurved tip. There is an equally attractive pure white form available which is far slower to multiply in the open garden. A meadow plant from NE Turkey. Height: 15cm (6in).

### M. botryoides

This species has fewer leaves than many, so the flower spikes are less hidden in the foliage. It is also a shorter plant with bright blue flowers, which are almost spherical, with white tips to the mouth. There is an equally attractive albino form commonly available, which has been called 'Pearls of Spain' or 'Album'. This *Muscari* is from S Europe to the Balkans, usually found in woodland or high meadows. Height: 10–15cm (4–6in).

### M. comosum

This plant is from a group of *Muscari* which is generally found in European countries where the summers are dry and hot and it does need a similar position in the garden, or even growing in a frame or pot to ensure a dry rest period. The group it belongs to are the aptly named tassel hyacinths, which have a tall stem with distinctly differing fertile and infertile flowers. In *M. comosum* the lower fertile flowers are olive-green or brown, and the upper infertile ones are a dark purplish blue; the flowers are held on long violet stalks. Height: up to 60cm (24in).

In **'Plumosum'** the inflorescence is much branched and consists of only mauve-blue infertile flowers and their stalks. It is very noticeable but not very beautiful.

### M. grandiflorum

This N African species from the Atlas Mountains, has dark purple-black constricted flowers, which have relatively large white tips to the segments. The leaves are greyish and quite wide. Height: 15cm (6in).

### M. latifolium (see picture also plate III, 1)

This plant has a bicoloured flowerhead with pale bluish lilac sterile flowers at the top of the inflorescence and larger dark indigo-purple fertile ones lower down. It usually has a single convolute leaf, which can reach 20cm (8in) long and 3cm (1¼in) wide at maturity. It grows well on a raised bed or at the front of a border in full sun, where it makes a pleasing impact. This plant is found in S and W Turkey. Height: 30cm (12in).

### M. macrocarpum (see pictures p.36 and plate III, 3)

This very attractive species has a dense raceme of tubular flowers, nearly 1cm (⅜in) long. Bright yellow fertile flowers are topped by only a small group of bluish purple sterile ones. The flowerheads are surrounded by many lax channelled glaucous grey-green leaves. The bulb is native to only a few localities, including E Crete, a few small islands and SW Turkey. A plant for a sunny raised bed or a large pot in a cold greenhouse. This species has perennial roots, an unusual feature for the genus and so requires extra space if potted. Height: 20cm (8in).

### M. muscarimi

This is often still found as *M. moschatum*, but under whatever name, this is a quietly attractive plant similar to *M. macrocarpum* but with shorter more deeply channelled leaves. This is the most sweetly scented *Muscari*, with a musk-like scent which gives the species its name. The flowers, held on a stout stem, are bluish white maturing to a greenish yellow. It will grow well in a sunny raised bed or in a deep pot. After a hard frost in late winter it may take a day or so to straighten, but the bulbs never seem to suffer in a cold spell. Like *M. macrocarpum*, it has perennial roots. Height: 20cm (8in).

### M. neglectum

A plant for a wild area or one which is confined, containing taller shrubs and trees which can be underplanted with this species. The plant has several thin leaves and purple-blue flowers with small paler blue sterile flowers at the top. The flowers have white tips to the constricted segments. The bulb produces numerous offsets that spread far and wide and so give the whole genus an undeserved bad name. It is widespread throughout Europe and W Asia, growing in a large variety of habitats. Height: 20cm (8in).

### M. pallens

The true *M. pallens* is a Caucasian plant from damper situations than most *Muscari*. It only has a slight restriction at the throat of the flower, which can be white through to a rich blue colour. The leaves are quite erect, green, with the typical hooded tip, which shields the flower bud. Height: 15cm (6in).

### M. pseudomuscari ♛ (see pictures p.144 and plate I, 5)

The open bells of this species are a sky blue and stand well clear of the glaucous green wavy leaves, which although produced in early winter are still in good condition in late winter and early spring when the flowers are at their best. This was originally called *M. chalusicum*, when introduced from Iran nearly forty years ago. In the wild, it is found in light woodland, amongst rocks and does well in a sunny niche and spectacularly well in a bulb frame, where the long roots are free to wander. Height: 20cm (8in).

*Muscari latifolium spreads only slowly by seed. It has attractive bi-coloured flowers – the lighter flowers at the top of the spike are sterile, the lower, darker flowers are fertile.*

### *M. tenuiflorum*

This tall plant has very contrasting flowers; the lower fertile set are violet in bud turning to light brown when open, whereas the infertile upper flowers are bright violet and very conspicuous. The raceme is of the loose type with each flower carried on a short stem. The leaves are long thin and wavy. This is a lowland species found from SE Europe, through south central Europe, Turkey, the Caucasus, to Iran. Height: up to 50cm (20in).

The true blue of *Muscari pseudomuscari* is framed by the prostrate grey-green leaves.

## NARCISSUS

### Amaryllidaceae

This bulb probably symbolizes spring more than any other, with its sparkling yellow blooms being among the first to brighten the garden. Along with the rose, the daffodil is the most easily recognized flower, by gardeners and non-gardeners alike. It can also be one of the most durable of plants, thriving in even the most neglected plots where all but the ivy have been taken over by weeds and other natives. This genus is not confined to spring flowering and can provide colour and beauty in the garden and greenhouse from mid-autumn through

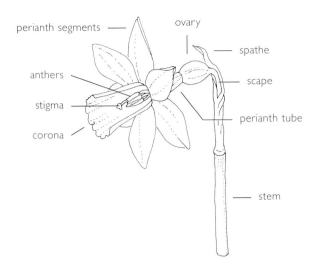

perianth segments — ovary
— spathe
anthers — — scape
stigma —
corona — — perianth tube
— stem

A typical daffodil flower – *Narcissus* 'Tête-à-tête'.

to mid-spring. And the flower colour is not just shades of yellow; there are white, orange and even pink flowers with bicoloured combinations of all of these available.

*Narcissus pseudonarcissus*, the Lent lily, and *N. obvallaris* the Tenby daffodil, are probably native to the British Isles, where once they were a common sight in spring, until agricultural methods changed in the twentieth century and much pasture was deep ploughed. Today conservation of these of naturalized *Narcissus* sites has ensured that they will delight the eye for generations to come in meadows, light woodland and hedgerows.

The numerous wild species are nearly all from Spain, Portugal and the Atlas Mountains in N Africa, with a few species found east and north through Europe as far as Turkey. *N. pseudonarcissus*, the traditional daffodil with the central trumpet, or corona, surrounded by the petals, or perianth segments, is found widely throughout Europe, with its origins in the Iberian Peninsula. This group is generally found in areas with moist soil and cool winters, followed by warm fairly dry summers. These plants are often found in light deciduous woodland, flowering and leafing long before the trees' leaves exclude the sunlight.

The Tazetta daffodils and their parent *N. tazetta* evolved from Spain and are found along the N Mediterranean coast as far as Israel and have even become naturalized in China and Japan. They are bulbs from milder winters and they will grow well in areas of little or no frost; elsewhere they will require the protection of a wall or cold glass cultivation in order to flower well.

Requiring similar treatment are the Jonquilla daffodils, a group from Spain and Portugal, which grow in damp grassy places, but require a sunny sheltered spot in temperate climates like that of Britain.

For the purposes of cultivation the groups like the Bulbocodium group, and the Cyclamineus and Triandrus daffodils, and all their hybrids, grow well if the winter is cool and moist and they have a dry resting time in summer. This just leaves *N. poeticus*, parent species of the Poeticus daffodils, and its forms; this is a plant from the southern mountains of Europe where it flowers later in spring in high, wet alpine pastures.

One aspect of cultivation shared by all *Narcissus* is their early root growth, often as early as midsummer if the conditions are damp. This is too early for commercial sales, but do buy and plant *Narcissus* as early as you can, so the roots can grow well into the earth before the soil temperature drops.

Daffodils have been hybridized for many years with over 20,000 *Narcissus* names being registered with the RHS, many of which have faded away or been replaced by finer cultivars. However the choice is vast with plants for many different positions and methods of growing. Before describing some of the daffodils available, I will outline some the different possibilities of growing *Narcissus* in a variety of situations.

### Naturalized in grass

This is one of the most natural and attractive ways to grow daffodils. When ordering the bulbs you must buy in bulk and from a reputable supplier, or you may introduce narcissus eelworm, which does quite quickly wipe out a colony and for which there is no chemical control available. It is better to plant a small area densely rather than spread the bulbs you have over a wide area, as a spotty effect can look rather pathetic. The lushness of the grass needs to be borne in mind too, as smaller cultivars and species which look so good in a naturalized situation, might be swamped by very long grass. In a small garden the large cultivars can look very overbearing, so the Cyclamineus cultivars and forms of *N. pseudonarcissus* are better for purposes of scale. At the RHS Wisley garden there is a famous meadow bank of naturalized *N. bulbocodium*, which are less than 20cm (8in) tall at flowering.

The bulbs of tall *Narcissus* need planting in holes some 15cm (6in) deep. This can be a hard task in late summer and early autumn after a drought, so you may need to hire or borrow a proper bulb planter with a 1m (3ft) handle with a foot bar. Many people advocate a random planting by scattering the bulbs by hand and planting

PLATE XI *Narcissus I*

4 *Narcissus* 'Navarre'

2 *Narcissus genuinus* × 'Jessamy'

1 *Narcissus minor* 'Cedric Morris'

3 *Narcissus* 'Minicycla'

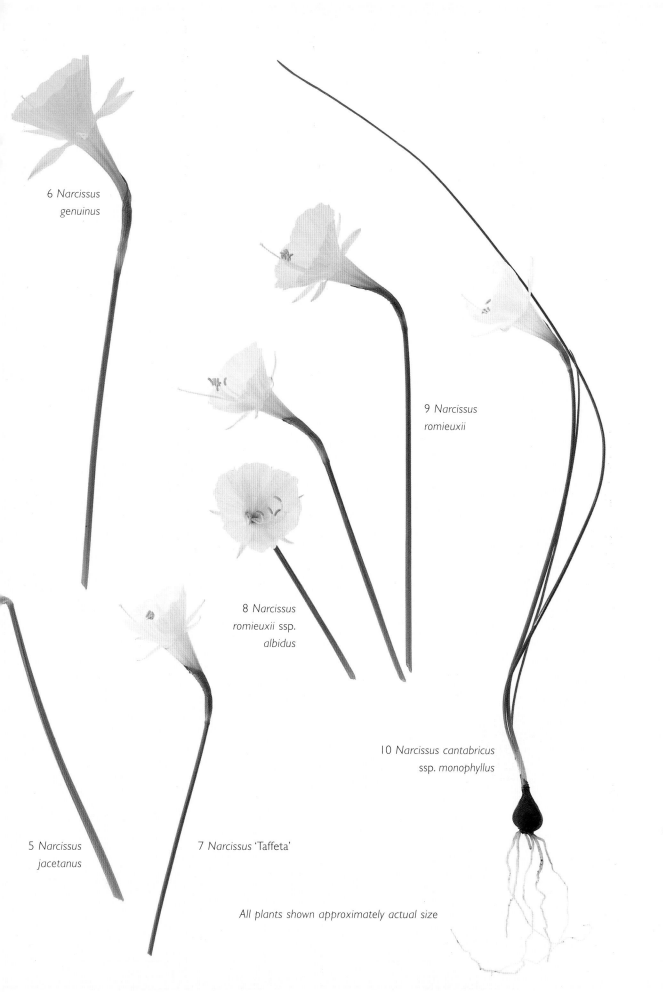

6 *Narcissus genuinus*

9 *Narcissus romieuxii*

8 *Narcissus romieuxii* ssp. *albidus*

10 *Narcissus cantabricus* ssp. *monophyllus*

5 *Narcissus jacetanus*

7 *Narcissus* 'Taffeta'

*All plants shown approximately actual size*

them where they fall. Certainly regimented lines do look out of place, as the effect is meant to be as natural as possible. Once the bulbs have flowered you must not be too impatient to cut the foliage; wait until early summer before mowing and then only make a light cut to remove the herbage. This depth of cut can be increased as the summer progresses, giving a short background for the emerging leaves in spring. It will be many years before flowering declines and summer thinning and replanting becomes necessary.

### Raised beds and rock gardens

Daffodils can be planted to great effect in these well-drained positions and many of the species will do as well as the miniature and small cultivars. They need to be carefully spaced, remembering that small though they are, they do produce abundant foliage, which needs space to develop in late spring. Here, spot-planting looks perfect as other flowering alpines and bulbs will surround the *Narcissus* to create beautiful cameo-like garden pictures. The species like *N. cyclamineus*, *N. bulbocodium*, and particularly the stronger forms like *N. b.* ssp. *bulbocodium* var. *conspicuus* and *N. b.* var. *obesus*, do well in these situations. It is best to avoid the early flowering forms because they can be damaged by storms in the depths of winter. The Cyclamineus cultivars like *N.* 'The Usurper', *N.* 'Little Englander' and *N.* 'Little Witch', which are smaller than most, look just right in these situations. There are traditionally shaped daffodils that fit the smaller scale too, like *N. asturiensis* and *N. minor* and their cultivars, as well as some varieties with smaller trumpets, like *N.* 'W.P. Milner', *N.* 'Little Gem', *N.* 'Little Beauty' and *N.* 'Topolino'. Among the small-cupped daffodils, *N.* 'Picoblanco', *N.* 'Xit' and *N.* 'Segovia' are ideal, as is *N.* 'Hawera', a widely available Triandrus daffodil.

### Shrubberies and mixed borders

In an area devoted to shrubs and trees large-flowered daffodils are quite suitable for planting under the deciduous specimens, where they can flower like a woodland plant. Once the flowers have faded the shrubs will soon burst into leaf and hide the abundant foliage, which must be allowed to die down naturally. Eventually the root density of the shrubs may impede the daffodils' develop-

*Narcissus* 'Topolino' is a reliable early season trumpet daffodil. It's ideal for any spot where you don't want too-large flowers to compete with other blooms.

ment and they may need moving to a new site. The choice of colour and size is great and must be left to the individual. Where herbaceous plants are grown for summer flowering, large-flowered daffodils can be interspersed, to bring some early colour to the border. Plant them deep enough to avoid any accidental damage to the bulbs from the tines of a garden fork when the border is worked over. The spring border at the National Trust garden at Sissinghurst Castle in Kent is stunning, with two parallel borders which for a few brief weeks in spring uplift the spirits. Here large daffodils provide the height at the back of the border, while smaller ones spill over the path.

### Bedding with daffodils

This is a labour-intensive form of gardening that requires the daffodils to be lifted as soon as the flowers fade and replanted immediately in a nursery row to recover for flowering again in two years time. Traditionally bulbs like hyacinths and tulips are used in bedding, but daffodils are equally effective and earlier flowering.

### Containers and window boxes

In autumn, the container will need to be cleaned and filled with new compost and the bulbs planted immediately, on their own or with other plants depending on the design. After flowering these can be removed, leaving the container ready for traditional bedding plants. The bulbs can be planted in a shady corner of the garden to rebuild as best they can. An alternative method is to grow the bulbs in half-pans and in late winter plunge the whole pot into the container. Once flowering has finished, this can then be removed and a new plant inserted to continue the season. The shorter daffodils are best for containers; firstly, because they will be less susceptible to wind damage, and secondly, because they will be more in scale with the whole container and the other plantings. N. 'Tête-à-tête', N. 'Golden Quince', N. 'Dove Wings' and N. 'Jumblie' would suit admirably.

### Indoor cultivation

For many years, there has been a tradition to pot daffodils very early in the dormant period (late summer) and place them in a cool position for the autumn, so that they flower indoors from just before Christmas onwards. The bulbs are best planted in a soil-based compost and in pots with drainage holes. The roots soon become active, but you must wait until the leaves are in strong growth before bringing them on to a windowsill or a shelf in the conservatory. The most popular are the prepared bulbs of the Tazetta daffodils like N. 'Paper White', N. 'Cragford' and N. 'Soleil d'Or', which flower in the depth of winter. They may need tying, as the growth is very etiolated due to the poor light in winter. Smaller daffodils that are not specially prepared for early flowering can be treated in the same way to extend the winter flowering into midwinter and late winter. The choice available is wide, but N. 'Sugarbush', a Jonquilla daffodil, and our old friend, N. 'Tête-à-tête', are hard to beat.

### Species under cold glass

It is possible for the small species Narcissus to be in flower from late autumn through to mid-spring without any forcing or heating if they are grown under cold glass. This will protect the stems from the elements and brighten up the greenhouse as the gardener escapes from the same winter weather.

In late summer, the bulbs are repotted in a soil-based compost to which has been added an equal amount of coarse grit. The pot is a matter of choice, clay is more attractive, but it is heavier than plastic; whatever you choose, keep the whole collection in one or the other, as the watering needs will vary. Cover the compost with a layer of grit, which helps stop any splashing of the flowers and also slows evaporation from the compost. It is also a good idea to plunge the pots in sand or similar, again to slow evaporation and also to lessen extreme temperature fluctuations that might effect the roots in winter and summer. They are thoroughly watered in late summer and kept moist until spring, when they need to be really wet. This is eased as summer approaches, when, as the leaves die down only the plunge is watered, making sure the bulbs are never really dried, just rested. In mid-spring a light shading is needed to keep the temperature down and all the lights and doors should be left open, whatever the weather. This cultivation method seems to suit most species with just the odd modification in compost for the acidity needed by a few trickier species. It is good practise to nip off the seed heads before they shed their seed or the plunge will become an alternative nursery for seedling Narcissus.

As I have said, the choice of daffodils is vast, and so the selection here is very much a personal one, based on those plants that have given me great pleasure during many a winter and spring in the garden and greenhouse. I have broken down the selection by using the recognized divisions of daffodils, beginning with the first two divisions together, trumpet and large-cupped daffodils.

## DIVISIONS 1 AND 2 – TRUMPET AND LARGE-CUPPED DAFFODILS

The trumpet daffodils have one flower to each stem and they have long trumpets. The large-cupped group have large cup-shaped coronas that are shorter than the perianth segments. The stems bear one flower. Unless stated otherwise, the daffodils in both of these divisions are 40–60cm (16–24in) tall.

**N. 'Binkie'**

This has a pale, almost white, cup-shaped corona and primrose-yellow perianth segments, making a very attractive combination.

**N. 'Cantatrice'**

A long-established cultivar with good shaped flowers that is still worth a place in gardens. Its clean pure white flowers have an almost waxy and velvety sheen to the long trumpet and pointed perianth segments.

**N. 'Gipsy Queen'** (see pictures p.37 and plate XII, 8)

This is an early trumpet daffodil, long-lasting but short in stature, and with a most distinctive habit and markings. The short foliage is curved at the ends and the very pale yellow trumpet is long and slim with a citrus-yellow margin. The perianth segments are a similar colour. Height: 15cm (6in).

**N. 'Ice Follies'** ♔

This has a wide frilled cup that opens as pale primrose, but soon fades to white. It has a very flattened appearance and is very durable.

**N. 'Kingscourt'** ♔

This is a very good golden daffodil of beautiful form and a good strong garden plant.

**N. 'Mount Hood'** ♔

This vigorous white daffodil, has an ivory-white trumpet, which opens as a pale primrose yellow. The plant lasts well and is among the best for garden decoration.

**N. 'Mrs R.O. Backhouse'**

This large trumpet daffodil was one of the first to have pink coronas. Although registered in 1923, it is rather special and still worth a place in the border.

**N. 'Passionale'** ♔

The purest white petals and an attractive pale pink flared corona with good stature, give this bulb a presence in the border. Although only just over forty years old, this selection is already hard to track down, but it is well worth the effort.

**N. 'Rijnveld's Early Sensation'** ♔

This is the earliest daffodil of these two divisions, often producing its first flower in the open garden in late winter, or even midwinter in a mild season. It is an egg-yellow throughout. It does need lifting regularly to maintain flowering, but nevertheless is a truly amazing bulb, flowering when there is so little about.

**N. 'Tosca'** (see picture plate XII, 1)

A short but very strong little trumpet daffodil with whitish segments and a contrasting pale yellow corona.

**N. 'W.P. Milner'** (see picture plate XII, 6)

Although first registered in 1890, this dwarf daffodil still holds its own for grace and freedom of flowering and is very useful in pots and containers. It has nodding creamy white flowers. Height: 25cm (10in).

## DIVISION 3 – SMALL-CUPPED DAFFODILS

The small-cupped varieties include some very distinct and beautiful selections. The smaller ones are often recommended for troughs or rock gardens, but because of the price you may decide to grow them as pot plants for a few years before risking them outside. The taller forms are good for the border and extend the season, generally flowering a little later than the trumpet daffodils. The cup-shaped coronas are less than one-third of the length of the perianth segments and just one flower is borne on a stem. Unless stated otherwise, they range in height from 40cm (16in) to 60cm (24in).

**N. 'Barrett Browning'**

This bicoloured daffodil, bred in 1945, has large white perianth segments and a small orange-red corona.

**N. 'Birma'**

This older bicolour has sulphur-yellow segments and a small orange cup.

**N. 'Segovia'** ♔

This cultivar has flat pure white petals and a flat lemon-yellow cup. It seems that *N. watieri* is one of the plant's parents – a rather capricious and beautiful species. Not only has the beauty has been transferred, but the challenging requirements for cultivation as well. Extra humus and a cool rest seems to help keep the plant in good condition. Height: 20cm (8in).

**N. 'Verger'**

This Dutch selection has white segments and a yellow cup with an orange rim. It is seen to good effect on Kew Green, just outside the Royal Botanical Gardens.

**N. 'Xit'**

A stunning plant of similar height to *N.* 'Segovia', this has crystalline white flowers. It also has similar cultural requirements to those of *N.* 'Segovia'.

## DIVISION 4 – DOUBLE DAFFODILS

A group you tend to either love, because you may find the petal formations intriguing, or hate, because you feel the grace and form of the daffodil has been lost. Double daffodils are not new, in fact one of the oldest cultivars, *N.* 'Eystettensis', better known as Queen Anne's double daffodil, has been grown since at least 1601. Nearly as old is *N.* 'Telamoneus Plenus', which was introduced into England from Florence in 1620. This is often grown as *N.* 'Van Sion' and has considerable vigour, maintaining its naturalization of a number of woods and fields in Britain. In Double daffodils, both the cup and the petals can be double. There may be one or more flowers to a stem. Unless stated otherwise, they are 40–60cm (16–24in) tall.

**N. 'Eystettensis'**
The flower, like a six pointed star, is composed of layers of narrow petals in several whorls, laid evenly one on the other. It is uniformly sulphur yellow. A very regular plant with sturdy stems, it is slow to increase, but not difficult to accommodate. Height: 15cm (6in).

**N. 'Golden Ducat'**
This was a sport from *N.* 'King Alfred' and it is just as rich a yellow; it's often used as a cut flower.

**N. 'Rip Van Winkle'**
This has been likened to an untidy dandelion with petals like crochet hooks. It certainly is fully double with masses of yellow petals just touched with green. Although short, it can be naturalized in short grass. Height:15cm (6in).

**N. 'Telamoneus Plenus'**
This is an extremely variable double in two shades of yellow; in some years the plant will have all double petals inside the trumpet, while in others it becomes almost dahlia-like without any discernible trumpet.

## DIVISION 5 – TRIANDRUS DAFFODILS

One of parent of this group is *N. triandrus*, more usually the rare *N. t.* ssp. *capax*, from near Finisterre in France. These *Narcissus* are among the most delicate looking and indeed early cultivars have mostly disappeared, although recent introductions are proving to be good garden plants. They have pendent flowers with reflexed petals that are usually borne two or three to a stem.

**N. 'April Tears'** ♛
First introduced by Alec Gray, back in 1939, this has

*Narcissus* 'Eystettensis' is a very neat dwarf double daffodil of great antiquity.

proved to be a first class *Narcissus*. The buttercup-yellow flowers are produced in two to five florets. Height: 20–25cm (8–10in).

**N. 'Hawera'** ♛
A similar cross to N. 'April Tears', this is an altogether stronger and taller plant, but very similar in other respects. It was registered a year before *N.* 'April Tears', in New Zealand. Height: 30cm (12in).

**N. 'Horn of Plenty'**
This large white Dutch selection has expanded coronas. Height: 30cm (12in).

**N. 'Liberty Bells'**
This has large rich lemon-yellow flowers, three to a stem. Height: 35cm (14in).

**N. 'Thalia'**
One of the tallest, but still with strong stems, it has pure white flowers and can have three or more per head. Height: 40cm (16in).

## DIVISION 6 – CYCLAMINEUS DAFFODILS

These cultivars usually have one flower per stem, set at an acute angle to the stem. The perianth segments are reflexed. They make very attractive garden plants, with good poise and delicacy. Unless stated otherwise they are 30–60cm (12–24in) tall.

**N. 'Beryl'**
A strong grower with primrose segments and an orange cup, this hybrid is over ninety years old but just as strong and prolific as ever.

**N. 'Dove Wings'** ♈
In this form the reflexed segments begin life as a creamy yellow, but age to white. The cup is a pale yellow.

**N. 'February Gold'** ♈
An old selection that usually just lives up to its name when it comes to flowering time. It has clear yellow perianth segments and a deeper yellow cup.

**N. 'February Silver'**
This white selection has pure white segments and a creamy white cup. Again, it is one of the first to flower.

**N. 'Jack Snipe'** ♈
A bicoloured hybrid with long creamy perianth segments and a yellow cup. Although quite short it will naturalize well in short grass. Height: 20cm (8in).

**N. 'Jenny'** ♈
This has a slightly crimped, lemon-yellow trumpet on opening, which quickly fades to a creamy white, but is always a shade darker than the perianth segments. As well as its AGM, it has also been awarded a First Class Certificate by the RHS.

**N. 'Jetfire'** ♈ (see pictures p.154 and plate XII, 9)
This is a quite new American hybrid with reflexed golden perianth segments and a bright red-orange trumpet. They only fade a little with age and are proving very amenable to cultivate in the garden.

**N. 'Minicycla'** (see picture plate XI, 3)
A cross made before World War I between *N. asturiensis* and *N. cyclamineus*, which produced one of the most perfect little daffodils. This short plant is a deep golden yellow with slightly reflexed outer segments and a neat trumpet. It is best grown in a trough or pot, as it would be overwhelmed in the garden. Height: 10cm (4in).

## DIVISION 7 – JONQUILLA DAFFODILS

These are the hybrids with *N. jonquilla* and its relatives. They are often scented with spreading petals and up to three flowers per head. Easy to cultivate, they thrive well in the open border, rock garden or grown in a pot under cold glass.

**N. 'Bell Song'**
This daffodil is often twin headed, with pure white segments and a bright pink cup. It is quite a new hybrid. Height: 30cm (12in).

**N. 'Bobbysoxer'**
A variety which has *N. rupicola* as one of its parents. The flowers are single with overlapping flat perianth segments of butter yellow, with a small bright orange cup. Height: 25cm (10in).

**N. 'Pencrebar'**
This is another very old variety that has survived because it is so distinct and attractive. It maybe likened to a yellow rose about 5cm (2in) in diameter. It is a double, which often has twin flowers. Height:15cm (6in).

**N. 'Rikki'**
The flowers of this selection are almost white with a small clear yellow cup. It makes an excellent addition to the rock garden or raised bed, being sturdy and free flowering. Height: 25cm (10in).

**N. 'Sundial'** (see picture plate XII, 7)
A neat garden plant, this daffodil has a flat outward-facing flower with a citron-yellow perianth and a flat cup that is slightly darker. It is an early vigorous form. Height: 20cm (8in).

**N. 'Sweetness'** ♈
This strongly scented variety has rich gold flowers with pointed petals. It has a long life as a cut flower. Height: 40cm (16in).

**N. 'Trevithian'** ♈
A tall variety with up to three flowers to the stem, it is excellent for in naturalizing in grass. It has short-cupped lemon-yellow flowers, which are highly scented. Height: 50cm (20in).

## DIVISION 8 – TAZETTA DAFFODILS

The flowers of this division are usually scented, with spreading saucer-shaped perianth segments and a short cup-shaped corona. There can be between three and twenty flowers to a stem. Already mentioned are those varieties prepared for indoor flowering around Christmas, but there are others for the open garden.

**N. 'Cyclataz'**
There are two to four flowers to a stem with yellow segments and an orange cup. It is probably too tender to risk in an unprotected environment, so is best grown in a pot. Height: 15cm (6in).

**N. 'Minnow'** ♈
Hardy enough for a sunny raised bed or rock garden, this

has flowers with crystalline white segments and a small lemon-yellow cup. Height: 15cm (6in).

**N. 'Silver Chimes'**

With up to ten flowers on stems, this typical Tazetta daffodil has pure white segments with a small delicate primrose-yellow cup, darkest at the base. It requires a sunny well-drained site in order to flower strongly. Height: 30cm (12in).

## DIVISION 9 – POETICUS DAFFODILS

The poet's narcissus, *N. poeticus*, which is widely distributed in S Europe from Spain to Greece and in the lower meadows of the Alps and Pyrenees, is one of the parents of this group. It is a very variable plant in the wild, with two forms regularly grown. *N. p.* var. *recurvus*, the pheasant's-eye narcissus, has one flower per stem with pure white segments which are curved back and a small corona with a green centre and a red rim above a yellow cup. It also has a spicy fragrance. In *N. p.* var. *physaloides* the spathe is enlarged to become a long oval shape, equalling the emerging bud in length. The hybrids in this group usually follow the form of the species with white perianth segments and small cup-shaped coronas.

**N. 'Actaea'** ♉

This is a Dutch-raised form with fine large white segments and a small yellow cup with an orange-red rim. It is often used as a cut flower.

**N. 'Cantabile'**

As with all these forms the perianth segments are white but here the cup is green with a fine red rim.

## DIVISION 10 AND 12 – SPECIES AND WILD VARIANTS AND MISCELLANEOUS

These two divisions concern the species and any plants with unusual combinations of parents that don't fit in other groups. These are all very important winter-flowering *Narcissus*. Many of these species are parents of garden hybrids, which have already been described, but there are a few naturally occurring hybrids, which are included here.

**N. alpestris**

Possibly the most exquisite of all daffodils, this is closely allied to *N. pseudonarcissus* ssp. *moschatus*, but shorter and unfortunately less easy to grow. It is native to a few sites

One of the Cyclamineus daffodils, *Narcissus* 'Jetfire' has the typical reflexed petals of that group. The bright colours of the trumpet and petals fade only a little with age.

in the Spanish Pyrenees, where it grows in acidic turf on rocky hillsides. The flowers are usually white, although there is a rare primrose-yellow form with flowers that hang very gracefully from dark green tubes, with the segments wrapped around parallel to the tube. The 3cm (1¼in) long tube is white and only slightly fluted at the end. This is a slow plant to increase, both from seed and vegetatively, but some beautiful examples can often be seen at Alpine Garden Society shows in spring. Height: 15cm (6in).

### N. assoanus

This charming miniature has up to three deep yellow flowers per stem. The flowers are short cupped, barely more than 1cm (⅜in) in diameter, with the segments up to 2.5cm (1in) across. The plant has typical upright Jonquilla type foliage. Height: 20cm (8in).

### N. asturiensis ♈

A miniature trumpet daffodil, this has uniformly deep yellow flowers and grey strap-shaped leaves. It grows well in a pot or sink garden, where the other planting is kept in scale with its size. Found in upland meadows in Spain and Portugal. Height: 10cm (4in) tall.

### N. bulbocodium

The *Narcissus* of the Bulbocodium group are known as the hoop petticoat daffodils; this species and its natural variants have small, almost rudimentary, perianth segments and large funnel-shaped coronas. The coronas vary from slim tubes to wide open trumpets which can also be flared. The flowers are solitary and usually held horizontally, with upturned stamens contained within the corona and a protruding stigma. The leaves vary in length and in their width; some are thin and lax, while others are wider and more stiff and erect. They are very variable and hard to classify, but all are very beautiful and quite easily grown in a cold greenhouse or bulb frame. The stronger varieties look very appealing in a rock garden, or naturalized in a damp spring meadow. They are found growing wild in mountain meadows from S France through the Iberian Peninsular and into the N African Mountains. Height: 5–15cm (2–6in).

If you try growing *N. b.* ssp. *bulbocodium* from seed you will soon realize the diversity of the plant. Even within a pot the range can be quite staggering, but it does give you the opportunity to select the best flower forms to grow on to form a colony. Typically, this *Narcissus* has deep yellow flowers with a little green suffusion at the base of the perianth segments. The leaves are dark green and narrow, less than 1.5mm (½in) wide. *N. b.* ssp.

*b.* var. *citrinus* is a pale form with large lemon-yellow flowers and more lax foliage. It is Spanish and grows very well in a bulb frame. It flowers in late winter. *N. b.* ssp. *b.* var. *conspicuus* is a fine strong-growing form that does well in the garden. The leaves are erect and numerous and seem to protect the flowers from the worst of the weather. The flowers are a deep yellow, long and fairly narrow, with some green on the reverse of the perianth segments. This one is found in W France and Spain. *N. b.* ssp. *b.* var. *graellsii* is a very distinct plant from Spain with slightly upward-facing pale yellow flowers, which are smaller than most. The stamens protrude beyond the corona mouth and the foliage is very reluctant to die away in summer. *N. b.* ssp. *b.* var. *tenuifolius* has quite straight prostrate foliage, with an evenly expanding bright yellow corona. It blooms a little later than many, and has distinct small, very dark brown bulbs.

*N. b.* var. *filifolius* has, as the name suggests, abundant fine foliage. It is produced early and becomes quite prostrate before the flowers open in early spring. They are smooth goblets of bright yellow and look very handsome when grown in a pot. *N. b.* var. *nivalis* is a small *Narcissus*, with tufts of stiff upright foliage. The flowers are slightly tapered from the base to the mouth and are usually a bright yellow, with a dark green staining on the reverse of the perianth. It is from Spain and Morocco.

A most eye-catching form, *N. b.* var. *obesus* is, as the name implies, a large plant. The deep yellow flowers can measure up to 3.5cm (1⅜in) across the corona. The foliage curls and hugs the ground. From Morocco, *N. b.* ssp. *praecox* flowers in midwinter, so it does need some protection. It is strong growing with pale yellow flowers.

If these bulbs are to be grown under glass they do need to be in their new compost by the end of late summer at the latest as rooting takes place very early, long before any leaves start to grow. They are susceptible to botrytis amongst the dense foliage, so ventilation must be adequate via louvres at bench level. This direct inlet of air does need careful control, especially if a gale is forecast, when these vents must be closed.

### N. cantabricus

Also part of the Bulbocodium group, this is a white-flowered hoop petticoat daffodil, which has a number of very select subspecies, all of which are from S Spain or N Africa. Height: 5–10cm (2–4in).

The form *N. c.* ssp. *cantabricus* var. *foliosus* has many narrow dark green leaves, with quite upward-facing milk-white flowers with a wavy margin to the corona.

They are large, up to 5cm (2in) long, and flower in late autumn and early winter. *N. c.* **ssp.** *c.* **var.** *petuniodes* has flowers with a flat corona which can be slightly reflexed and over 3cm (1¼in) across. This makes a beautiful pot plant in the depths of winter. *N. c.* **ssp.** *monophyllus* (see picture also plate XI, 10) should have just one leaf per bulb, but not all them get it right and some have two, very narrow dark green leaves. The crisp white flowers appear in midwinter.

### N. cordubensis (see picture plate XII, 4)

A Jonquilla type of daffodil, this has quite large bright yellow flowers of some substance. There are up to four flowers to a stem with segments that are broad and touching, without overlapping. The slightly darker yellow cup is bell-shaped and slightly corrugated. This is a recent introduction from Spain. Height: 30cm (12in).

### N. cyclamineus

This most distinctive species has deep yellow perianth segments that are reflexed tightly backwards, leaving the trumpet completely exposed. These trumpets can be up to 2cm (¾in) long. The bulb seems to like acidic conditions and looks very special in damp meadows or among shrubs. If you live in an alkaline area they can be grown in acidic compost that is kept very moist in spring. Native to moist alpine meadows in Portugal and Spain, it used to be collected from the wild in large numbers, which has thankfully stopped. Height: 30cm (12in).

### N. fernandesii

A Jonquilla type of daffodil, with long quite narrow dark green foliage, which ascends and when mature tends to bend downwards from the halfway point. There are up to five flowers to a stem of the typical rich yellow of the Jonquillas. It is very good in pots, flowering in late winter. Height: 15cm (6in).

### N. gaditanus

About the smallest Jonquilla, this has up to three flowers per stem, which are only about 1.5cm (½in) across; they are yellow with a darker yellow dumpy cup. The very thin dark green leaves reach 20cm (8in) in length. It is from S Spain and Portugal. Height: 12cm (4¾in).

### N. genuinus × 'Jessamy' (see picture plate XI, 2)

A typical Bulbocodium group daffodil with quite substantial flowers with green markings at the base of the corona. It has the vigour of a hybrid and grows well in a pot or frame. Height: 20cm (8in).

### N. hedraeanthus

Part of the Bulbocodium group, this very strange *Narcissus* has unusual flowers in that the anthers reach far beyond the corona. It is small and often grows at an angle of forty-five degrees to the ground. The flowers are pale yellow. The leaves are dark green and often spreading, but short, to 8cm (3¼in) long. It is best grown in a pot or bulb frame. Height: 5cm (2in).

### N. jacetanus (see picture plate XI, 5)

A rather small trumpet daffodil with a mid-yellow corona that shades into a distinctive green tube. From limestone areas in N Spain. Height: 15cm (6in).

### N. jonquilla ♡

This has a very strong perfume, so strong in fact that a just few flowers will scent a whole room. The flowers, up to five to a stem, have a small cup and are a bright deep yellow. The rush-like leaves are dark green and nearly cylindrical in section. It occurs in damp and even very wet conditions in S Europe. Height: 30cm (12in).

Although a smaller scale form of the species, var. *henriquesii* has flowers that can be of greater diameter.

*Narcissus cantabricus* ssp. *monophyllus* is an excellent winter-flowering species for pot culture.

The strong-growing wild daffodil, *Narcissus nobilis*, growing in a Suffolk garden.

### N. longispathus

A very variable species which is notable for its very long spathe and pedicel, both of which can reach 5–6cm (2–2½in) in length. It is a trumpet type of daffodil with bright yellow perianth segments to 3cm (1¼in) long and corona of similar length. Height: 25–30cm (10–12in).

### N. minor ♛

This plant is rather like a taller *N. asturiensis*, with the dividing line between them hard to define. It has flowers that are 4cm (1½in) long, which are more funnel shaped than *N. asturiensis*, and a greater number of thinner leaves. Height: 25cm (10in).

### N. nevadensis (see picture plate XII, 3)

The channelled leaves of this species are held erectly to 25cm (10in), with the flowers just topping them. These flowers face slightly upward and have parallel coronas of pale yellow, with slightly darker yellow margins. The perianth segments are cream reaching 5cm (2in) in diameter. A very neat and attractive *Narcissus*. Height: 30cm (12in).

### N. nobilis

This is a fine tall-growing bicoloured *Narcissus* for a dampish position. The perianth segments are cream with a strongly contrasting golden yellow flared trumpet. The pedicel is quite long, but the flowers are held horizontally, making it a fine sight in the garden in early spring. Height: 30cm (12in).

### N. obvallaris ♛

This is the Tenby daffodil, a small trumpet daffodil found in Wales with similar plants located in Central Spain. The horizontal tube is yellow with green stripes and about 1cm (⅜in) long; the twisted golden yellow segments are some 4cm (1½in) in diameter. It is one of the sturdiest and longest lasting daffodils, good for naturalizing and planting in a shrub border. Height: 20cm (8in).

### N. pallidiflorus

This is a trumpet daffodil from woodlands in the French Pyrenees, with large drooping flowers early in the season. The very pale yellow tube is slim and only slightly flared, with green suffusions which can be variable. The perianth segments are a pale yellow, twisted and are held forward around the tube. The plant is quite short and the flower can look a little too large for the height of the stem, which lengthens with age. Height: 20cm (8in).

### N. papyraceus

This is commonly encountered as *N.* 'Paper White' and is notable for its ability to flower in the depths of winter; it is often grown in bowls and pots for this purpose. The species is very variable and is found all around the Mediterranean basin, usually at low level and growing over limestone. The form grown has pure white Tazetta-type flowers 3–4cm (1¼–1½in) across, with up to twenty to a stem. They do become etiolated in winter and need staking to keep them upright. Height: 30cm (12in).

### N. poeticus

A species of the wet meadows from the Pyrenees to Greece, this has solitary upward-facing flowers with white segments, some 7cm (2¾in) across. The corona is small and cup-shaped, and often yellow with an orangey margin. Height: 35–40cm (14–16in).

### N. pseudonarcissus

This is a very widespread and variable species, that can be argued to include *N. nevadensis*, *N. nobilis*, *N. pallidiflorus*

*Narcissus minor* 'Cedric Morris' will do well if lifted every few years and given a fresh position.

and *N. obvallaris*. Gardeners can choose their reference and name accordingly, as long as they are aware of the pitfalls. Luckily the plants still look as distinct and, whatever it says on your label, look just as beautiful. The typical form in cultivation has pale yellow segments, with the coronas just a few shades darker. It has solitary nodding flowers up to 6cm (2½in) in diameter. Native to SW Europe and probably naturalized in N and E Europe. Height: 20–35cm (8–14in).

A dwarf form from E Spain, **ssp. *eugeniae*** is only 10cm (4in) tall in the wild, but more in cultivation, with an upward-facing yellow corona and lighter coloured segments, up to 7cm (2¾in) in diameter. The leaves are a bluish green, to 12cm (4¾in), but longer in a pot. The **ssp. *moschatus*** (see pictures pp.56–57, 163 and plate XII, 5) runs *N. alpestris* a close second as the choicest medium-sized daffodil. It has the advantage in being a true garden plant, thriving in a partially shaded area, but still slow to multiply. The solitary white trumpet flowers

PLATE XII *Narcissus 2*

1 *Narcissus*
'Tosca'

2 *Narcissus*
*rupicola*

3 *Narcissus*
*nevadensis*

4 *Narcissus*
*cordubensis*

*All plants shown approximately actual size*

8 *Narcissus* 'Gipsy Queen'

9 *Narcissus* 'Jetfire'

5 *Narcissus pseudonarcissus* ssp. *moschatus*

6 *Narcissus* 'W.P. Milner'

7 *Narcissus* 'Sundial'

hang, as do the drooping segments, at a steep angle to the stem. At some some 30cm (12in) tall, it is about twice the height of *N. alpestris*. Although this daffodil has been in cultivation for a long time, over three centuries, the supposed wild locations have lost any trace of this plant and it may now only exist in gardens.

**N. romieuxii** ♛ (see pictures p.164 and plate XI, 9)
Although close to *N. bulbocodium*, this differs in having a very short pedicel and protruding anthers. These plants are variable in colour and time of flowering, from late autumn through to early spring. Height: 10cm (4in).

One of the most vigorous and showy forms is **ssp. romieuxii var. mesatlanticus** with large pale yellow flowers early in the new year. Among the vigorous hybrids of *N. romieuxii* and *N. cantabricus* made nearly fifty years ago by Douglas Blanchard, are those named after fabrics. Most commonly found is the early flowering, pale yellow **Nylon Group**, which is a must for the cold greenhouse in late autumn. A fortnight later, **'Taffeta'** (see picture plate XI, 7) with white flowers, takes over.

**N. rupicola** (see picture plate XII, 2)
This very attractive dwarf Jonquilla has solitary flowers on a long green tube. The flowers are mid-yellow and 2.5cm (1in) across with a little flared cup facing upward on thin stems. The rather sparse foliage is narrow and a grey-green colour. It seeds around on a sunny raised bed or in a bulb frame. Height: 15cm (6in).

From Morocco, **ssp. marvieri** has an even longer perianth tube and green leaves.

**N. tazetta**
This species has up to twenty, small bicoloured highly scented outward-facing flowers to each stem. The segments are white and the small cup yellow, but there are variants with yellow segments. A tall species from Central and W Mediterranean, it needs a very sunny warm position to flower well in Britain. Height: 40cm (16in).

**N. 'Tête-à-tête'**
This ubiquitous plant was the result of a self-sown seed of *N.* 'Cyclataz' found by Alec Gray. It occasionally carries two flowers per stem and has a strong constitution, with the golden yellow flowers slightly darker in the trumpet, which is a little flared. Height: 30–60cm (12–24in).

**N. triandrus** ♛
These are beautiful dwarf daffodils but they are not easy to grow well, seeming to require acidic well-drained compost, and even then they are not long lived. They all have one to three goblet-shaped cups and twisted, drooping and recurved perianth segments. Height: 20–30cm (8–12in).

In **var. triandrus** the segments are pale yellow and the corona white. In **var. cernuus** the flowers are all one colour and can be white or pale cream. Lastly, the very beautiful **var. concolor** has flowers that are a uniform golden yellow.

**N. watieri**
This is a pure white species, rather like an albino *N. rupicola*. From the High Atlas Mountains in Morocco, it grows as a snow-melt plant between 2400–3400m (7870–11150ft) on north-facing slopes in acidic turf. It makes a very attractive pot specimen, when grown in free-draining acidic compost which is just kept moist in summer. Height: 10cm (4in).

## ORNITHOGALUM

### Hyacinthaceae

This is a very large family of plants found in Europe, Africa and W Asia, of which only a few fall within the remit of this book. Many gardeners are familiar with the star of Bethlehem, *Ornithogalum umbellatum*. This is a British native and is a fast colonizer of gardens, as the bulb produces numerous bulblets rather like *Muscari neglectum*. However even this plant can, in a confined space, look quite effective, particularly around the middle of the day, when the flowers are open wide. The flowers are star- or cup-shaped, usually white with a median green line down the outside of the segments and held in a flat or pyramidal raceme. These plants prefer a sunny well-drained position, but will often seed themselves in the most unlikely positions and proceed to flower very well; we may think we know what conditions plants need, but the unexpected keeps us in our place, showing us that we still have much to learn. The list below does not include any of the tall, late spring- and summer-flowering ornithogalums, that can be such a feature later in the year.

**O. collinum**
This plant begins to flower at ground level and only gradually lengthens with age. The many starry flowers nestle amongst thin hairy leaves, which lengthen after flowering. The flowers are 3cm (1¼in) in diameter and green in bud, opening to white. It is a very prolific grower, which has a short, but very effective period of

*Narcissus pseudonarcissus* ssp. *moschatus* is one of the most graceful of daffodils.

*Narcissus romieuxii* ssp. *albidus* is a white form from Morocco which flowers in winter.

flowering in a pot or in a sunny very well-drained position, such as on scree, looking particularly attractive before the leaves lengthen. It is native to the Mediterranean region, where it grows in stony lowland areas.

### O. fimbriatum

White flowers, with a thin dark green median line, appear in late winter. They are held in a flat umbel, initially quite close to the ground but etiolating with age. This species has a number of lax thin leaves, which are hairy beneath, and some 12cm (4¾in) long at flowering time. A plant from SE Europe and Turkey, it will grow on a sunny scree, but is safer in a pot or bulb frame, as early slugs find the foliage irresistible. Height: 10cm (4in).

### O. nutans ♛

This very attractive plant can easily be overlooked at a quick glance, as it is so perfectly camouflaged. The flowers are composed of pale green and white pointed segments that droop and on closer inspection have a silvery sheen about them that is quite beautiful. The leaves begin to die back at flowering time, but even so, the plants make an interesting feature in sun or shade. Native to the Balkan Peninsula. Height: 30cm (12in).

### O. oligophyllum

This species is native to NE Turkey and the adjacent Caucasus, where it grows in alpine meadows. In cultivation it is easy to grow in well-drained soil in sun or semi-shade. The flowers are quite large, over 2cm (¾in) across, and pure white, with wide green median stripes on the outside of the segments. The flowering stem is held between two or three, deeply channelled bright green leaves. It flowers in late winter and early spring. Height: 10cm (4in).

## OXALIS

### Oxalidaceae

The shamrock-like leaves of this genus disguise a huge diversity of adaptations. Some *Oxalis* are too successful and become pernicious weeds, while others are quite demanding of the gardener. They are nearly world-wide in their distribution, with some unfortunately naturalizing huge areas as alien weeds, such as *O. pescaprae*, the Bermuda buttercup, that has blighted many Mediterranean landscapes. That said, many are beautiful, none more so than the winter-growing South African species, which flower with greenhouse protection in spring. These species come from the SW Cape, which has a Mediterranean type of climate with most of its rainfall in winter. The flowers of this genus are five-petalled and more or less funnel shaped.

There are many other SW African *Oxalis* which look very beautiful, to judge from photographs and paintings. They would be very desirable additions to any cool greenhouse, should they become available, but are best kept in a pot until they can be assessed for vigour.

### O. pescaprae

Although a weed in warm temperate climates this is a handsome plant for a pot, leafing in autumn and flowering in late winter. The flowers are bright yellow, above bright green clover-like foliage. The buds are held erectly, but as they open the flowers droop and hang downward. They flower from small scaly bulbs and even in Britain are best confined to a pot, as in SW England they have managed to naturalize themselves. There are double forms of the plant in cultivation. Height: 30cm (12in).

### O. purpurea

This widespread and variable species from SW Africa has white, pink, rose, purple and even yellow forms, depending upon the locality. Although from a warm temperate area this plant flowers very well in an unprotected bulb frame in late autumn and early winter, or can be grown in a pot just as successfully. The clover-like foliage is light green and looks rather like velvet; the bright rounded yellow flowers are held just above the foliage. It seems to flower best if late summer is very wet, or at least the watering is regular and truly soaking during this period. Height: 20–30cm (8–12in).

In Britain, it is the yellow form, **'Ken Aslett',** that is most usually cultivated.

### O. versicolor (see picture p.44)

From the Cape Peninsula this is too tender to risk outside, but makes a perfect winter-flowering pot plant for the frost-free greenhouse. The leaves have been reduced to three tufts of narrow square-ended leaflets, which appear in late autumn with the flower buds. The buds gradually lengthen to 2cm (¾in) and when there is sufficient light unroll like a spiral to reveal the red edges to the white flowers above a pale yellow tube; the common name of candy cane is very apt. They last for two months or more, as long as they are kept quite cool. Height: 10–15cm (4–6in).

## PUSCHKINIA

### Liliaceae

A small genus from the Middle East, where they grow on mountains by melting snow, these plants are very similar to *Scilla* and *Chionodoxa*, but have a small cylindrical corona surrounding the stamens and style. In the wild, they flower from mid-spring to midsummer depending upon the altitude, but in temperate countries like Britain, they are among the earliest flowers of the new year. The first flower opens at ground level, and then gradually the raceme extends, opening more flowers as it grows to its full height by early spring.

### P. scilloides var. libanotica (see picture plate III, 4)

The pale blue flowers have a blue median line, which is visible on both sides of the segment. As the six segments are joined at the base they never open fully, but are held in a wide cup. A very easy and prolific bulb, it needs regular dividing to look attractive, otherwise the bulbs become too congested. From the Caucasus, S Turkey, N Iraq and Iran through to the Lebanon, where it grows in alpine meadows and scrub. Height: 20cm (8in).

There is a pure white form available, 'Album', which is just as easy and attractive. There is also a green variant with more bell-shaped flowers.

## RANUNCULUS

### Ranunculaceae

A widespread and diverse family of which only a few have storage organs that could be included in a bulb book, and of those fewer still are early into flower. Those that do fit our category are particularly beautiful plants with buttercup-like flowers in many colours. The tuberous and rhizomatous species require differing cultivation techniques, depending upon their native homes. They are all plants centred around the Mediterranean basin, although *Ranunculus ficaria*, the common celandine, is widespread from W Europe to W Asia.

### R. asiaticus

This species is native to N Africa, SE Europe, including the islands, and SW Asia, where it grows on gentle slopes in full sun, which are wet in spring and dry in summer. The colours vary from white, pink, red and yellow. In

exposed sites, the flowers are the same size, but on dwarf stems. In cultivation they do require a dry summer and some frost protection in winter. I have seen a few gardens where raised beds have brought the tubers through most winters, with the spring flowering that followed matching the height and intensity of the Mediterranean plants. In general, it is safer to grow the tubers in pots, planted in early autumn in a well-drained soil mix. Keep this pot just moist until growth appears in winter, when the compost must never be allowed to dry out. The plant may be placed in a saucer and the water level maintained as a reservoir, until flowering is over, then the plant can be rested for the summer, under a bench in the greenhouse. Height: 30cm (12in).

This species has given rise to some florists' plants of great antiquity, first introduced into Europe from Turkey in 1580 by Carolus Clusius. These are the **Turban Ranunculus**, fully double selections that are still grown today; such as *R. asiaticus* **Turban Ranunculus** 'Hercules', a greenish white double, and 'Rosalie' with China-pink doubles with a black centre. The **Persian Ranunculus** from Turkey, introduced in about 1700, are both single and double and generally smaller than the Turbans, but exhibit a great range of colour. In the late 1800s the French bred a semi-double group of plants with a black eye. These so-called **French Ranunculus** have been improved by many nurseries in the last one hundred years. This leaves the last group, the **Peony-flowered Ranunculus**. They were introduced at the Ghent Floralies in 1923 and have proved to be the most free-flowering doubles and semi-doubles available. They are a little taller than the French and flower for a longer period. These unusual and dramatic flowers are often available as cut flowers, or in small pots in spring, which can be used for bedding once the threat of frost is passed.

### *R. calandrinioides* ♉

At first glance, this plant does not appear to have the storage organs that will help with early growth, but on closer inspection the root stock is thick and the roots fleshy. This beautiful *Ranunculus* is from high in the Atlas Mountains in Morocco and grows in winter to flower very early in spring. This species will grow very well in a sheltered sunny scree, but can be damaged by high winds, so consequently is often given a deep pot and grown in a cold greenhouse. The long wavy glaucous leaves are attractive and enclose a stem topped with two or three white or pale mauve buttercup-like flowers, some 5cm (2in) in diameter. Height: 15cm (6in).

### *R. creticus*

A tuberous-rooted plant that breaks into leaf in autumn and which, rather like *R. asiaticus*, must not dry out again until next summer. The plant can be grown in a scree but is often grown in a pot in a cold greenhouse, where the many 3cm (1¼in) wide bright yellow flowers open above wavy edged kidney-shaped leaves. Found on Crete in mountainous regions. Height: 20–30cm (8–12in).

### *R. ficaria*

Although in some situations *R. ficaria*, the lesser celandine, is a weed or wild plant, in selected forms it can be a very attractive plant for a shady spot in the garden. This little tuberous plant is widespread from Britain eastwards to Siberia, where it is found in shady or grassy banks and woods. With such a wide distribution, it is inevitable that eagle-eyed gardeners would find varieties for the garden. All are very easily propagated, by just separating the tubers and planting each little piece straight back into the bed, where it will flower the next spring. Height: 10–15cm (4–6in).

The selections are very varied, with double flowers in white, bronze and cream and singles of white, cream and every variation of yellow. There are popular forms with particularly interesting foliage, like 'Brambling' with olive-green and brown-streaked leaves and 'Brazen Hussy' (see picture also plate II, 4) with dark brown-purple foliage. If you grow a mixture of these you do need to nip out any seedlings that revert to the wild form, or the special forms will soon be lost. It is also worthwhile sorting through the colonies to look out for your own interesting sports. For instance it is common to find 'Brazen Hussy' producing white-flowered offspring, while still retaining the attractive foliage. The wild variant **ssp. *ficariiformis*** is a large S European form with big yellow flowers and stature to match.

### *R. kochii*

This is a very compact and low-growing celandine, from the bare and stony mountains of Turkey, Iran and Iraq. It is a snow-melt plant from 3000m (9840ft), which flowers very early in the year. It is best in a frame or pot, although it will grow in a sunny raised bed, but can be mud splashed by bad weather. In a frame the bright buttercup-yellow flowers are produced near ground level above the round shiny leaves. After flowering the plant needs a dry rest in summer. Height: 5cm (2in).

*Ranunculus ficaria* 'Brazen Hussy', an eye-catching selection by Christopher Lloyd, has both striking flowers and foliage.

## ROMULEA

### Iridaceae

This genus can be found on the northern and southern sides of the Mediterranean Sea, then in a few mountain localities in tropical Africa, with a large and attractive group in South Africa. The flowers are funnel shaped and rather like stiff crocuses in appearance, appearing from late winter until spring, depending upon the species. Some have multi-coloured flowers, with a range of white, pink, red, purple, yellow and blue segments. They need strong sunlight to open and then do so only for a few hours in the middle of the day. The storage organ for these plants is a corm which is often quite small. The leaves are long thin and wiry. They usually set seed, which nestles in a three-sided capsule and invites collection; this is a prudent undertaking, as some species self-sow in all the wrong places and are hard to remove.

The Mediterranean plants need careful choosing to avoid the species with small dowdy flowers. However there are a few that are underrated that are easily grown and can make an impact in a bulb frame or a sunny raised bed. Those *Romulea* from the SW Cape of South Africa, where they have winter rainfall and flower in the spring, are best grown in pots of sandy loam in a cool greenhouse, which are watered in autumn and kept frost-free during winter. In warm temperate areas they grow very well in sunny borders.

### R. amoena

A most striking species from the Cape this has crimson to deep rose-pink flowers. In the centre of the flower is a mixture of white and dark purple markings. The leaves are long and channelled, to 30cm (12in) in length. Height: 15cm (6in).

### R. atranda

This species has large flowers of pale magenta or violet with a purple zone above a yellow throat and black or purple anthers with yellow pollen – a very stunning combination of colours. It has the usual long narrow leaves but with conspicuous ribbing. A South African native. Height: 10cm (4in).

### R. bulbocodium

The most commonly cultivated European species, this has cup-shaped violet or lilac flowers with a yellow or white throat, with one or two flowers to each stem. When open the flowers are 3cm (1¼in) across, with the pointed segments over 3cm (1¼in) long. The narrow quite stiff plain leaves arch outward to reach 30cm (12in) in length and are well developed at flowering. They do not decay but remain as thin brown wires until removed in summer. This plant is common in the Mediterranean region in sandy and rocky locations from sea level to 1000m (3280ft). Height: 10–15cm (4–6in).

There are several distinct varieties of this variable species that need describing: **var.** *clusiana,* from the Iberian Peninsula, has larger flowers of lilac with a yellow centre and makes a good garden plant; **var.** *crocea*, with bright yellow flowers with darker streaks of brown on the outside of the segments, is from Turkey and Syria and needs a dry summer to succeed; **var.** *leichtliniana* is the Greek form with white flowers and a yellow throat, and

var. *subalpestris* is a stunning form from the Greek islands with violet flowers with white centres.

### R. flava

A widespread plant in the Cape region, which can have yellow, white, purple or pink flowers. The outside of the segments is, however, always greenish or greenish brown. It is a robust plant with slightly glabrous wider leaves. Height: 25cm (10in).

### R. requienii

This species has deep violet purple, rather globular flowers, without any inner markings. It is found growing wild in Corsica and Sardinia and, rather surprisingly, proves to be hardy in more northerly countries like Britain. Height: 3–5cm (1¼–2in).

### R. rosea

This variable Cape native has the typical stiff leaves of the genus, which are long, reaching 35cm (14in) or more. The flowers are a distinctive yellowish green with dark lateral stripes in bud, opening to expose segments of pink, rose or lilac. This plant has become naturalized in the Channel Islands. Height: 15cm (6in).

The most delicate shade of pale pink, the starry flowers of *Scilla bifolia* 'Rosea' appear in early spring.

The flowers of **var. *reflexa*** are pink through to magenta with a darker throat, and slightly reflexed. The leaves are very thin.

### R. sabulosa

Known as the satin flower because of a satin sheen on the flower's inner segments, this has large blooms that vary from bright salmon to glossy scarlet, with some dark blotches within the throat. The leaves are grooved, dark green, and reach up to 20cm (8in) in length. Native to hills in the NW Cape where it grows in sandy loam. Height: 5–10cm (2–4in).

### R. tempskyana

The very attractive, dark purple starry flowers begin to flower just above ground level in early spring and lengthen later. It grows very well in a pot or the bulb frame. From the E Mediterranean islands and mainland Greece. Height: 5–8cm (2–3¼in).

## SCILLA

### Hyacinthaceae

A bulbous genus of some forty species of which a few, like *Scilla siberica*, are well known and easily grown. However, there are many others that are just as garden worthy but seldom seen. These spring-flowering plants are at home in a rock garden, border or even under shrubs, where the soil will dry a little during summer. The scaly bulbs are perennial and slowly extend by producing offsets. They don't require a thorough baking over summer and prefer a slightly damp rest, once the leaves die down. These plants are prodigious seeders, and colonies are best built up by letting them self-sow, or in the case of rarer species, sowing in a pot as soon as they are ripe and growing on for two years before planting out.

The flowers have six segments that are free at the base and make open cup shapes or starry bells, depending on the species. They are usually blue or violet with some striping, but there are occasionally albino or pink forms to be found.

Looking back at descriptions of *S. bifolia* from sixty years or so ago we seem to have lost many excellent garden forms of this hardy little bulb. Today the RHS *Plant Finder* lists just two forms available, whereas earlier this century there used to be sixteen. It is probable that a number were duplicates, but nevertheless there is a loss of diversity for the gardener. The whims of fashion or poor plant constitution may have caused the decrease in a particular plant's availability, but whatever the reason it is beholden upon gardeners to propagate and distribute rare garden plants for generations to come. In the case of *Scilla*, seed exchanges are an excellent and easy method of keeping all the species available to gardeners. Some species previously included in *Scilla* are now found in *Ledebouria* and *Hyacinthoides*.

### S. amoena

In cultivation since the eighteenth century and naturalized in SE Europe, the origins of this species are unknown. It has strong affinities with *S. bithynica*, but does not have any bracts at the base of the pedicels and the flowers are erect on the raceme, rather than horizontal to upright as in *S. bithynica*. There are three to six starry mid-blue flowers to a stem, each about 2cm (¾in) across. It is an easy garden plant that produces the flower stem and the long linear leaves at the same time, growing well in any border that is not too dry. Height: 20cm (8in).

### S. bifolia ♔

This little species is from the mountains of S Europe and Turkey and is often found near melting snow. It is a very good plant for spreading in a semi-shaded area in a rock garden or raised bed. The one-sided raceme bears starry flowers that are usually a bright turquoise-blue, although pink and white forms are also cultivated. The leaves are usually green, fleshy, keeled and held just below the flowers, but in some of the forms the edges of the leaves are red and the staining extends below ground. Height: 5–10cm (2–4in).

'Alba' is good pure white form while **var. *praecox*** is an early strong-growing variety with bright blue flowers. 'Rosea' (see pictures p.168–9 and plate I, 8) is a pink form that fades rather quickly once the flowers open. There is an older form in gardens with brighter and longer lasting pink flowers but it is not generally available. The flowers of **var. *taurica*** are large and blue with conspicuous purple anthers; its leaves are edged red. It is slow to increase and does not seem to set seed.

### S. bithynica (see picture also plate I, 2)

An early flowered species from north and south of the Bosporus, which soon spreads in most ordinary garden situations. Up to twelve, starry mid-blue flowers are held upright or horizontally on the raceme. Purple anthers make a pleasing contrast to the white filaments beneath. There are small bracts at the base of the flower pedicels. The flower stem is surrounded by a few narrow green linear leaves. Height: 20cm (8in).

*Scilla bithynica* thrives in a sunny border and flowers during late winter.

### S. cilicica

A species from the E Mediterranean, which needs a sheltered site to do well. The open cup-shaped lavender-blue flowers are only slightly reflexed and are well spaced on a stem which is stained with a little of the flower's colour at the top. The long linear leaves are formed in winter and can be a little ragged by the time of flowering in early spring. Height: 15–20cm (6–8in).

### S. griehuberi

The many lilac-blue cup-shaped flowers open more widely than others and are slightly reflexed. The narrow leaves develop during the winter. Native to Iran. Height: 10–15cm (4–6in).

### S. hohenackeri

The stems of this species hold a loose raceme of pendent lilac-blue flowers. They are an open reflexed cup shape with protruding stamens. The narrow linear leaves are not formed until spring and then only reach 10cm (4in) in length. This is an Iranian species, which grows well in a shady damp position. Height: 10cm (4in).

### S. italica (see picture also plate III, 5)

This neat-growing plant has a rosette of dark green narrow leaves around a compact umbel of starry bell-shaped blue flowers. It is found in stony places in Italy, France, Spain and Portugal. It is a versatile plant in cooler climes, flowering well in sun or part shade. The white form is especially attractive, cropping up regularly in colonies that are allowed to self-sow. Height: 15cm (6in).

### S. liliohyacinthus

Although this may flower a little after most early bulbs have finished, by early spring the broad shiny leaves, some 3cm (1¼in) wide, are very evident as a feature in the shady rock garden or border. The starry mid-blue flowers can be rather a let down after such attractive foliage. This French and Spanish bulb also has a widely grown white-flowered form. Height: 10–15cm (4–6in).

### S. melaina

This relatively newly described species produces its three or four narrow strap-shaped leaves in the spring; they are about 15cm (6in) long. The starry bell-shaped flowers are a sky blue with up to four in a small raceme, but none the less, it is an effective garden plant which seems suited to a well-drained but shady bed. It is from S Turkey and found in woods and subalpine meadows to 1400m (4590ft). Height: 10–15cm (4–6in).

### S. messeniaca

This is mainly found in Greece, in the Peloponnese, where it grows on rocky hillsides at 1000m (3280ft) and flowers in early spring. It has dark green leaves, which are neat and which frame the flowering stem that has between eight and fifteen, slightly upward-facing, pale blue, starry bell-shaped flowers. It soon colonizes under shrubs and semi-shady places in the open garden, where it makes an attractive sheet of blue in early spring. Height: 10–15cm (4–6in).

### S. mischtschenkoana

This plant has open reflexed cup-shaped flowers with relatively large pale blue segments, each with a dark blue stripe on the outside. The flowers appear as they push through the soil and continue to extend until the stem is some 15cm (6in) tall with many flowers. The glossy green leaves follow the flowers out of the ground and reach about 10cm (4in) in length. It is a very adaptable plant, growing well in sun and shade, with the first blooms appearing just after Christmas. It is from N Iran and the Caucasus where it is found growing on stony hillsides. Height: 15cm (6in).

### S. monophyllos

A species that just begins to flower in early spring, it has a well-spaced raceme of starry bell-shaped blue flowers. It has just one leaf that is quite wide and clasping at the base. This species is from sandy heaths and pine woods in SW Spain and Portugal, so needs drier conditions to grow well, liking a bulb frame or very well-drained soil in the full sun. Height: 15cm (6in).

### S. persica

From wet meadows in Iran, N Iraq and SW Turkey, in cultivation this plant needs a wet spring in a well-drained sunny position. Many flat starry mid-blue flowers are held horizontally on 1–2cm (⅜–¾in) long pedicels. The upright channelled leaves, to 15cm (6in) long, encase the flowering stem. The plant does not seem to increase much in cultivation and seedlings need growing on to increase a grouping. Height: 30cm (12in).

### S. puschkinioides

This species has a raceme composed of a few pale blue or white, 1cm (⅜in) wide, starry bell-shaped flowers with a darker stripe down each segment. The leaves are quite long and thin with a white central stripe. A Central Asian species, where it grows as a snow-melt plant above 1000m (3280ft). In cultivation it is proving to be quite easy. It is a quietly attractive plant, not often grown. Height: 10–15cm (4–6in).

### S. ramburei

This tall *Scilla* has bluish starry flowers, up to 1.5cm (½in) across, held in a loose upward-facing raceme, with as many as thirty flowers to a flowerhead. The narrow lance-shaped leaves gradually taper to a sharp point and are grey-green on the upper surface. Native to Portugal, SW Spain and N Africa, where it grows at low levels in sandy places, it thrives in full sun in a well drained position in cultivation. Height: 50cm (20in).

### S. rosenii

One of the most challenging species of *Scilla* to get to

An under-rated *Scilla*, the white form of *S. italica* has neat foliage and a conical flower spike.

flower in character, this is a high snow-melt plant from NE Turkey, Georgia and Armenia, where it flowers in late spring or early summer. In temperate climates, mild winters can induce the plant to grow and then, when it comes to ground level, the poor light levels and inclement weather stop the growth and it blooms at ground level, spoiling this beautiful flower. It is best grown in the coldest part of the garden, where frost lingers, or in a pot which is housed in a north-facing frame. I know of a grower who keeps the potted bulb in a refrigerator until it shows growth. He takes it out in the

early spring so that the plant lengthens in the strong light to show its true stature. There are one or two flowers with reflexed segments up to 3cm (1¼in) long. They are a light blue with a white centre and are worth the effort. There are two or three quite broad green leaves. Height: up to 15cm (6in).

### S. siberica ♈

The well-known and easily grown Siberian squill is ideal for the rock garden or a semi-shaded border. It is a short plant with two or three shiny green leaves with a hooked tip, which lengthen after flowering. The flowers are very variable in colour and size. They are pendent and bell shaped, up to 1.5cm (½in) long. Found in S Russia, the Caucasus, the Crimea and NW Iran, in meadows and woodland. Height: 5–10cm (2–4in).

'Alba' (see picture plate I, 11) is a pure white selection of equal vigour and beauty. The darkest blue form is **'Spring Beauty'** (see picture plate I, 6), although the same colour can be found in the wild. From S Turkey comes **ssp. *ingridae***, a pale blue *Scilla* of unique colour, which is spreading in cultivation. This is said to be just a southern form of the species.

### S. verna

Native to W Europe, this squill, although a treasure of shoreline areas, does not have quite enough presence for the garden. The Spanish equivalent may be worth including in a collection; it is larger and has star-like blue-mauve flowers with brighter blue ovaries and anthers. Height: 5–20cm (2–8in).

## SPARAXIS

### Iridaceae

This South African genus of cormous plants are winter growing and spring flowering. From the SW Cape area, which has most rain in winter, they are not frost tolerant, so need greenhouse protection. The corms should be planted in large pots of sandy loam in early autumn and kept moist until growth begins. The watering should be increased and the pots placed in full sun to keep them from etiolating. Once they have flowered the foliage will die down in early summer, so the watering must be reduced and then stopped to let the corms rest during the summer. The brightly coloured, six-petalled flowers are star shaped. There are packs sold for summer flowering; these have been cold stored to control the flowering time, but will revert to normal the following year.

### S. bulbifera

This species has aerial bulbils, found in the branches of

the stem. The large flowers, up 6cm (2½in) in diameter, are cream or white with a yellow or green base. The sword-shaped leaves are shorter than the flowering stem. Height: 40cm (16in).

### S. elegans

The attractive flowers, on unbranched stems, are occasionally white, but most usually salmon-pink with coiled purple-maroon anthers and a dark centre. This species also has bulbils in the leaf axils and sword-shaped leaves to 30cm (12in). Height: 25–30cm (10–12in).

### S. grandiflora

This tall species has flowers in white, rose and purple. The sword-like leaves are about half the height and form bulbils in the axils after flowering. Height: 40cm (16in).

A yellow form, **ssp. *acutiloba*** has many large trumpet-like flowers. The flowers of **ssp. *fimbriata*** are cream with the three outer segments a dusky purple beneath. It is a robust plant. Less than 20cm (8in) tall, **ssp. *violacea*** has varying amounts of purple and white markings.

### S. tricolor

The most common *Sparaxis* in cultivation, this shows many variations of colour. In the Cape, it is known as the harlequin flower and is becoming scarce. The flowers are bright orange, purple or pink with a yellow throat and a band of dark blackish purple at the bases of the segments. There are five to ten leaves which are shorter than the flowering stems. The commercial stock with this name is usually of hybrid origin and has a great colour range. Height: 35cm (14in).

## TRILLIUM

### Trilliaceae

A group of woodland rhizomatous plants from N America and E Asia, most of which fall outside the remit of this book, but there are just a few that are very early and demand a place, on account of their form and beauty. They are very distinct in having, as the name suggests, three leaves, single flowers with three petals and three smaller but very noticeable sepals. The seeds are slow to germinate, but early sowing before they dry at all seems to speed the event. Otherwise the rhizomes can be divided in early spring or in late summer. As woodland plants, they do best in semi-shade in humus-rich soil that is sheltered from the strongest winds.

### T. albidum (see picture pp.108–109)

An early large-flowered white trillium from California and Oregan, this grows very well in the shady garden. Height: 30cm (12in).

*Trillium rivale* is a small but effective plant in a shady bed or trough.

### T. chloropetalum var. giganteum ♈

This is an early flowering plant with upward-facing purple flowers, surrounded by dark green mottled leaves. In time, an attractive colony will develop that precludes weeds and regularly sets abundant seed. There is a white form that is equally attractive. Native to central California. Height: 40–50cm (16–20in).

### T. ovatum

The flowers are more open and are a pure white above green unmarked leaves. From California northwards to Canada, growing in light woodland and forest glades, it is easy to grow in any shady border. Height: 20cm (8in).

### T. rivale ♈

A smaller species with upward-facing white or pink flowers that may have some pink flecking. The flowers are held clear of the leaves on short stems and make a very showy sight in a small border or deep sink or other container. Found in wet areas of woodland in Oregon and California in spring. Height: 5cm (2in).

## TRITONIA
### Iridaceae

A genus that has affinities with *Crocosmia*, this is found in tropical as well as S Africa. Only a few of the Cape cormous plants will be described as they are winter growing and spring flowering. They all have cup-shaped flowers that face upward on thin wiry stems. The segments are not always regular and begin to open from the base of the raceme. They can be grown in a frost-free greenhouse in a sandy loam, which is watered in autumn. In more temperate climates the intensity of light is far less than they are used to in Africa and so the stems will lengthen, possibly needing some support.

### T. crocata

A slender inflorescence carries many orangey red flowers, with the three lower segments bearing a yellow line. The lance-shaped leaves are 30cm (12in) long. The corms are small. This species is declining in the wild because of the expansion of agriculture into the clay flats where it grows. Height: 50cm (20in).

There are two popular hybrids that may have *T. crocata* as a parent; **'Orange Delight'** and **'Prince of Orange'** are very effective and produce long-lasting cut flowers.

### T. securigera

A very attractive plant with apricot to yellow flowers, but always with yellow in the throat. It blooms early in the year, with up to fifteen flowers on a stem, above the lance-like foliage. Height: 35cm (14in).

### T. squalida

This fine species has regular wide cupped flowers that have pinkish segments with darker veins, and a yellow or pink base. It has lanceolate leaves, shorter than the flowering stem. Height: 50cm (20in).

## TULIPA
### Liliaceae

*Tulipa* is one of the major bulbous families, and one that people can immediately name and visualize. These are one of the earliest bulbs introduced into our gardens, first recorded in the sixteenth century and coming from Turkey. The genus is found in the Mediterranean regions, the Middle East, the Caucasus and eastward as

far as China. They are nearly all plants of a long hard winter, followed by a short spring and a hot dry summer, so correct positioning in the garden is crucial for success. If they are planted out, the site must be well drained and in full sun; in wetter areas it may be necessary to lift the bulbs in summer and replant in late autumn each year. Alternatively, they grow very well in a bulb frame or deep pot in a sunny frame or greenhouse, where they can have a dry rest in summer. Most just fall outside the season covered by this book, but by no means all. Some of the small species flower in early spring and have finished by the time spring is really underway.

### T. biflora

This small species has few starry white flowers with a yellow centre and a greenish exterior that is marked with purple. There are two grey-green leaves that are slightly hairy. It makes a good perennial feature for a sunny raised bed or rock garden. It is native in rocky places from SE Europe to S Russia, where because of its range there are small variations. Height: 10cm (4in).

One such variation is *T. turkestanica*, which has up to twelve flowers on a stem about twice the height of *T. biflora*. It is a good garden tulip, lasting and increasing for many years in a sunny situation.

### T. cretica

Native to Crete, this small tulip is best grown in a pot in a cold greenhouse or frame. The dark green leaves with a fine purple edge show early in the year. The flowers are bright green in bud, opening to reveal white segments with a small yellow eye and, once opened, the reverse has a faint pink tinge to the browny green background. Not as strong a grower as other Cretan tulips, it makes a very beautiful display in a clay pot. Height: 15cm (6in).

### T. humilis

This name covers a large group of beautiful dwarf tulips for the raised bed, bulb frame or for a pot. All the forms need to be grown in full light to keep the flower stem as short as possible. The flowers are all very bright in the pink to magenta range and can measure 7cm (2¾in) across when fully open. The species itself is a pink-magenta with a yellow eye. They all have quite narrow grey-green leaves that can lie almost flat on the ground in some forms. All are found from S and E Turkey, Iraq, Iran and eastward into W Asia. Height: 10–15cm (4–6in).

The flowers of **var.** *pulchella* are a paler purple with a

A delicate little beauty from Crete, *Tulipa cretica* requires pot cultivation to flower well.

*Tulipa tarda* is readily obtainable and easy to please in a sunny spot.

blue centre with a white margin. The **Albocaerulea Oculata Group** is the stunning white form with a bluish purple eye. The flowers of **Violacea Group** are purple with a yellow or blackish centre.

### T. kaufmanniana

This is the famous water lily tulip, which when crossed with *T. greigii* produced an array of colourful short tulips for an early display. The species is well worth growing, with large flowers that open completely flat in good light. They are white or yellow with some crimson markings on the outside, but can be very variable in their native mountains in Central Asia. It has a strong stout

stem and broad, mostly basal leaves. Height: 30cm (12in).

**Kaufmanniana hybrids**

These hybrids of *T. kaufmanniana* and *T. greigii* are widely available and will brighten any sunny spot from early spring onwards. The leaves are strongly mottled and striped, a character inherited from *T. greigii*. *T.* 'Alfred Cortot' ♛ is a deep scarlet with a black base. *T.* 'Gluck' is a strong yellow with bands of carmine red on the outside. *T.* 'Heart's Delight' is carmine with a paler edge on the outside, a paler carmine inside and a yellow base. *T.* 'Shakespeare' is a mix of salmon and scarlet with a yellow base and well-marked leaves. *T.* 'Stresa' ♛ has deep golden yellow flowers with an orange-red stripe on the outer segments and inside, the deep yellow base has some red veining. *T.* 'The First' is an ivory white form with a yellow base that has a little red flushing on the outside. A very early variety and close to the species.

**T. kolpakowskiana** ♛ (see picture plate III, 8)

This tulip has slim yellow flowers suffused on the outer three segments with pink and green. There is no basal blotch, but it has a darker yellow centre. The undulate leaves are quite narrow and grey. From the mountains of Central Asia, it grows well in a well-drained sunny position. Height: 25cm (10in).

**T. kurdica** (see picture plate III, 10)

Closely related to *T. humilis*, this tulip is bright brick-red to orange-red. From NE Iraq, found at 2400–3000m (7870–9840ft) near melting snow. Height: 10cm (4in).

**T. maximowiczii**

A short-growing, brilliant scarlet tulip which is very perennial if grown in a raised bed. Height: 15cm (6in).

**T. montana**

A small species with brilliant red flowers that have a small purple-black basal blotch and very prominent yellow anthers. It has deeply channelled leaves about 15cm (6in) long. It grows well in a sunny raised bed, flowering in early spring. From N Iran. Height: 15–25cm (6–10in).

**T. neustreuvae** (see picture plate III, 7)

This plant used to be very rare in cultivation but thanks to modern propagation techniques it is now widely available at a modest price. The flowers are bright yellow, with the outer segments having a broad green band and the three inner ones with greenish lines. The two bright green leaves are up to 10cm (4in) long and 1cm (³⁄₈in) wide. It is an early flowering tulip and seems best in a

Despite its long name, *Tulipa maximowiczii* has a simple beauty and is ideal for a raised bed.

*Tulipa sylvestris* is widespread in Europe but can be shy in flowering in some gardens.

cold frame or greenhouse. Native to Central Asia. Height: 10–15cm (4–6in).

**T. praestans**

The flowers of this distinct plant can number five and are a plain orange-red. The nearly upright grey-green leaves clasp the stem for three-quarters of its length. It is a persistent garden plant. A tulip from the mountains of Central Asia, where it grows on steep earthy slopes and in light woodland. Height: 30cm (12in).

Often seen gardens is 'Van Tubergen's Variety', a strong selection from the Dutch nursery.

**T. saxatilis**

Lilac-pink flowers with a conspicuous white-edged yellow eye and about 5cm (2in) long, appear in late winter. The broad shiny leaves appear before the flowers. It spreads by stolons and soon makes a good colony in the garden, although it should be excluded from bulb frames or raised beds for this reason. From Crete and SW Turkey. Height: 20cm (8in).

**T. sylvestris**

A widespread tulip naturalized in N Europe, it has yellow flowers that have a greenish suffusion on the outside. It is very easy to establish in a sunny spot, but is not a prolific flowerer. Height: up to 40cm (16in).

The shorter **ssp.** *australis* has a red suffusion on the outer segments and is more reliable at flowering.

**T. tarda** (see picture p.177)

A small, easily grown tulip from Central Asia. The yellow segments have a broad white tip. Height: 10cm (4in).

## FLOWERING TIMES

This chart is a general guide to the flowering period of all the genera described in the A–Z section of this book.

| GENUS | Late autumn | Early winter | Midwinter | Late winter | Early spring |
|---|---|---|---|---|---|
| Amana | | | | | ■ |
| Anemone | | | ■ | ■ | ■ |
| Arisaema | | | | | ■ |
| Arisarum | | | | | ■ |
| Asphodelus | | | | ■ | |
| Babiana | | ■ | ■ | ■ | |
| Bellevalia | | | | | ■ |
| Bulbocodium | | | | ■ | |
| Chasmanthe | | ■ | ■ | ■ | |
| Chionodoxa | | | | ■ | |
| × Chionoscilla | | | | ■ | |
| Colchicum | | | ■ | ■ | |
| Corydalis | | | | ■ | |
| Crocus | ■ | ■ | ■ | ■ | ■ |
| Cyclamen | ■ | ■ | ■ | | |
| Cyrtanthus | | ■ | ■ | ■ | |
| Eranthis | | | ■ | ■ | |
| Erythronium | | | | | ■ |
| Fritillaria | | | | ■ | |
| Gagea | | | | ■ | |
| Galanthus | ■ | ■ | ■ | ■ | ■ |
| Haemanthus | | | ■ | ■ | |
| Herbertia | | | ■ | ■ | |
| Hermodactylus | | | | ■ | |

| GENUS | Late autumn | Early winter | Midwinter | Late winter | Early spring |
|---|---|---|---|---|---|
| Hyacinthella | | | | ■ | ■ |
| Hyacinthoides | | | | ■ | |
| Hyacinthus | ■ | ■ | ■ | | |
| Ipheion | | | | ■ | ■ |
| Iris | | ■ | ■ | ■ | ■ |
| Korolkowia | | | | | ■ |
| Lachenalia | | ■ | ■ | | |
| Ledebouria | | | | ■ | |
| Leucojum | | | | ■ | |
| Massonia | | | ■ | ■ | |
| Melasphaerula | | | | ■ | |
| Merendera | | | | ■ | |
| Muscari | | | | ■ | ■ |
| Narcissus | ■ | ■ | ■ | ■ | ■ |
| Ornithogalum | | | | ■ | |
| Oxalis | ■ | ■ | ■ | ■ | ■ |
| Puschkinia | | | | ■ | |
| Ranunculus | ■ | ■ | ■ | ■ | |
| Romulea | | | | | ■ |
| Scilla | | | | | ■ |
| Sparaxis | | | | ■ | ■ |
| Trillium | | | | | ■ |
| Tritonia | | | | ■ | ■ |
| Tulipa | | | | ■ | |

## PROPAGATION TECHNIQUES

Please note, hybrids are unlikely to produce identical offspring if propagated by seed.

1 only those with scales
2 only forms of *F. imperialis*
3 only *R. asiaticus*

| GENUS | Seed | Division | Scales | Chipping | Twin-scaling | Cutting & scopping | Cuttings |
|---|---|---|---|---|---|---|---|
| *Amana* | ● | ● | | | | | |
| *Anemone* | ● | ● | | | | | |
| *Arisaema* | ● | ● | | | | | |
| *Arisarum* | ● | ● | | | | | |
| *Asphodelus* | | ● | | | | | |
| *Babiana* | ● | ● | | | | | |
| *Bellevalia* | ● | ● | | | | | |
| *Bulbocodium* | ● | ● | | | | | |
| *Chasmanthe* | ● | ● | | | | | |
| *Chionodoxa* | ● | ● | | | | | |
| × *Chionoscilla* | | ● | | | | | |
| *Colchicum* | ● | ● | | | | | |
| *Corydalis* | ● | ● | | | | | |
| *Crocus* | ● | ● | | | | | |
| *Cyclamen* | ● | | | | | | |
| *Cyrtanthus* | ● | ● | | | | | |
| *Eranthis* | ● | ● | | | | | |
| *Erythronium* | ● | ● | | | | | |
| *Fritillaria* | ● | ● | ● 1 | ● | | ● 2 | |
| *Gagea* | ● | ● | | | | | |
| *Galanthus* | ● | ● | | | ● | | |
| *Haemanthus* | ● | ● | | | | | |
| *Herbertia* | ● | ● | | | | | |
| *Hermodactylus* | ● | ● | | | | | |

| GENUS | Seed | Division | Scales | Chipping | Twin-scaling | Cutting & scopping | Cuttings |
|---|---|---|---|---|---|---|---|
| *Hyacinthella* | ● | ● | | | | | |
| *Hyacinthoides* | ● | ● | | | | | |
| *Hyacinthus* | ● | ● | | | | ● | |
| *Ipheion* | ● | ● | | | | | |
| *Iris* | ● | ● | | | | | |
| *Korolkowia* | ● | ● | | | | ● | |
| *Lachenalia* | ● | ● | | | | | |
| *Ledebouria* | ● | ● | | | | | |
| *Leucojum* | ● | ● | | | | | |
| *Massonia* | ● | ● | | | | | |
| *Melasphaerula* | ● | ● | | | | | |
| *Merendera* | ● | ● | | | | | |
| *Muscari* | ● | ● | | | | | |
| *Narcissus* | ● | ● | | ● | ● | | |
| *Ornithogalum* | ● | ● | | | | | |
| *Oxalis* | ● | ● | | | | | |
| *Puschkinia* | ● | ● | | | | | |
| *Ranunculus* | ● | ● | | | | | ● 3 |
| *Romulea* | ● | ● | | | | | |
| *Scilla* | ● | ● | | | | | |
| *Sparaxis* | ● | ● | | | | | |
| *Trillium* | ● | ● | | | | | |
| *Tritonia* | ● | ● | | | | | |
| *Tulipa* | ● | ● | | | | | |

# Appendix I *Conservation*

Conservation is a thorny issue with some famous bulbous sites endangered through over-collecting. It is probably true to say that everything seen on a holiday can be bought from nursery stock in this country, making collection unnecessary. Many countries are outlawing indiscriminate collecting and it is now illegal to bring into Britain many plants without a licence, including cyclamen and snowdrops. Collection of the seed of bulbous plants is not usually so detrimental to the population, and anyway, it requires practice and skill to find a drying crocus capsule on a brown Greek hillside in early summer. Native flora is not only under threat from collecting but also by the ever-increasing use of herbicides as farming practices change and more land is intensively cultivated throughout the world.

The society Flora and Fauna International, publishes the *Good Bulb Guide*. This lists suppliers of bulbs who have agreed to never knowingly sell wild-collected bulbs or at least label those that are from a wild source, so the buyer can make a choice. The majority of these bulbs are imported via Holland, who in the 1980s imported about 300 tonnes a year of dry bulbs from Turkey alone. As these were mostly small bulbs like crocus, iris and snowdrops the number of bulbs involved must have been vast. Over forty companies have signed up to this agreement and a new list is published annually. Flora and Fauna International have themselves initiated a nursery scheme for snowdrops with the aim of getting Turkish farmers to cultivate snowdrops and other indigenous bulbs, so maintaining the quality for the gardener and relieving the pressure to keep on collecting. This started in 1996 and does need the support of gardeners everywhere. In 1997, I purchased some *Galanthus elwesii* from this scheme and have been very pleased with the results so far. One bulb in particular is by far the largest and most eye-catching selection I have ever seen. This scheme and other conservation measures have begun to reduce wild-collected exports, but as the demand is so great these cultivated exports do need all the help we gardeners can give them. It is to be hoped that one day these cultivated exports will entirely replace the commercial digging of wild-collected bulbs.

# Appendix II *Where to See Early Bulbs*

In a quiet winter period there is nothing better to lift the spirits than a garden visit to admire the precocious small flowers, whether in large drifts in parkland or in sheltered corners of cottage gardens. In Britain, there are a growing number of hardy gardeners opening their gardens to the public for just such delights. The Yellow Book, or more properly *Gardens of England and Wales Open for Charity*, is an excellent source of information. Although not published until early spring, you can look in the previous year's edition for details of winter openings. There are of course, large gardens like RHS Wisley, the Royal Botanic Gardens at Kew, Harlow Carr, the Royal Botanic Garden in Edinburgh, and many others, which are open to the public and that have winter areas or gardens where bulbs are an integral part of the display.

## SNOWDROPS

Snowdrops are enjoying something of a renaissance and many gardening societies are organizing visits to gardens and collections not normally open to the public. Local specialist nurseries often arrange events. For instance, Foxgrove Plants of Enborne in Berkshire always have a garden opening in February, when their snowdrops look the best, in aid of their local church. The Cottage Garden Society Snowdrop Group, run by Daphne Chappell of Cinderdine Cottage Snowdrops, organizes events like the annual snowdrop gala, where talks are given in the mornings, and in the afternoons visits are made to famous gardens where snowdrops are a feature.

The weekend gardening section of national newspapers is often very useful in highlighting new and established gardens open to the public. The following gardens regularly open and attract large numbers of people in late winter, the hardy vanguard for the new season. Anglesey Abbey, near Cambridge is a National Trust property, open for snowdrops and recently for a large new winter garden. Benington Lordship, Benington, in Hertford-shire, has a Norman moat where snowdrops have been naturalized. Brandy Mount House, Alresford, in Hamp-shire, is a private garden which houses one of the National Collections of *Galanthus* and is open for a few days in February when the snowdrops can be seen at their best in a woodland setting. Colesbourne Park, south of Cheltenham, in Gloucestershire, was the home of Henry J. Elwes, who gave his name to *Galanthus elwesii*. The garden is open on selected weekends in late winter. Fountains Abbey, Ripon, in Yorkshire, is a National Trust Property with near daily opening. Kingston Lacy, Wim-bourne Minster, in Dorset, is another National Trust gar-den. It has special openings for snowdrops which are advertised in winter, prior to opening. Laycock Abbey, near Chippenham, in Wiltshire, is again a National Trust property that opens specially for the woodland spring bulbs at weekends in late winter. Painswick Rococo Garden, Painswick, in Gloucestershire, is a private his-toric garden restoration that has a wonderful snowdrop dell. It is open daily. Walsingham Abbey, Little Walsing-ham, in Norfolk, has a snowdrop walk through acres of woodland next the River Stiffkey. The openings vary to suit the season for the single and double *Galanthus nivalis*.

## DAFFODILS

In early spring, the *Narcissus* becomes the focus for the gardener and many openings are planned to see these harbingers of spring. Their attraction is nothing new, for many hundreds of years the scattered colonies of the Lent lily, *N. pseudonarcissus*, have delighted the eye and inspired many poems and paintings. Most famously, William Wordsworth wrote in 1807, in his poem 'I wan-dered lonely as a cloud', about the naturalized daffodils on the banks of Ullswater in the Lake District. Nearly two hundred years later, there are still beautiful drifts to be seen next to the lake.

In the 1930s, the Great Western Railway ran 'daffodil specials' from London to see the naturalized *N. pseudonar-cissus* found on the Gloucestershire and Herefordshire borders. The trains have gone, but thankfully the *Narcis-sus* are as good as ever and a circular 'daffodil way' has been opened, giving views of them in meadows, wood-land and by the lanes. In Yorkshire, the valley of Farndale

is another mecca for the public to see naturalized *Narcis-sus* in a beautiful and wild setting. This site is again is served by a well-marked and maintained footpath. There are other sites throughout S England, often in the care of societies and trusts, which should mean their future is assured. Even some banks along the M5 motorway are home to scattered colonies, although probably unseen by the speeding motorist.

The Tenby daffodil, *N. obvallaris*, was first recorded in the late eighteenth century in Pembroke, in Wales, from the coast around Tenby, north to the Preseli Mountains. Colonies were greatly depleted by collecting until the latter part of the twentieth century when the remaining stocks were augmented by fresh planting. This *Narcissus* differs in having a uniformly deep yellow flower, whereas *N. pseudonarcissus* ssp. *pseudonarcissus* has bicoloured flow-ers. There are many public footpaths in Dyfed which are lined with naturalized daffodils in spring.

## FRITILLARIES

Another early bulb to evoke public interest is the snake's head fritillary, *Fritillaria meleagris*, the beautifully muted flower of damp water meadows. It used to be a locally common plant in S and E England, where rivers flooded land in winter that was used for grazing or a hay crop. Today, carefully managed sites are viewed by thousands every year, appear on local television regularly and seem to be assured of a place in our flora. Two areas in partic-ular are quite spectacular in early spring, firstly the famous site in Magdalen College Meadow in Oxford, and also in the Thames valley, the largest concentration of all is found in the North Meadow at Cricklade, which is now a National Nature Reserve.

## TULIPS

In early spring many tulips also begin to show their sparking colours, often used in bedding schemes in parks and gardens. If you would like something a little more subtle, then the species are often a little smaller, although they can be just as bright. The Cambridge University Botanic Garden, which is open daily, houses the National Collection of species tulips and some hybrids and is well worth a visit in early and mid-spring. Two famous gar-dens, Hadspen Gardens near Castle Cary in Somerset and Pashley Manor near Ticehurst in E Sussex, also have famous displays of tulips open to the public.

## PLANT COLLECTIONS AND SOCIETIES

The National Council for the Conservation of Plants and Gardens is an umbrella organization that has drawn together many diverse growers with the aim of cataloguing and growing garden-worthy plants from many genera as National Collections. There are many holders of these National Collections who occasionally open their gardens to the public and these include some growers of early bulbs. The National Plant Collections Directory gives full information about the collections, opening times and other visitor information. Other opportunities to view them are at flower shows, like the monthly RHS shows at Westminster in London. The winter and spring shows often have stands devoted to one genus of plants like snowdrops, fritillaries and cyclamen. Often great care has been taken to construct a beautiful mixed display of winter and early spring plants, which can be viewed in the comfort of a dry cool show hall. There is the added attraction of being able to buy many of these choice plants from nurseries, which come from the length and breadth of the country.

The Alpine Garden Society and the Scottish Rock Garden Club have some shows early in the year where many early bulbs are exhibited in perfect condition and again specialist nurseries are on hand to tempt the gardener with many unusual plants. These Saturday shows are always open to members of the public.

## BULBS IN THE WILD

For those who want to see bulbs in the wild, there are all sorts of holidays available, from spartan camping expeditions to luxury cruises that take in ports near gardens and sites of interest. Many early bulbs are snow-melt plants so spring is the time to pull on the walking boots and head for the hills, camera at the ready. Spring begins early around the Mediterranean basin and in midwinter, you can often get relatively cheap package tours to Cyprus. Not long after, S Spain and the Atlas Mountains of N Africa begin to bloom; however, both areas have varied weather at this time of year and can be wet and quite cold. In the true months of spring the choice is vast

and you can hunt bulbs up mountains as the snow melts well into early summer in places like Switzerland. In N America, spring and the bulbous plants that emerge can be followed from S California's coastal ranges via the Sierra Nevada and the Cascades from March through to August. In the Northern Cascades Mountains some areas have so much winter snow that it takes until August to melt, effectively making any visit in summer a spring holiday. There are many small tour companies organizing such trips with experienced botanists and gardeners leading the visits. If you really wish to see a variety of plants, local knowledge is vital as seasons vary, as do the flowering times. These tours nearly all have the tour industry's bonding but it is always advisable to check.

## BULBS IN NORTH AMERICA

North America also has many wonderful gardens that feature bulbs in the late winter and early spring. Of course, the large botanical gardens and arboretum have extensive bulb collections, though you might try the following in particular: Wave Hill in the Bronx, New York; the U.S. National Arboretum in Washington D.C.; Longwood Gardens in Kennett Square, Pennsylvania; Chanticleer in Wayne, Pennsylvania; the Atlanta Botanical Garden in Atlanta, Georgia; Callaway Gardens in Pine Mountain, Georgia; the Chicago Botanical Garden in Glencoe, Illinois; the Morton Arboretum in Lisle, Illinois; the University of California Botanical Garden in Berkeley; and the Butchart Gardens on Vancouver Island, Canada.

Winterthur Gardens, in Winterthur, Delaware, feature the March Bank, the oldest part of the garden, where planting of snowdrops, crocus, daffodils and other bulbs began in 1914. At the Brooklyn Botanic Garden in New York, March finds the Daffodil Hill ablaze in yellows and golds. Many early bulbs are naturalized along the walk to the Rock Garden and also in the Jane Watson Irwin Perennial Garden at the New York Botanical Garden in the Bronx. The Missouri Botanical Garden in St Louis has three dedicated bulb gardens and has also placed bulbs in its woodland, rock and cutting gardens. The Dallas Arboretum Botanical Garden in Texas boasts over 200,000 bulbs and celebrates their blooming through the month of March.

Some growers open their fields to the public. Brent and Becky's Bulbs in Gloucester, Virginia, features a wide variety of bulbs, while Old House Gardens in Ann Arbor, Michigan, specializes in heirloom bulbs. The outstanding display of early bulbs at Fernwood, in Niles, Michigan, climaxes in late February and early March with tens of thousands of snowdrops and aconites, though the lavish show continues through the spring.

In Virginia you can find several historical sites with noteworthy early bulb displays: the Publick House in London Town; Virginia House in Richmond; Mount Vernon near Washington, D.C.; Monticello in Charlottesville; and Colonial Williamsburg in Williamsburg.

Tulips are also very popular and three communities that celebrate them with annual festivals are Holland, Michigan; Pella, Iowa; and the Skagit Valley in Washington State.

# Appendix III  *Where to Buy Early Bulbs*

## UK AND EUROPE

**Avon Bulbs** Bath, BA1 8ED, UK

**Rupert Bowlby**
Gatton, Reigate, RH2 0TA, UK

**Broadleigh Gardens**
Taunton, TA4 1AE, UK

**Bulbes d'Opale** Boerenweg
Ouest, F-59285 Buysscheure, France

**Cambridge Bulbs**
Newton, CB2 5BH, UK

**Carncairn Daffodils Ltd.**
Co. Antrim, BT43 7HS, UK

**P.J. Christian**
Wrexham, LL13 9XR, UK

**Groom Bros. Ltd**
Pecks Drove Nurseries,
Spalding, PE12 6BJ, UK

**Michael Hoog**
Huize Zwanenburg, Postbus 3217,
NL-2001 Haarlem, Holland

**P. de Jager & Sons Ltd.**
Marden, TN12 9BP, UK

**La Pivoine Bleue**
'A Sechan Dessus',
32 550 Montegut, France

**Monocot Nursery**
Clevedon, BS21 6SG, UK

**Potterton & Martin**
Nettleton, LN7 6HX, UK

**Janis Ruksans**
Bulb Nursery, LV-4150 Rozula,
cesu apr., Latvija

**R.A. Scamp**
Falmouth, TR11 4PJ, UK

**Tile Barn Nursery**
Benenden, Kent, TN17 4LB, UK

**Van Tubergen UK Ltd.**
Diss, IP22 2AB, UK

## USA

**Brent & Becky's Bulbs**
7463 Heath Trail,
Gloucester, VA 23061

**International Bulb Society**
Membership Director
550 IH-10 South, Suite 201,
Beaumont, TX 77707

**The Bulb Crate**
2560 Deerfield Road,
Riverwoods, IL 60015

**Scott Kunst**
Old House Gardens,
536 Third Street,
Ann Arbor, MI 48103-4957

**Van Bourgondieu Brothers**
245 Farmingdale Road,
PO Box 1000, Babylon, NY 11702

**Nancy Wilson Species and Miniature Narcissus**
6525 Briceland-Thorn Road,
Garberville, CA 95542

## AUSTRALIA

**G. and S. Reid**
R.M.B. 6270 via Wodonga,
Victoria 3691

Societies with seed exchange programs that include bulbous plants

**Alpine Garden Society**
Pershore, WR10 3JP, England

**North American Rock Garden Society**
PO Box 67, Millwood, NY 10546,
USA

**The Scottish Rock Garden Club**
Poynton, SK12 1NT, Scotland

# Appendix IV *Glossary of Terms*

**Alternate** Leaves borne singly to a node, so they alternate along the stem.

**Applanate** Flat leaves, as seen in *Galanthus nivalis*.

**Anther** The upper part of the stamen, that produces pollen.

**Axil** Where the leaf joins the stem.

**Basal plate** The compressed stem at the base of a bulb, from which roots and leaves develop.

**Biternate** Divided into threes.

**Bract** A modified leaf.

**Bulb** see pp.16–17

**Bulbil** A small new bulb-like organ borne in the leaf axil or, sometimes, flowerhead of the parent plant.

**Bulblet** A small new bulb produced at the base of the mature parent bulb.

**Convolute** Leaves that they are rolled or wrapped around each other.

**Corm** see p.17

**Corolla** The petals of a flower.

**Corona** A cup- or trumpet-shaped part of a flower, as found in the genus *Narcissus*.

**Dicotyledon** A plant with two seed leaves, or cotyledons. The largest group of flowering plants.

**Entire** Leaves with untoothed edges.

**Falls** The three outer segments (tepals) of an iris, which usually hang outwards.

**Filament** Part of a flower stamen, the stalk that supports the anther.

**Filiform** Threadlike.

**Glabrous** Smooth, or hairless.

**Glaucous** A grey-blue colour or a white or grey bloom

**Globose** Round, globe-like.

**Inflorescence** A cluster of flowers, a flowerhead.

**Involucre** A whorl of leaves or bracts surrounding a flower or flowerhead.

**Lanceolate** Spearhead-shaped leaves.

**Linear** Narrow leaves with parallel edges.

**Monocotyledon** A plant with a single seed leaf, or cotyledon. This includes most bulbous plants.

**Nectary** A nectar-producing gland in the flower.

**Panicle** A loose flower cluster.

**Perianth** The outer parts of a flower, usually when petals and sepals are indistinguishable.

**Opposite** Leaves borne two to a node, opposite each other on the stem.

**Ovary** Part of the flower containing embryonic seeds.

**Pedate** Leaves that have lobes or divisions, which are in turn divided.

**Pedicel** The stalk of an individual flower.

**Perianth** See Tepals.

**Plicate** Folded or pleated leaves.

**Raceme** An unbranched flowerhead, with many individual stalked flowers borne along the main stalk.

**Rhizome** see p.18

**Scales** A bulb part; either the swollen leaf base of aerial foliage or thick fleshy scale leaves which never grow upwards.

**Scape** The leafless flower stem.

**Segments** See Tepals.

**Sessile** Without a stalk.

**Spadix** A fleshy flower spike bearing numerous small flowers; a particular characteristic of the Araceae family.

**Spathe** A bract that surrounds a flower bud or spadix.

**Stamen** The pollen-producing part of a flower, consisting of the filament and anther.

**Stigma** That part of a flower which receives the pollen during pollination.

**Stolon** A spreading stem which, on contact with the soil, roots at its tip to produce a new plant.

**Stoloniferous** Spreading by means of stolons.

**Tepals** The floral leaves of the monocotyledon flower, equivalent to the petals and speals of a dicotyledon and often called the perianth segments, or just the segments.

**Tessallated** Chequered; a regular mottling, as in the flowers of some *Fritillaria* and *Colchicum*.

**Trifoliate** With three leaves or leaflets.

**Tuber** see p.18

**Tunic** The coat covering bulbs and corms.

**Umbel** A round or flat-topped flower cluster, where the individual flower stems arise from a central point.

**Undulate** With waved or crimped edges.

# Bibliography

Anderson, E.B., *Dwarf Bulbs for the Rock Garden*,
  T. Nelson & Sons, 1959

Barnes, D., *Daffodils for Home, Garden and Show*,
  David & Charles, 1987

Beckett, K.A. (ed), *Encyclopaedia of Alpines*,
  Alpine Garden Society, 1993-4

Blanchard, J., *Narcissus: a guide to wild daffodils*,
  Alpine Garden Society, 1990

Bryan, J.E., *Bulbs,* Christopher Helm, 1989

Davis, P.H., *Flora of Turkey*,
  Edinburgh University Press, 1986

Elliott, J., *Bulbs for the Rock Garden,* Vista Books, 1963

*The European Garden Flora* Vol. 1,
  Cambridge University Press, 1986

Grey, A., *Miniature Daffodils*,
  W.H. & L. Collingridge, 1955

Grey-Wilson, C., *Cyclamen: a guide for gardeners,
  horticulturists and botanists,* Batsford, 1997

Grey-Wilson, C., and Mathew, B., *Bulbs: the bulbous
  plants of Europe,* Collins, 1981

Jeppe, B., *Spring and Winter Flowering Bulbs of the Cape*,
  Oxford University Press, Cape Town, 1989

KAVB *International Checklist for Hyacinths and
  Miscellaneous Bulbs*, Hillgom, 1991

Liden, M., and Zetterlund, H., *Corydalis*,
  A.G.S. Publications Ltd, 1997

Mathew, B., *The Smaller Bulbs*, Batsford, 1987

Mathew, B., *The Iris*, Batsford, 1981

Mathew, B., *The Crocus*, Batsford, 1981

Mathew, B., and Baytop, T., *The Bulbous Plants of Turkey*,
  Batsford, 1984

Phillips, R., and Rix, M., *Bulbs*, 2nd ed.,
  Pan Books, 1989

Royal Horticultural Society, *RHS Plant Finder*,
  Dorling Kindersley, 1999

Stern, F., *Snowdrops and Snowflakes*,
  Royal Horticultural Society, 1956

Synge, P., *Collins Guide to Bulbs*, Collins, 1963

Turrill, W., and Sealy, R., *Studies in the Genus* Fritillaria,
  Bentham Moxon Trustees, 1980

Wells, J., *Modern Miniature Daffodils*, Batsford, 1989

# Index

## ACKNOWLEDGEMENTS

I would very much like to thank the following for their
kind help and support:
Richard Ayres
Sarah Buckeridge
Keith and June Davis
Ronald Mackenzie
John Morley
Wol and Sue Staines